For when were
hiking

Love,
sed

colin

THE HUNGRY HIKER'S
BOOK OF GOOD COOKING

BOOK OF

Illustrations by Susan Gaber

THE HUNGRY HIKER'S GOOD COOKING

by Gretchen McHugh

Alfred A. Knopf   New York   1991

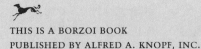

THIS IS A BORZOI BOOK
PUBLISHED BY ALFRED A. KNOPF, INC.

Grateful acknowledgment is made to the following for
permission to reprint from previously published material:

Garden Way Publishing: *Garden Way's Guide to Food
Drying*, with permission from Garden Way Publishing,
Charlotte, Vermont.

Pierce School: recipes for Banana Bread, Date-Nut Bread,
and Apple Bread from *The Pierce Pantry*. Copyright © 1975
by Pierce School.

Charles Scribner's Sons: From Ernest Hemingway, "Big
Two-Hearted River" and "The Last Good Country" in *The
Nick Adams Stories*. Copyright © 1972 The Ernest
Hemingway Foundation. Reprinted with the permission of
Charles Scribner's Sons.

Library of Congress Cataloging in Publication Data
McHugh, Gretchen, [date]
The hungry hiker's book of good cooking.
Bibliography: p.
Includes index.
1. Outdoor cookery.   I. Title.
TX823.M36   641.5'782   81-48131
ISBN 0-394-51261-8   AACR2

Manufactured in the United States of America
Published June 22, 1982
Reprinted Four Times
Sixth Printing, December 1991

to the memory of Fred Lewis

Contents

Acknowledgments

Although it would be impossible to name everyone who participated in this book, I would like to thank a number of interested souls, hikers and non-hikers, who contributed ideas, recipes, and enthusiasm: Nancy Barker, Chantal Clesca, Jim Hewins, Maureen Keating, Anne Lalas, Meredith Mazer, Gene Perrin, Sarah and Lydia Porter, Shirley Sarvis, Janet Smith, Anne Stanley, Luanne Sukenik, Dick Tucker, Carolyn Verbecke, and the staff of Chang's Fruit and Vegetable Market. For helping me to learn about backpacking stoves, I'd like to thank Ray Kalio.

Much gratitude is due Toni Mueller, Susan Hufford, Max Casey, Beth Ronka, and Mary Barker, whose prudent and quizzical reading of the manuscript in its various stages was invaluable.

Ken Moody, good friend, supplied guidance, moral support, and hikers to feed. To the hikers ("Algoma '80"), I am grateful for helping me to cull recipes by carrying, cooking, and tasting them.

I especially thank my children, Jennifer and Murray, whose tasting of strange foods, and good humor in the face of other trials connected with the book, were a splendid help.

One more acknowledgment is in order, to Judith Jones, whose wisdom, instinct for teaching, and love of good food were in evidence throughout the time she patiently guided the book to its final shape.

Introduction

When I first began to backpack, the food I ate didn't seem to fit at all the way I felt—exhilarated, healthy, and at peace with nature. I tried various freeze-dried meals and soon abandoned them as expensive and eventually unpalatable; their fancy names didn't hide the fact that they all began to taste alike. It's true that supermarkets offer many clever quick meals, and I thought about things like "pasteurized processed cheese spread," "bacon bits," and "hamburger helpers." But I don't eat that sort of food at home, and I really didn't want to eat it on the trail, when, if anything, my taste buds are more sensitive than ever.

So I started searching for good backpacking food. As I did, I fell into conversations with many hikers, and the more we talked, the more I saw that they shared the same dissatisfactions.

The foremost gripes about the food we could buy were its expense and the numerous chemicals it contained. If only we could dry our own food, I thought, we'd avoid both of these drawbacks; and we'd have a wider choice of foods, besides. But the trouble with purchasing a food dryer is that it's an expensive item—upwards of $100—and that's a lot for a backpacker who's already invested in expensive gear like a packframe, tent, sleeping bag, and boots.

About the time I was personally confronting this obstacle, I happened to ask a favorite hiking friend-and-mentor, Fred Lewis, for his recipe for jerky stew. This tasty dish made from home-dried jerky, parsnips, mushrooms, carrots, and green peppers endeared itself annually to the campers whom Fred led into the Canadian wilderness for a week of bushwhacking and gastronomical rewards.

Fred said, "I can't give you a recipe."

(One of these cagey fellows who won't part with his secrets, I thought.)

"There really isn't a recipe for jerky stew," he went on, "but you do need a dryer."

Whereupon the cagey fellow, mentor at heart, made me one.

I've learned since that Fred's dryer costs $30 or less to make, depending on what materials you already own, and that he designed it to be made in a few hours with simple home tools.

With the dryer problem solved, so many things then became possible. In fact, a whole new world of hiking gastronomy opened. The first thing my family did, of course, was to pack our own version of jerky stew. Sometimes we made nifty trail tradeoffs for it, like grilled Lake Superior trout, and exchanged lore, too: how to catch the big ones, how to make jerky. News of the dryer elicited interest and excitement among the hikers we met, young and old.

Other possibilities began to emerge. I found many uses for the vegetables that dried so beautifully over Fred's single light bulb; and mushrooms, parsnips, carrots, beans, cabbage, corn, zucchini, and eggplant began to find their way into our wild soups, omelets, and pilafs.

If I could do that, I could do more, I decided. I knew that carbohydrates that include pasta, rice, grains, pan breads, and homemade breads were the mainstay of the hiking menu. They're a wonderful source of energy, and wonderful foods besides. But I wanted to show how these foods could be used in many ways, with all the delicious embellishments they encourage. And besides, I saw in my travels that backpackers didn't always know how to cook these simple foods. I was horrified more than once to see a camper with a supermarket package of rices-mixed-with spices, thinking it would be "convenient"—and then having to cook for 50 minutes a mishmash of awful stuff that his dog wouldn't eat. This really bothered me, since I knew that a pot of plain white rice cooks in 15 minutes and is the perfect complement to numerous trail meals.

I also observed pasta overcooked—or cooked again and again into the same old "macaroni" and "spaghetti with meat sauce," when there is a wide range of great simple pasta dishes. In fact, one of my favorite dinners is a plate of properly cooked linguini tossed with a bit of sautéed fresh garlic and a grating of fine Parmesan, and that's certainly easy to do in the wildest of kitchens.

As I thought about sauces and meats to accompany basic pastas, rice, and other grains, I realized that I was simply going to apply the same standards I do to meals at home. Along with its lightness and imperishability, my wilderness food would have to taste good, look good, and offer an exquisite texture contrast now and then.

After some trials and errors, I found ways to dry a few basic sauces at home; on the trail, you combine these with the chosen pasta or grain, grate a good cheese over the top, and add condiments or seasonings to taste. There are several Mexican and pasta dishes that can be made this way. Exercising a flexible attitude toward these basic components—and all the hikers I know do—you can invent dinners to your heart's content.

I also like to combine home-dried jerky and vegetables to make stews. And once I have such ingredients on hand, I get hold of some dried mushrooms, and add stir-fry dinners to my menus. These are terrific trail meals. While the jerky and vegetables soak, you cook the rice; the stir-fry itself takes minutes; it includes fresh garlic (a wonderful food) and ginger, if you like it; the crunchy, fresh nuts and a mixture of lovely colors are complemented by a heap of fluffy white rice.

A thick soup made up at home out of barley and lentils, home-dried vegetables, seasonings, and a hearty stock thickened with instant potato powder, bouillon, or tomato paste is a one-pot feast, good for cold-weather camping, especially with dumplings cooked on top of it.

I'd much rather dry my own hamburger (overnight, in the oven, after browning it) than pack "soy granules" or other tasteless substitutes for meat I've seen. When you do this, you're ready to store a package of dried hamburger with other dried foods in the refrigerator as a more or less permanent stock of hiking provisions, ready to go when you are. You can add to these reserves at convenient times—for instance, when cooking large batches of food like refried beans, spaghetti sauce, or chili.

Prepared at odd moments when you've got time, trail meals set aside like this make those rushed moments before a trip much easier. There is nothing more frustrating than realizing you have to delay for hours getting into the fresh air, just to assemble provisions. Think how nice it would be to have enough things on hand for a weekend trip so that you didn't even have to cross the threshold of a store! I did this once, and took off down the path wearing a ridiculous grin. Although this kind of food packing might not happen very often—if only because you have to stop in at a good cheese store—it makes sense to aim for it.

The directions in the book are divided into two parts: preparation ahead at home, and trail directions. The more carefully you prepare at home, the less you have to do on the trail, when you're hungrier and your stove is smaller. But I must hasten to add that this isn't a book of fancy cooking. I've had two goals: to prepare delicious food, and to keep everything as simple as possible. These goals are by no means mutually exclusive.

Since the wilderness cook isn't known for his slavish following of recipes, I've indicated many possible substitutes for various foods, from meats to seasonings. Some recipes, like Super Soup, positively invite substitutions. Granola, fillings for pita and tortillas, and stir-fry dinners are like this too. But with things like rice, pasta, and grains that need a specific method of cooking, pay attention to the recipe at first, until water ratios and cooking times become familiar. Knowing how to cook these basic foods right will make future cooking on the trail much easier.

It only takes a moment to jot down your own shorthand version of my trail directions; and I advise you always to do so—or to Xerox the recipes, if that's convenient. Although you think you may remember the details of a recipe, it's surprising sometimes how grateful you can be for a few scrawled directions tucked in with the packets of ingredients. And sometimes you may want to turn over the cooking to someone less experienced.

With some recipes, you can choose between two different methods, depending on how simple you'd like to keep your cooking procedure. For example, white sauce can be made either from separately carried flour, butter or margarine, and dry milk, or from a bit of dry homemade mix. Aware of the differences in the way hikers pack food, I've usually presented cheese in two ways: as an extra treat to add to a dinner ("added from the lunch supply") or as a specific ingredient to be pre-grated and packed in with the other ingredients.

I'm sure this book doesn't exhaust the supply of good home foods that can be adapted to the wild kitchen. But as I've explored some of the basic ways they can be adapted, I hope I've inspired you to do the same. If the book uncovers possibilities for backpacking foods that haven't occurred to you, or that you assumed were impossible, I'll be happy.

I wish you many fine walks, and many fine wilderness repasts to celebrate them with.

THE HUNGRY HIKER'S
BOOK OF GOOD COOKING

1

THE WILD KITCHEN

*Equipment / Heat for
cooking: stove or fire?*

EQUIPMENT

The ideal backpacking kitchen combines minimum weight with maximum efficiency. To equip the wild kitchen in this spirit is to engage in a continuous process of paring away nonessentials. The best way to pare away nonessentials is to decide on specific cooking gear for each trip only after you have your menus planned and food assembled.

Another good way is to improvise. If you haven't got an oven, use a frying pan with a lid instead. If you haven't got a frying pan lid, use squares of aluminum foil that you have cut to size and folded at home. If you haven't got a frying pan, cook biscuits by steaming them as dumplings, or roast them over the fire on a stick. Lacking a ladle, use a drinking cup. To make an instant pitcher for powdered drinks, use a Ziploc bag. Grass and sand make the best pot scourers. And so on, *ad infinitum*. I haven't seen a wild cook yet who hasn't invented something in the culinary line (and who isn't duly pleased with himself).

This doesn't mean that there isn't an intriguing array of culinary inventions to woo the eager wild cook, who may be outfitting himself initially or simply updating his equipment. Backpackers, depending on gear as they do, are perpetually fascinated with it in a spirit that is as prudent as it is adventurous.

While much equipment can be found economically by browsing through your own kitchen and through department stores, the best place to shop for certain long-term items, like cookpots that must withstand the rigors of wild kitchen use, is in a backpacking store or catalog. (See page 274.)

Gear includes each camper's personal utentils, cooking equipment, fire and stove gear, dishwashing items, and the food-packing materials.

If the list of gear that follows looks impossibly spare, that's good. How little you need to carry into the woods to cook delicious, hearty meals might astonish even Thoreau.

WHAT EACH CAMPER CARRIES—PERSONAL FOOD GEAR

1 bowl   A plastic cereal bowl is better than a plate for several reasons. Its high sides keep food warmer longer than a flat plate; its smaller size makes it easier to pack; it can be found in any supermarket; it's lighter than the lightest aluminum; and it will never burn your hands.

1 cup   The backpacker's cup, the one with the measuring lines and that weighs next to nothing (somewhere between $\frac{1}{3}$ and $\frac{1}{2}$ ounce), is my favorite. Plagued by eternally freezing fingertips, I consider it an essential function of a cup to warm me as, with much shivering, I grasp my morning tea and evening soup. Because a metal cup would be too hot, I have never even faintly considered using one and wish to remain aloof from other considerations in the plastic/metal cup controversy, such as the status advantage of wearing a genuine Sierra cup at one's belt, or the fact that this popular receptacle can double as a dinner plate, salad plate, or egg poacher. The plastic cup doubles as a measuring cup, which is quite enough versatility for me.

1 spoon   The knife-fork-spoon sets sold for about $2 in camping stores are irresistible. But soon you find that the knife is redundant (you're already carrying a sharp knife); the fork is redundant (because you have a spoon);

and if there is a plastic carrying case, it hoards germs and moisture before it finally tears or mercifully gets lost.

1 sharp knife   The camper's choice of a sharp knife is one of those delightful personal choices, like hats, around-camp loafing shoes, and walking sticks, that reflect not only his personality but the whole range of activities in which he has used this implement. The fisherman, for example, is apt to have been in touch with the very best of cutlery from the inception of his angling career.

The size of the knife, its shape, the array of blades, scissors, tweezers, corkscrews, files, pliers, fish scalers, vegetable graters, and scalpels that might bristle from it; its safety features, signature, color, case, and even its weight—all are secondary to two things: the sharpness of its edge and how much you like it.

My favorite knife is the Swiss army model so serenely simple it's not even popular. Not being given to surgery, bartending, or complex tailoring while backpacking, I consider the 5-ounce, multi-equipped officer's army knife a contraption-ridden nuisance. But the simplest model, the New Pocket Pal, is a wonderful knife. It costs $5.95 and is usually found hovering unobtrusively in the back of the case in a backpacking store. There are cheap imitations that are not in the Swiss army line: beware. The blade of the authentic model is sharp and stays sharp. It is of modest length, but perfectly adequate for most camp uses, as it cuts bread, garlic, moleskin, wood, line, and fish. (I consider a knife that can clean bluegills as having passed the ultimate test.)

A one-quart water container that doesn't leak
The Naglene polyethylene wide-mouth plastic bottle found in backpacking stores is a good choice. It's rugged, the top works easily, and it's a nice-looking vessel, too. Whatever make or shape of water receptacle you choose, though, be sure to test it for leaks before use.

GENERAL EQUIPMENT

Stoves, fuel, grills   See pages 15–22.

Cookpots   There are many camping cookpots to choose from. Some come in sets, with nesting pots and lids that can be used as frying pans or plates. (See the note on Sigg cook kits that fit Peak I and Svea stove modules, page 16.) When choosing, consider the number you'll be cooking for and the type of stove you have; for instance, high, tippier stoves shouldn't have wide pans set on them. Buy the best you can afford, as good cookware will earn its keep by wearing well and conducting heat efficiently.

Our standard cookpot is a Sigg 2-quart aluminum vessel. (It can be bought in backpacking outfitting stores and through the Eastern Mountain Sports catalog; see page 274.) Its ¾-inch-wide handle will lock into an upright position. To pry the lid off takes an extra tool or two—a knife, and a couple of asbestos fingers, for example. After ten years of devoted service, it has a few minor dents; it is stable and easy to pour from, and it conducts heat well. At $20, this is no cheap pot, but it is an excellent long-term investment.

Our 1-quart pot is not a smaller version of the 2-quart Sigg vessel (although we could have bought a 1-quart Sigg pot); therefore, it doesn't nest into it or otherwise contribute to packing "style." This small cookpot came rather in a kit with a frying pan, with which it shared a handle. Because the flat lid has a small "lifting" triangle, it can be removed easily with a stick, knife, or other handy implement. This feature compensates for the pot's slight instability, which is due to its straight sides and tall shape.

Carry two pots if you plan to serve soup as a dinner's first course, to make a pasta dish, or to have hot water on hand for hot tea and other elixirs.

If your pots don't nest together or fit into a stove kit, save pack space by carrying food inside them.

Frying pan   A 7-inch size is standard, though the size depends on the number in your party. What you cook in it matters, too: I find myself taking our larger, 8½-inch, 6-ounce pan more and more these days, both because we are making more stir-fry dinners and because my son's fishing skill is increasing. Its handle, once shared by the 1-quart pot, is gone, so we make do with a pot gripper. For stir-fry dinners, cooking pan breads, and frying fish, the frying pan is essential. Look for a Teflon coating, or use a little vegetable oil to keep things from sticking.

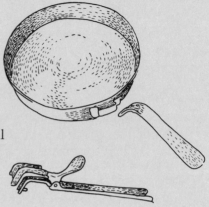

Frying pan lid   In order to "bake" in a frying pan, you need a lid for it. Most frying pans don't come with lids, so improvise with the lid from a cookpot, or cut 12-by-12-inch squares of aluminum foil, fold them, and carry them in a side pocket of your pack.

Note: It is possible to save money, and time spent scouring pots at the end of a trip, by making pots to last the entirety of one trip out of number 10 cans. (One quart 14 ounces of tomato juice comes in this size can.) These will not replace a frying pan, of course; and they are best carried tied to the outside of your pack, where they quickly dispel any notions that you are a stylishly outfitted hiker.

Punch two holes opposite each other at the top of the can and tie strong but flexible wire, like picture wire, in secure knots through the holes to make a handle. The resulting pot can be suspended from a tripod over a fire (using a chain that ends with an S-hook), or it can sit on a grate.

My collection of pots and pans doesn't have the élan of a cook kit; my frying pan isn't Teflon and is a little on the heavy side. But I rather enjoy sampling the different ingenuities of these various cookpieces; and I hope to pass them along to my children.

OTHER USEFUL ITEMS

Spatula   Essential for turning eggs, pan breads, fish, and stir-fry meals.

Large spoon   Useful particularly when cooking over a wood fire, to enable you to stir things without scorching your wrist or hand.

Ladle   A very elegant tool to use for serving soup and other hot things. The less elegant alternative, which works as well in a congenial group not afraid of each other's germs, is to use someone's drinking cup for ladling.

Pot gripper   This handy item, half spring, half pliers, and referred to affectionately as the "magic tool," is essential for lifting a heavy pot off the fire or stove by clamping onto its rim.

Potholder   An oven mitt or other kind of potholder is helpful.

Small whisk   Useful when you cook flour and butter for a white sauce, and to dispel lumps from "instant" sauces and gravy. Small ones are available in most hardware stores; Early Winters catalog offers a small collapsible whisk (see page 274).

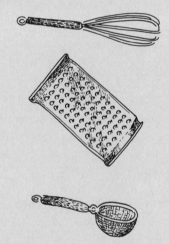

Tiny grater   In a store you may find one that will fit easily in your pack and be useful for grating cheese.

Strainer   To strain tea into your cup after you've brewed it in a pot from tea leaves (see page 67).

FOOD-PACKING MATERIALS

Plastic bags   A friend and I, packing together for joint family trips, used to look up at each other periodically over heaps of food and equipment to query incredulously, "How did anybody ever backpack without Ziploc bags?"

The Ziploc sandwich bags are a little flimsy for camping purposes. But the uses for the next two sizes of this plastic bag, the quart and gallon sizes, are numerous.

Airtight, they can really be trusted to enclose tubs of margarine, hunks of salami, or other foods whose unrestrained presence would wreak unmistakable havoc in the pack. (I wrap salami first very well in plastic and use the Ziploc bag as an outside cover.) They are useful as makeshift pitchers—measure enough powdered drink such as lemonade into the quart-capacity bag. Then on the trail fill it with a quart of cold water, mix, use, and re-use. Using a Ziploc bag rather than your water container for this purpose will keep the inside of your water container from picking up a motley assortment of sweet smells that will bother you in time (in a short time, probably).

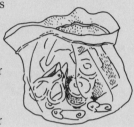

Most dry foods like granola, cereals, rice, mixes, and home-baked bread are best carried in the less-expensive plastic bags of about 12-inch-square size, with ties. Double-bag these as a matter of habit for extra protection. Ziploc bags do not work for gorp, because after they have been opened and resealed several times, with the possibility of nut skins, salt, or other little bits of stuff getting into the groove, they won't work anymore. Package components of dinners to be cooked on the trail in small, sandwich-size bags.

Any time you pack anything in a plastic bag, squeeze all the air out of it before fastening it shut.

Always bring extra plastic bags. The only sure way to keep your food safe from varmints, big and little, while you sleep, is to tie it all in a "bear bag" and hoist the resulting cache over the limb of a tree. (For details, see page 270.) For this you need two large plastic bags, of the kitchen-trash-bag size, to put one inside the other for extra strength, plus 20 feet of nylon line, sometimes called backpacker's line, which you can find in a backpacker's store or in a marina. (The line is essential anyway, for clothesline, improvised handrails for river crossings, extra help in unexpected steep climbs, and extra tent rigging on those confounded "platforms" found in eastern U.S. camping areas.)

Large plastic bags are also good pack covers at night, to keep rain and dew off.

Extra Ziploc bags are very handy for repackaging food from bags which have got a puncture; packing out trash; carrying wet clothes; carrying first aid, sewing, and writing kits. A Ziploc bag is a nonpareil for keeping maps and other vital printed matter dry and intact.

Assorted containers   There are several ways to carry food staples such as sugar, flour, honey, peanut butter, and sauces:

• Wide-mouth polyethylene bottles in various sizes are excellent for both gooey and dry staples.

• There are squeeze tubes made out of polyethylene which have a screw cap at one end and a crimp clip at the other. While many hikers find these useful, I find them a menace because they do *not* hold food safely. It can escape from the rolled-up end, and therefore these gadgets should always be enclosed within a Ziploc bag. (Back to the wide-mouth bottle.)

• Save plastic vitamin bottles for spices, small amounts of flour or vegetable oil, or brandy. Test these carefully before using to make sure they are leak-proof.

• Plastic 35-mm film cans are excellent small-food carriers, too, and I haven't used one yet that leaked. They are therefore also good leakproof containers for matches.

• Self-sealing plastic bags (similar to Ziploc bags) as small as 5 by 8 inches, which are good for spices and clarified butter, can be bought through the Recreational Equipment, Inc., catalog (see page 272).

Dishwashing equipment   Camp dishwashing equipment need be no more than a simple scouring net and a modest amount of soap—detergent powder in a small plastic bottle with a screw top, a tube of biodegradable soap, or a bar of soap in a soap dish. Pre-soaped scouring pads are a nuisance in the wild, as their exuberance at producing suds is bad, ecologically speaking, for the innocent dishpan you are scouring. Sand is one of the best scouring materials ever; grass, pine needles, and leaves are excellent, too, and they have the advantage of being eminently biodegradable.

But no soap is biodegradable, no matter what claims are made for it. While doing dishes at the lakeshore at sunset is one of backpacking's unsung pleasures, be sure that at the same time you are enjoying this serenity you are not also dumping soap into Nature's pure waters. Rinse dishes by pouring water over them *away from* the lake or stream.

HEAT FOR COOKING:
STOVE OR FIRE?

Whether the brisk crackling of a compact wood fire or the sudden imperti-
nent roar of a tiny backpacking stove breaks the silence of the wilderness
as you begin dinner preparations, that first swallow of hot soup at the end
of a day's hiking seems to reach straight to your weary feet. That fragrant
hot swallow makes the difference between misery and the glowing sense
of comfort you later try to explain to skeptical nonbackpackers who think
they are upholding civilization by staying home.

Arguments about which we *should* cook over, stove or wood fire, are
really outside the scope of a cookbook. In general, the ethical/ecological
question is hard to answer (and it hasn't been). Is the burning of firewood
an important phase of the forest's chemical life; or do campfires throw
Nature off balance? Though there are times when no one but a moral
degenerate would build a fire, there *are* situations when it hardly seems
more offensive to burn wind-thrown sticks or sea-thrown driftwood than
to consume fossil fuel that had to be mined, refined, packaged, transported,
inventoried, purchased, repacked, and toted to the campsite.

Wood fires have practical, as well as aesthetic, advantages. The small
grill you need for fire cooking certainly weighs and costs less than stove-
plus-fuel. You can heat two pots simultaneously over a longish fire, whereas
a stove will heat only one at a time. While some campers complain about
soot-blackened pots ruining the interior of their packs, I haven't been much
bothered (it's a rather dry soot, in contrast to the grill's messy grease). I
haven't researched how long a wood fire takes to boil a quart of water in
72° F. weather (the chart-making empiricist's test), but I suspect that a
properly built fire is the granddaddy that taught all the little stoves how.
And, to ascend from matters purely practical, the aesthetic attributes of a
wood fire cause us to put up with smoke in our eyes, burned knees, and
sooty paws, in order to enjoy the way it warms those paws, wet clothes,
and soul.

But to get back to that larger question . . . Unless the area specifically
bans campfires (more and more areas do this now), you need to use your
own judgment. If the landscape is almost treeless, a decent respect for the
stuff that's there will cause you in all good conscience to let it lie. The

conditions might be so dry that one zephyr-carried spark could set off a conflagration of proportions entirely larger than needed to heat your pot of soup. As a result, most of us now lean heavily toward using a stove rather than building cookfires, as the world's wild places shrink.

Allow me to introduce a humble little machine, a metal contrivance no bigger than a geranium pot, over whose flame a vast and complicated array of foods can be cooked. My Svea, plodding calmly into its tenth year of reliable service, is the stove to which I refer, and I refer to it fondly, for it is dependable, if not refined. It is not the easiest stove to cook over (its blowtorch qualities make it one of the hardest), but even after comparison with newer stoves on the market, I find myself loyal. One's choice of stove is a very personal matter—one depends on it so.

My Svea travels in a grubby, soot-blackened bag in which rattle around together several cigar canisters of wooden matches, two or three half-empty disposable lighters, a funnel, a medicine dropper, a little handle which can turn the metal cover into a miniature cookpot, and the stove's key.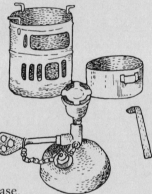

The steps involved in lighting a stove comprise a ritual just as the ancient art of firebuilding does. The ritual isn't the same but the importance attached to it is.

Having extricated the stove from its traveling case, I twist off its windscreen, unscrew the tank lid, and peer into the inside to see if any gas is visible. If not, fuel goes from a Sigg fuel container through a funnel into the stove. Returning the windscreen, I arrange a few small tools within easy reach: these are the key, a medicine dropper, and matches. I fit the key into the spindle and turn it all the way to the right and back again, whereby a little metal spear comes up and cleans the hole. I transfer half a medicine dropper of gas from the Sigg bottle into the circular cavity around the stove's spigot. Lighted, this exposed gas warms the gas inside the tank, which expands to escape in a jet from the hole. That is the signal to give the key a small turn, and Pouf! the escaping gas, ignited by the burning gas around it, begins to burn fiercely. The nifty little stove is lit.

In windy weather, it is necessary to use something as a windscreen. Rather than depend on natural objects like large rocks for this purpose, you might want to build a simple windscreen at home that you can unfold as needed. In the absence of any objects, block the wind as much as possible with your body.

Dampness also seems to affect the alacrity with which the stove lights. And in cold weather, a mini-pump must be employed to prime the fuel sufficiently. If the first try fails, as it sometimes does, I begin again, by dropping more gas into the declivity and repeating the process.

The Svea's best feature is its reliability. It certainly is not a subtle cookpiece, as its range of heat hovers between the white intensity of a blowtorch and its low setting, Super Hot. This is a good stove to use when writing a cookbook, however—any recipe I cook over a Svea anybody can cook over anything. (See "Cooking tips for stoves," page 20.)

WHICH STOVE FOR YOU?

The discussion becomes again both subjective and practical, simultaneously. There are many backpacking stoves; ten of the most available I will chart and discuss briefly. They all do the same thing—burn fuel to heat food—but they differ in format, weight, the severity of the conditions under which they work, the type of fuel they burn, and the subtlety of their heat controls.

In choosing your stove, you need to consider the number in the party you're cooking for, the temperature, the altitude, the availability of the fuel your stove burns, how heavy the stove is, how quickly it heats up, how reliable it is under the conditions you're going to be using it, how easy it is for *you* to operate, and whether you want it to be infinitely adjustable between hot and simmer or if you want it just to be hot, period. The major stoves available offer differences in design, and they range imaginatively among all these possibilities.

Stoves can be divided into two basic types:

Stoves that use liquid fuel   When white gas, kerosene, or other fuels are carried in liquid form, they must be warmed, or primed, before they will ignite. Once learned, though, this extra step, performed variously depending on the stove's design, is a small factor, considering these stoves' dependability and economy.

Cartridge stoves   These burn butane or L-P gas (liquefied petroleum), which is packaged into cartridges under pressure. These stoves win the prize for convenience—all you do is plug in the cartridge and light. But certain inconveniences nearly cancel their simplicity: cartridges are expensive in the long run; they must be packed out; and they do not perform well in the cold or when half empty (and GAZ cartridges can't be changed until empty).

(Propane, a second kind of pressurized gas which must be carried in heavy steel cartridges, is unsuitable for backpacking. Propane stoves are used in campers and boats.)

Consult the two charts that follow for an overview of the most popular stoves.

Liquid Fuel Stoves

Model	Approximate price	Weight (sans fuel)	Advantages	Disadvantages
Svea 123	$42	1 lb. 2 oz.	Small, compact, light, dependable, economical.*	Noisy, no heat control, clumsy to fill, wind-affected.
Optimus 8R	47	1 lb. 8 oz.	Small, compact, reliable.	Slow, unsuitable for winter use.
Optimus 111B	78	3 lbs. 8 oz.	Rugged, quiet, dependable; Good for big groups.	Heavy.
Optimus 00 (kerosene)	46	1 lb. 11 oz.	Kerosene widely available, cheap; stove, stable and light.	Kerosene is hard to light and smelly.
Optimus 96	46	1 lb. 8 oz.	Smaller version of Optimus 00.	
Peak I	36	1 lb. 12 oz.	Built-in windscreen; reliable, pump-primed, quiet, clean. Fast; has simmer control.*	A little heavy.
Mountain Safety Research Model G/K	75	15 oz.	Very light, reliable. Burns many fuels.	No simmer control.
Optimus Purist 1	40	1 lb. 9 oz.	Stable	

*A Sigg cook kit consisting of 2 pots, a lid/frying pan, potholder, and windscreen, to fit with each of these two most popular stoves, can be bought for about $30.

Cartridge Stoves

Model	Approximate price	Weight (with cartridge)	Advantages	Disadvantages
GAZ Bluet S-200: butane cartridge	$18 *(11-oz. cartridge is $2.20)*	1 lb. 11 oz.	Easy to use, fuel found worldwide, works well in high altitudes.	Slow, won't work in cold. Cartridge not changeable until empty; doesn't burn well half empty.
Hank Roberts Mini: wick-fed butane cartridge	$23 *(9-oz. cartridge is $1.10)*	1 lb. 1 oz.	Easy to use, very compact, light, tiny.	Slow, inefficient in cold weather.

OTHER NOTES ON STOVES

Fuel availability   Bluet cartridges and kerosene are the only fuels readily available worldwide, in case you are off to see fjords or veldts. White gas can be bought easily anywhere in North America. The Mountain Safety Research multi-fuel stove will burn any kind of liquid fuel ever invented, from the looks of its possible fuel list, in case you need to purchase fuel in a place like the Himalayan foothills. (It will burn white gas, leaded and unleaded automobile gasoline, kerosene, aviation fuel, Blazo, Stoddard solvent, diesel fuel, and stove oil.)

Heat controls   Consider your cooking style. Some stoves burn like blowtorches (Svea and Mountain Safety Research stoves), while others are both quick to heat and have wonderfully sophisticated simmer controls (like the Peak I). A few stoves (Optimus) come in both small and large versions to accommodate a small or a large group. Look at the heat base. Is it tiny, as the Optimus burners are, or is the heat distributed in a wide circle, as in the Peak I and Purist? Even heat distribution over the bottom of the pan helps to prevent burning.

Safety   Camping stoves are very safe when they are used properly (see pages 19–20 for safety tips). If you want a particularly stable stove, look for the ones with flatter designs, like the Peak I and the Optimus Purist. Kerosene is the safest fuel to use if you worry about spilled fuel lighting accidentally—kerosene won't.

Cleanliness   Cartridge stoves are ultra-neat, while certain gas-burning stoves (like the Svea) need to be contained neatly so they don't get other things in your pack grimey.

Noise   Some stoves burn with a noisy roar (Svea), while others are quiet and genteel (Peak I and cartridge stoves).

STOVE SUGGESTIONS BY NEED

Stoves for small-group use (up to 4 people), 4-season

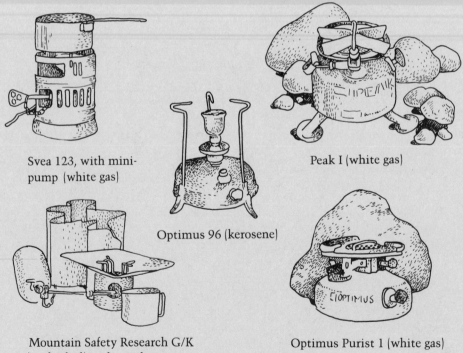

Svea 123, with mini-pump (white gas)

Optimus 96 (kerosene)

Peak I (white gas)

Mountain Safety Research G/K (multi-fuel) with windscreen

Optimus Purist 1 (white gas)

Small, light stoves for small groups, nonwinter

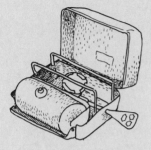

Optimus 8R (white gas)

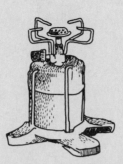

GAZ Bluet S-200 (cartridge)

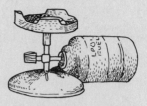

Hank Roberts Mini
(cartridge)

Big stoves for big groups, 4-season

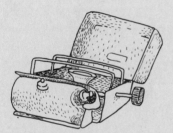

Optimus 111B (white gas)

Optimus 00 (kerosene)

GENERAL SAFETY PRECAUTIONS WHEN USING STOVES

Follow the directions that come with the stove.

Practice at home with a new stove before first using it on a trip.

Use only the fuel specified for that stove.

Before using the stove, clear a space in case spilled fuel is lighted accidentally.

Level the stove, using a small stick or other handy object.

Have the food, water, and pots ready before lighting your cookpiece. Do not leave a burning stove unattended.

Do not use big, overhanging pots on the Optimus 111B or 8R, to avoid over-heating problems.

Do not refuel a hot stove.

Keep the air space around cartridges free. Do not block ventilation by building an extensive windscreen, or by trying to hold up a big pot with rocks.

Screw fuel cartridges in completely. Feel the cartridges periodically to see if they're hot. If they do feel hot, turn the stove off immediately.

Spilled white gas is flammable. Try not to spill it.

Never light a stove inside your tent.

If inclement weather forces you to use the stove inside your tent, light it out-side, then take it in. *Be sure to ventilate properly!* Carbon monoxide, a by-product of burning gas, will kill you: it does not give warning signals such as a funny smell, nor does it affect your senses before you keel over.

Keep your stove clean and in good working order. Carry spare parts if that seems indicated.

COOKING TIPS FOR STOVES

A stove has room for only one pot at a time, in contrast to a wood fire, over which you can set two pots. Juggling cookpots to produce a two-pot meal over one stove can be less of a problem than you might think, however.

For instance, with a pasta meal, first heat up the sauce. Then let it sit, allowing its flavors to intermingle and "marinate," while you cook the pasta in another pot. Then reheat the sauce briefly, while you drain the pasta, and it will taste better than it would have at first heating. (Directions for one-pot pasta dishes are on page 199.)

There are a few things you can do to get water to boil faster. Cover the pot, and refrain from adding salt, which does *not* make water boil faster. A good windscreen is indispensable in most situations. And water will boil faster in a black pot than in one unsullied by soot, as the black absorbs heat. (Mountain Safety Research in Seattle [see page 274] makes black pots; you can make your own black pots by not scrubbing them off after cooking over a fire.)

Most of the recipes in this book can be cooked on a backpacking stove. One exception is a meal like jerky stew, whose cooking time stretches into an hour; in some situations or over certain stoves, it would be impractical to keep a stove going for an hour. (The Peak I, however, could easily manage the hour's simmer required; and one relaxed weekend when fuel was plenteous, we even cooked jerky stew over a Svea, which is like cooking over a Bunsen burner.)

Nor can you grill with much *élan* over a stove.

But, while the essential function of a stove should be to boil water as fast as possible, you can do quite a bit of fancy cooking over even the most intractable little powerhouse, when you keep two things in mind.

Unless the stove was designed to distribute heat generously under the surface of your pot, you'll need to shift the pot around in order not to burn one spot while the others languish uncooked. (Since some badly designed home stove burners present the same problem, you might already be very good at this.) This adaptive technique is especially valuable when cooking with a frying pan—pan breads, stir-fry dinners, and fish for example.

Second, realize that there is another way to turn the heat down besides twisting a knob (or having the wind blow the flame out). Like the photographer who compensates for dim light by opening the lens or by slowing the shutter speed, you can simply lift the pot away from the heat for a moment; or, with a little exquisite patience, *hold* it off the flame when you see that scorching is imminent. Do this especially when making a roux for white sauce or when making pudding.

As you learn to handle the cookpot cleverly over nonadjustable heat, you will increase your cooking repertoire. It will grow to include pancakes, omelets, puddings, pilafs, curries, stir-fry dinners, pan-fried trout, and biscuits. It will open up new vistas of international cuisine and reintroduce home dishes you hadn't considered as wilderness fare. It will, in short, let you *cook* in the wildest kitchen imaginable—what a discovery!

WOOD FIRES

What to pack   When you plan to do all your cooking over a wood fire, you need to bring only a grill and matches. The grill needs to be packed in a sturdy plastic bag to keep the inside of your pack from acquiring that unwanted charred look and greasy feel; and the matches need to be kept dry. I confess to carrying a small lighter, as well, for insurance.

The basic backpacker's grill offered in stores and catalogs is

a $6 nickel-plated, free-standing device whose supports will fold under it for flat packing. It weighs 12 ounces, stands 6 inches high, and is 13 inches long, which is long enough to accommodate two pots at once over a longish fire.

Another possibility for a grill design is one you work out yourself, starting with two cake-cooling racks which you can buy in the hardware store. These are cheaper and lighter than the "formal" grill. At camp, set the racks on six rocks of similar size, or on two logs. The racks may end up closer to the fire than six inches, but they will still work very nicely.

Suspending pots over a fire involves using downed wood, which is not available everywhere, and certainly not to be used in popular camping areas—which have probably long since been denuded of foliage anyway. Although I am no advocate of fancy woodcraft in most situations, it is still possible to use it ethically in areas where downed wood really abounds and you're not going to disturb the landscape by borrowing some.

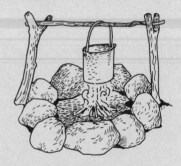

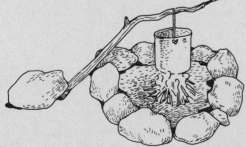

A pot can be suspended over a fire if it has an over-the-lid handle. Put through the handle a stick which you have (a) suspended between two forked sticks at either side of the fire, or (b) stuck into the ground at an angle and held down with a big rock. The big-rock arrangement is a little riskier for pot stability, but it is a handy technique to have in the back of your mind in case you find yourself for some reason suddenly without stove or grill.

A third way to suspend pots over a fire is by means of a tripod. Find three long sticks (4- or 5-foot-high poles) and lash them together at the top to make a tepee. From the lashing, suspend a chain with an S-hook at the end of it, and hang a pot or two from the S-hook.

How to build a fire   The popular image of the campfire is of a huge blazing tepee of eagerly burning thick logs. A good cookfire, on the other hand, is a compact, efficient steady conflagration of rather small sticks—the biggest not much thicker than your thumb. These usually are obtained from whole downed (*only* downed and dead) branches that have been hauled into camp and broken into 12-inch lengths. A good cooking fire is longer than it is wide, if you want to set two pots over it, and is kept steadily stoked from each end.

Before starting a fire, collect tinder and wood, to have it ready. Clear a space about three feet square of all leaves, twigs, and needles so that your fire will stay in its own safe spot. If possible, surround your fireplace with rocks as further insurance of safety.

If the day is windy and the forest tinder-dry, don't build a fire at all. Rather than unleash a series of devilish sparks upon the innocent landscape, use a stove or eat a cold supper.

In conditions of extreme wet, you can still get a fire going if you have much dry tinder and exquisite patience—but here again a stove will be a welcome sight as you pull it out of your pack.

Fallen birch bark makes the best tinder (*never* peel trees), followed closely in conflagration potential by dry pine needles, dead grass, dead leaves, and paper. Over a core of tinder, build a tepee out of the tiniest dead sticks you can find. Add some slightly larger sticks, still keeping the tepee shape. Being sure more wood is handy, light the tinder from the upwind side, blowing on it a little if necessary to enlarge the flame; only begin to add more sticks, gradually working up into the larger sizes, when the fire is going nicely. (Some of the more talented fire tenders I have known love to sit and make neat heaps of various-size sticks. Such people are ideal trail companions, whose interest in backpacking should be carefully nurtured.)

Extinguishing a fire   We have all been admonished tirelessly to put our fires out before we leave a campsite or retire into our tent for the night. To that earnest chorus I will add my voice, with the practical note that, if you are short of water, dirt will help to smother the fire. But truly *suffocate* it, and stamp around to extinguish any stubborn sparks.

Fire cooking tips   As with a very hot stove, hold the pot off the heat if you need to for a moment when the fire gets too hot. The flame of a wood fire will vary in intensity depending on the dedication of its stoker. In other words, be flexible yourself in light of the inflexibility or unpredictability of a fire, and you can turn out a very successful white sauce or pan of biscuits.

To "bake" over a fire, see page 175.

The hot coals left after a well-tended fire has burned down are excellent for cooking in. Foil-wrapped fish and vegetables or a covered pan of camp bread cooks beautifully when pushed into a bed of hot coals.

Soot-blackened pots supposedly are an unwelcome contribution to the inside of one's pack. Several recourses are available. You can ignore the problem by ignoring the black, which is what I do. Or, if you are more fastidious, you could pack all pots in plastic bags.

I have also been admonished by accomplished young trail fellows to soap the bottom of a pan before putting it over a fire. Then, they say, I can just wipe off soap and soot afterward, and pack the pot, pristine, into my clean pack, without a second thought. Well, I have a few second thoughts. I would have to bring extra soap and extra paper towels; I would have to burn the used soapy-black paper towels in the fire, if it hadn't been extinguished by dishwashing time, or pack them out or to the next campfire, if it had. I put up with sooty pots.

Besides, in a black pot, water boils faster.

2

GETTING READY

Home food drying/Dried foods you can buy/Valuable foods in the wild kitchen/Bake-ahead bread, cakes, and cookies

HOME FOOD DRYING

Dried foods are the mainstay of the wilderness menu. The backpacker, already familiar with raisins, jerky, herbs, hard tack, and leathers, is always eager to try new dried foods.

But commercial sources (except for the "ethnic" ones which rely on centuries of drying practices) are unreliable as well as expensive. Anyone who has bitten into a dried peach and found himself with a mouthful of chemicals (bringing to mind the famous query "Do I dare to eat a peach?") knows the perils of depending on store-bought dried fare. The sulfur employed to preserve the color of dried fruits ruins their taste. A freeze-dried dinner can cost nearly $3 per serving and taste little better than cardboard. And who knows the food value of something which is unidentifiable by the time it's been frozen, dried, and vacuum-packed?

The best way to have dried foods is to dry them yourself. Home food drying is one of those ancient practices, like quilting and bread baking, that is coming back into fashion. It is quiet, it uses little or no auxiliary power, it is aesthetically pleasing, and easy. The fact that it cannot be rushed, as quilting and bread baking cannot be rushed, further endears it to backpackers, whose favorite mode of travel in the jet age is walking.

Home drying expands the wilderness menu to include any kind of favorite fruit or vegetable. Flavorful, *real* stews are possible in the remotest woods. Dried homemade meat sauces made from ground meat and seasonings can be reconstituted and heated up in ten minutes; if flour has been added, they'll make their own gravy. Puréed fruits, dried into leathers, make ideal snacks. The range of foods that can be dried to use for backpacking is great, and the equipment needed and the process of preparing them are minimal.

All you need are access to a good market (if you haven't got a home garden), a tiny corner of space, and a simple dryer to put in it. Your oven comes in very handy too. In other words, you could dry foods in a studio apartment or even in a college dormitory room. Most foods need no pretreatment, but if you choose to use one, you are in control of what benign, or beneficent, additives there are, like vitamin C, lemon juice, honey, or salt. Drying removes almost none of a food's nutrients, in contrast to canning and freezing.

Home drying also means an amply stocked cupboard of food when you most need it, the night before leaving. We're all familiar with the last-minute crises involving cotter pins, tent stakes, moleskin, maps, boots, rain gear, bug juice, Band-Aids, lens filters, and the possibility of leaking feathers. When equipment matters are threatening to crowd out gastronomic concerns, it is nice to have your own mixes and dried meals at hand so you do not have to depend on store-bought convenience items.

Much drying can be done in the regular course of home cooking. For example, when making spaghetti sauce, you can double the recipe and dry the extra half, removing it from the dinner half before you add water. It isn't any trouble to brown a pound of hamburger while cooking dinner, to drain it, and put it into the oven to dry overnight. Thick soups and leftovers all lend themselves to drying and can be set aside as you have them. Meanwhile, your little dryer can be steadfastly rendering sliced fruits and vegetables packable and delicious, and drying as much jerky as you can eat.

What happens to a food when you dry it?   It will lose between 95 and 75 percent of its water, depending on what it is, and weigh $\frac{1}{12}$ to $\frac{1}{2}$ of its original weight. Dried food keeps because bacteria which cause spoilage can't grow in a dry medium. The enzymes in the food might continue to be active, though, which causes discoloring in some fruits; this can be avoided by dipping them in one of several possible solutions.

What are the optimum conditions for drying food?   The food itself should be in excellent condition. The temperature of the drying agent (dryer or oven) should be between 100 and 140 degrees. The air should circulate. Food should be easy to get at so that it can be checked. It should be easily removable from the racks or pans upon which it is dried.

To get these conditions, we advance slightly beyond the ancients, who laid foods in the sun or over the fire in cave, igloo, or tepee, to the wonders of the light bulb and the oven.

THREE WAYS TO DRY FOOD

A simple food dryer   The drawing and accompanying instructions on the opposite page are for a homemade dryer that can be made easily by the home carpenter.

It's a simple dryer without a thermostat or a fan. Using a 200-watt bulb, it generates a temperature of 100° F., and it can dry fruits, vegetables, meats, and herbs. It is inexpensive to build and to run; the total cost of the materials is about $30.

Because small-cut foods will fall through its metal cake-cooling racks, you need to lay such foods on cheesecloth. Another answer to this problem is to make your own racks out of screens in wood frames. In that case, you could change the dimensions of the dryer—but if you expanded the drying space by very much you would also have to add more light bulbs to provide enough heat. The temperature should not fall below 100° F. (Use an oven thermometer to measure it.)

If you want to buy a dryer, plan to spend $100 or more. Since dryers are not (yet) common household items, you probably won't be able to walk into your neighborhood department store and pick one out.

The dimensions of this dryer will fit the kind of metal racks that you cool cakes on, that is, 10½-inch square racks. Buy the racks first, and if they are a different size, adjust the dryer's dimensions accordingly, allowing ⅛-inch clearance for the racks on the sides.

Materials may be freely substituted.

Do not paint.

Directions:

1. Read the drawing and become familiar with the dryer parts and their positions.

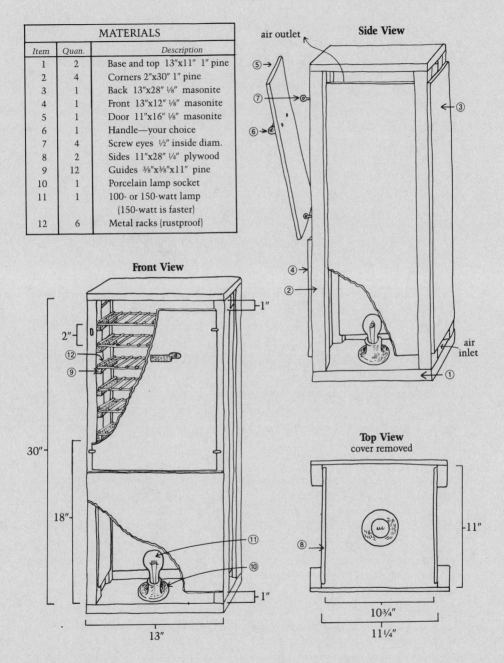

MATERIALS		
Item	*Quan.*	*Description*
1	2	Base and top 13″x11″ 1″ pine
2	4	Corners 2″x30″ 1″ pine
3	1	Back 13″x28″ ⅛″ masonite
4	1	Front 13″x12″ ⅛″ masonite
5	1	Door 11″x16″ ⅛″ masonite
6	1	Handle—your choice
7	4	Screw eyes ½″ inside diam.
8	2	Sides 11″x28″ ¼″ plywood
9	12	Guides ⅜″x⅜″x11″ pine
10	1	Porcelain lamp socket
11	1	100- or 150-watt lamp
		(150-watt is faster)
12	6	Metal racks (rustproof)

Side View

air outlet

Front View

2″

30″

18″

13″

1″

1″

Top View
cover removed

air
inlet

10¾″

11¼″

11″

2. Construct the base and top (item 1) by cutting two pieces of 1-inch pine to 13 by 11 inches.
3. Cut out the two sides (item 8) by cutting two pieces of $\frac{1}{4}$-inch plywood to 11 by 28 inches.
4. Cut out the four corners (item 2).
5. Cut out the front, back, and door (items 3, 4, and 5) from Masonite or $\frac{1}{4}$-inch plywood.
6. Cut rack guides (item 9) from $\frac{3}{8}$- or $\frac{1}{2}$-inch square stock.
7. Using the dimensions on the drawing, glue and nail rack guides to the inside of the sides.
8. Glue and nail the corners (item 2) to the outside of the sides. (*Note:* the corners must extend 1 inch beyond the top and bottom of the sides, to allow for air passageways.)
9. Mount the lamp socket (item 10) in the center of the base (item 1).
10. Nail and glue the sides to the top and bottom of the dryer. Wood screws are excellent to secure the top and bottom to the corner pieces.
11. Nail and glue the back and front to the side corners. Remember to leave the 1-inch air passages on the top and bottom.
12. Install $\frac{1}{2}$-inch screw eyes on the front corners and install the door. (Turn the eyes to hold the door in place.)
13. Place the racks in the dryer and plug a 200-watt light bulb in the socket.

The area of this dryer is $4\frac{1}{2}$ square feet, which may be small for your needs. Other food dryers, which can be bought through the mail, are:

Waring Dehydrator. Electric; has a circular design, five trays; a fan forces 140° F. air upward from the base. Cost: about $75. Bazaar de la Cuisine, Inc., 1003 Second Avenue, New York, NY 10022.

Equiflow Dehydrator. The air flow is horizontal and is between 80° and 140° F. Ten trays in a 15-by-15-inch frame have 14 square feet of drying space. (There are also models available with 5 and 41 square feet of drying space.) Cost of the middle model: about $200. Burpee Seed Company, Warminster, PA 18991; Clinton, IO 52732; and Riverside, CA 92502.

Solar Food Dryer. Uses natural convection, is solar-powered, and can be used in a sunny inside area. Cost: from $152 to $358. Stow-A-Way, 166 Cushing Highway, Cohasset, MA 02025.

Excalibur Dehydrator. Has a thermostat, a fan, and a recirculating device to reuse warm air and vent moisture-filled air; 12 square feet of drying area. Cost: $149. Stow-A-Way (see above).

The oven   As a complement to the simple dryer, use the oven to dry foods that need to be spread in a shallow pan, like fruit for leathers, soups, sauces, groundbeef dishes, canned beans, and puréed vegetables.

Grease a flat pan—a cookie sheet or a pizza pan with low sides—and spread the food out in as thin a layer as possible. Set the oven temperature at its lowest setting, 140° F. Set the pan in the middle of the oven, open the door a little,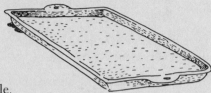
and put a utensil, like a large spoon, crosswise to hold it open. This will let the air circulate. Foods will take 6 to 8 hours to dry this way, which means that you can dry them overnight and avoid tying up the oven during the day when you might need it.

The sun   Sunshine, of course, is the time-honored drying agent—if you live in a climate that supplies lots of it. When you dry food outside, put it on racks or screens so that air can circulate around it, and, if necessary, protect it from insects and pets. Bring incompletely dried food inside at night, if you expect dew, rain, or marauders.

BASIC EQUIPMENT NEEDED FOR DRYING

A sharp knife   The thinner you slice food to be dried, the quicker it will dry and the quicker it will cook on the trail. The best knife to use for slicing food is a large (10-inch) chopping knife made of high carbon steel that will take and keep a truly sharp edge.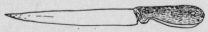
(A sharpening steel is an essential companion.) It is an expensive purchase, but such a knife is really an essential part of a good cook's kitchen, and it will earn its keep.

A cutting board   This should be 9 by 13 inches at least.

Cheesecloth   Unless your dryer racks are screened, you'll need cheesecloth to keep tiny foods from falling through the racks.

Scale   Use a kitchen scale, a cast-off postal scale, even a small letter scale of the type found in stationery stores.

Pans   Flat pans like cookie sheets and pizza pans with rims are necessary to dry purées and other food mixtures in the oven.

Nonstick spray   Although greasing pans with shortening or margarine works well, using spray is faster when you've decided to fit a little pre-backpacking cooking into the course of regular dinner preparation.

Paper and pen   Keep a pen and a stack of small pieces of paper handy for labeling dried foods as you package them. To be really organized, make up labels ahead of time that look something like this:

| DATE |
| FOOD |
| TRAIL DIRECTIONS |
| NO. OF SERVINGS |

Storage containers   Plastic bags, jars, clear plastic wrap for leathers.

Blender, food mill, or potato masher   For puréeing foods.

DRYING VEGETABLES

Vegetables are easy to dry. Mostly they need no pretreatment—only to be scrubbed, possibly peeled, and cut thin. The chart on pages 36–7 lists individual vegetables, and it's not an exhaustive list; for example, I haven't tried to dry okra yet. Experiment with your own favorite vegetables.

Tiny vegetables—peas, sliced mushrooms—have to be dried on a piece of cheesecloth to keep them from falling through the dryer racks.

When you have a choice of how to cut a vegetable, think of how you might use it. Julienned vegetables are excellent in stir-fry dishes. Carrot "flakes," which you can make with a grater or a vegetable peeler and then cut into smaller pieces, are good for stews, soups, and lentils dishes. Sliced vegetables are good in stews.

Note that peas and green beans are better dried after blanching, and that potatoes should be dipped briefly in lemon juice and water to keep them from discoloring.

To cook dried vegetables on the trail, see Chapter 5, page 245.

How to purée and dry squash   Dry a butternut squash—that plain-looking tan-skinned winter squash—and be prepared for a stunning metamorphosis. You lift from a round pan a golden filigree medallion, which is too delicious, however, to remain in a purely aesthetic capacity for long. It reconstitutes into a tasty purée in a few quick minutes, and it makes an excellent soup and a tasty snack. Cut a medium squash (about 2 pounds), unpeeled, into about 8 or 10 pieces, discarding the seeds and fibers. Drop the pieces into a large pot of boiling water and simmer for 20 to 25 minutes, until tender. Drain  and cool them, then peel and mash with a potato masher or a fork. Season with 2 teaspoons Butter Buds or 2 tablespoons butter, and a generous pinch of salt. Spray flat pans with nonstick spray and spread the squash out in a thin continuous layer. Dry it in a 140° F. oven for 6 to 8 hours, leaving the door propped open. This will make 4 to 6 servings when reconstituted with an equal amount of water. (See page 248; and see page 161 for Squash Soup.)

Note: When you dry a huge squash (3½ pounds), it will make 4 cups of mashed squash before you dry it; then you'll have enough for both snacks (simply eat the dried squash plain) and a hot dinner vegetable.

VEGETABLES THAT CAN BE DRIED STRAIGHT OUT OF THE CAN

Tomato paste   Dried tomato paste, or tomato "leather," is good to add to stew or soup for flavoring. It can be used as the basis for a camp-made tomato sauce (see page 203).

To make a tomato leather, spread canned tomato paste over a greased cookie sheet to a depth of no more than ¼ inch, and set it in the oven at the lowest setting (140° F.). Prop the door open slightly and leave the tomato paste for 6 hours or until you can pull the dried paste from the pan and roll it up. *Be very careful not to overdry a tomato leather* as that will result in a strong, rather unpleasant taste. Wrap the roll in clear plastic wrap.

This leather will turn back into tomato paste when you add water to it. For each can of dried paste, add 2 cups of water. The tomato leather is as handy as powdered bouillon for flavoring meals: tear off small hunks as you need them.

Concentrated tomato paste can be bought in a tube, like toothpaste. It is very convenient, but expensive. Also, I've tasted some that had an "off" flavor.

Dried canned beans   Drain a 16-ounce can of navy, kidney, pinto, or black beans. (A good brand to use is Goya.) Either mash the beans with a potato masher or leave them whole.

Consider drying mashed beans after you cook them in a little garlic first: Lightly sauté 2 cloves finely chopped garlic in 2 tablespoons oil. Fry the mashed beans, turning once to cook the other side, over medium heat. Season to taste with salt and pepper.

Spread the beans on a greased flat pan and dry in the oven at 140° F. with the door propped open a crack, for 6 to 8 hours, until they are crumbly. Pack in a plastic bag, labeled "Refried Beans. Reconstitute with an equal amount of water."

See page 221 for Burritos recipe, and pages 238–9 and 160 for other bean recipes.

See page 237 to cook dry beans and then dry them.

Vegetable Drying Chart

(Drying time varies between 12 and 14 hours)

	Pretreatment	*If properly dried*	*Amount fresh and dried*
Beets	Peel, slice thin	Curled and leathery	1 pound = ³⁄₄ cup
Butternut squash	Cut, cook, peel, and purée *(page 35)*	Dry, like filigree	1 medium squash = ¹⁄₂ cup
Cabbage	Slice thin	Wispy	1 small head (1¹⁄₂ pound) = 1 cup
Carrots	Slice lengthwise or julienne; or grate, then chop fine for carrot flakes	Leathery, still orange; somewhat curled	6 carrots = 1 cup

	Pretreatment	*If properly dried*	*Amount fresh and dried*
Celery	Slice	Very dry and shrunken	1 bunch = 1 cup
Corn	Cook in boiling water 2 minutes, cut kernels off ears	Hard, pebbly; slightly darker	Corn from 6 ears = 1 cup
Eggplant	Peel, slice thin	Pale and leathery, very light	1 medium eggplant = 1 cup
Green beans	Cook in boiling water 10 minutes	Shrunken and leathery but not brown	1 pound = 1 cup
Green pepper	Slice thin	Shriveled but still green and pliable	2 green peppers (1 pound) = 1 cup
Kohlrabi	Peel, slice thin	Curled and leathery	1 pound = $\frac{3}{4}$ cup
Leeks	Wash well, slice well up into the green part	Like parchment; not brittle	1 medium leek = 1 cup
Mushrooms	Wash well, slice thin	Crinkled, but not too shrunken	1 pound = $1\frac{3}{4}$ cup
Parsley	Chop	Dry, almost powdery	1 bunch = $\frac{1}{2}$ cup
Parsnips	Peel, slice lengthwise or julienne	Dry and leathery	1 pound = $\frac{3}{4}$ cup
Peas	Cook in boiling water 10 minutes	Hard as pebbles	1 package frozen peas = $\frac{2}{3}$ cup
Potatoes	Slice and soak for no more than 10 minutes in lemon juice dip *(page 35)*	Will almost crack in two	1 pound = $\frac{3}{4}$ cup
Tomatoes	Slice "through equator" and coat with olive oil	Leathery and still red	$\frac{3}{4}$ pound = 1 cup
Turnips	Peel, slice thin	Curled, dry, and leathery	1 pound = $\frac{3}{4}$ cup
Yellow summer squash	Slice across or lengthwise	Curled edges, leathery; not brown	1 medium squash = $\frac{1}{3}$ cup
Zucchini	Slice across or lengthwise	Curled edges, leathery; not brown	1 medium squash = $\frac{1}{2}$ cup

DRYING FRUIT

Fruit to be dried should be ripe but in very good condition: it shouldn't be bruised or mushy.

Some fruits can be dried simply by peeling them if necessary, slicing them, and laying them on the dryer racks:

apples	berries and cherries	pineapple
figs	lemon and orange peel	

You may prefer to dip certain fruits into a solution of either salt, ascorbic acid, or fruit juice to keep them from discoloring:

apricots	peaches	pears

A honey dip will make these fruits into sweet snacks:

rhubarb	apricots	strawberries
bananas	pineapple	

The dips, which I have borrowed from *Garden Way's Guide to Food Drying* by Phyllis Hobson, are:

Salt dip   Dissolve 6 tablespoons salt in 1 gallon lukewarm water. Allow the sliced fruit to stay in this solution no more than 5 minutes.

Ascorbic acid dip   Dissolve 5 grams of vitamin C tablets (this would be ten 500-mg tablets or 2 tablespoons vitamin C crystals or powder) into 1 quart of lukewarm water. Slice the fruit into this solution and let it sit no more than 5 minutes, then remove and drain this batch and add a new one.

Fruit juice dip   Add ¼ cup lemon juice to 1 quart lukewarm water. Or use undiluted pineapple juice as a dip.

Honey dip   Dissolve 1 cup sugar in 3 cups hot water. Cool to lukewarm, then stir in 1 cup honey. Using a slotted spoon, dip the fruit into the solution, then drain it well.

FRUIT LEATHERS

A fruit leather is a cooked purée of a single fruit or of some combination, which has been dried.

Applesauce is the easiest—you can dry canned applesauce as your first leather—though homemade applesauce is far tastier.

First coat with nongrease spray a cookie sheet or a pizza pan with rim. Spread the applesauce over the bottom surface of the pan to a depth of no more than ¼ inch. Set the pan in the oven at the lowest temperature, propping the door to stay open a crack, for 6 to 8 hours. Pull the dried fruit from the pan, roll it up, and wrap the roll in clear plastic wrap. A fruit roll should keep for 6 months in the cupboard, and much longer if you refrigerate it.

Making your own fruit purées is very easy, using a food mill, a blender, or a potato masher.

Cut the fruit into pieces without peeling it. Take the pits out of peaches, plums, and apricots. Cook the fruit in water to cover until soft but not mushy, for 15 to 20 minutes. Then purée it, using one of the above three utensils. Flavor the purée to taste with sugar, honey, lemon, or cinnamon. You might want to combine it, too, with another fruit—like blueberries with peaches, or applesauce with plums, pineapple, pears, or strawberries. The possible combinations are wonderfully various. Then dry the purée as described for applesauce.

DRYING MEATS

Beef jerky It may surprise you to learn how easy it is to make jerky. But then, when you think that our progenitors must have made a lot of jerky every time they killed animals too big or too plentiful to eat all at once, like bears or buffalo or whales, the idea of jerky loses in complexity what it gains in mystique.

Eat jerky plain as a snack. Grind it up and combine it with dried fruit for pemmican (an Indian food). Grill it over the fire, cook it for stew, stir-fry it, or invent some other use for it; it can't be beat for travelability and taste. It is a protein staple in the wilderness diet.

Homemade jerky not only tastes better than the store-bought stuff, it is extraordinarily less expensive.

To make jerky, take a raw piece of beef round or chuck, quite lean, and slice it thin, across the grain. Lay the slices across the racks of the dryer for two days and nights and then test it by breaking a piece. It is dry enough if it cracks in two when you break it.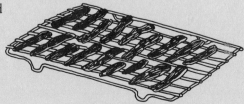

The smaller and thinner you cut

the pieces of meat before drying them, the quicker they will get tender as you soak and cook them. If your use for jerky will be primarily as a snack, all you have to do is slice it very thin. But for a stew or a stir-fry, cut beef into very thin strips, 3 or 4 inches long. It is much easier, incidentally, to slice beef or any meat when it's partially frozen.

One pound of sliced beef dries to 4 ounces of jerky, making a ratio of undried to dried meat of about 4 to 1.

Before drying the meat, you can season it with some combination of the following spices: paprika, pepper, salt, or other concoctions like "lemon pepper" or seasoned salt. Garlic is wonderful on jerky; I recommend rubbing the meat with cut cloves of garlic before slicing it. (Garlic "powder" is an unsatisfactory substitute.)

A marinade will change the taste slightly and cause the meat to take longer to dry. Marinating tenderizes the meat, however—acid, in soy sauce and wine, the principal ingredients of the two marinades that follow, breaks down the tissues of the meat. Remember that drying will intensify whatever flavors you soak the meat in.

A Simple Marinade for Beef Jerky

For 3 pounds of lean beef:

2 tablespoons soy sauce
¼ teaspoon salt
2 drops of Tabasco, or cayenne
    pepper to taste

Ground pepper
1 fresh clove garlic, minced

Slice the beef across the grain as thin as you can.

Mix the marinade ingredients, put the meat in the mixture, and refrigerate (or keep it somewhere at about 50° F.) for at least 12 hours, 2 days if possible.

Pat the meat dry and set it on the dryer racks for 2 or 3 days. It's dried enough if a piece will snap in two when you bend it.

Wine Marinade for Beef Jerky

For 2 pounds of lean beef (chuck, round, or sirloin):

½ cup red wine
1 tablespoon red wine vinegar
1 tablespoon olive oil
2 fresh cloves garlic, minced
2 tablespoons minced onion

1 bay leaf
Ground pepper
Pinch each of thyme, oregano, and
marjoram

Slice the beef across the grain as thin as you can.

Mix the marinade ingredients, put the meat in the mixture, and refrigerate (or keep it somewhere at about 50° F.) for at least 12 hours, 2 days if possible.

The meat is dried enough if a piece will snap in two when you bend it.

Note: Before stir-frying jerky, soak it 30 minutes. Before using it in a stew, soak it as long as you can—at least an hour.

I am reminded here to urge you to pack dental floss or toothpicks when you carry jerky. A piece of sinew lodged stubbornly between your teeth will cause considerable discomfort. (I began to wonder what the Indians used for toothpicks—porcupine quills? bone splinters?—and not long after happened to browse through Caswell-Massey, a fancy soap emporium in midtown Manhattan, which claims to be "Manhattan's oldest pharmacy." There I spied individual goose-quill toothpicks, each wrapped in its own paper wrapper, and straightaway considered these a clue in the great Indian toothpick question.)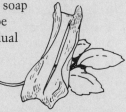

Ground beef   To increase your supply of dried foods for happier last-minute packing, brown a pound or two of hamburger while you are making dinner at home. Then drain its fat off and dry it for 6 to 8 hours or overnight in the oven at 140° F. Label it and store it in the refrigerator. One pound of ground beef dries to 6 ounces, about 1⅓ cups.

Other ground meats, like lamb, pork, or veal, can be dried similarly.

Note: Although in normal cooking some fat in the meat adds flavor to a recipe, it's important to get rid of fat when drying ground meats; the fat might become rancid before the meat itself spoils. Pour the fat off after the meat has browned; or refrigerate the browned meat, fat and all, whereupon the fat rises to the top and you lift it off.

By flavoring the meat and adding a little flour, you can make a delicious dried mix that is the basis for several quick trail dinners (see pages 195–8).

Sliced cooked pressed beef   Like the chipped beef we used to have when we were kids, this salty sliced beef that you buy in 2½-ounce packages in the lunchmeat section of the supermarket tastes very good with white sauce, or mixed with gravy on mashed potatoes.

But it still must be dried further for backpacking purposes. A package typically contains 13 slices, which are thin enough to dry overnight in the food dryer or within 6 hours in the oven (at 140° F. with the door propped open—spread the slices on a cookie sheet). Crumble the dried slices to make about ¼ cup, enough to serve 2 or 3, as in Creamed Chipped Beef and Mashed Potatoes (see page 186). See also Quick Beef Hash (page 185) and Pemmican (page 151).

You can carry this meat undried, in its original package, for a day or so, but like other lunchmeats, except hard salami, it doesn't keep well.

Bacon   There is simply no comparison in flavor between commercial "bacon bits," which aren't bacon at all (are they food?) and your own home-dried product, which is. You can store dried bacon in the refrigerator or freezer until you are ready to use it. Dried bacon keeps well on the trail. It is excellent flavoring for many foods.

To dry bacon, chop a pound or ½ pound into small pieces with a sharp knife. Fry these in a big pan until crisp, then drain well on paper towels. (It's easiest to remove them from the pan with a slotted spoon.) Dry for as long as you'd dry jerky, about 2 days in the dryer or 6 to 8 hours in the oven. The pieces will be brittle when dry enough.

One pound of bacon dries to 1 cup of bacon pieces.

FREEZE-DRIED MEATS

Chicken   Chicken needs to be cooked before drying, and drying toughens it so much that even after soaking for an hour you can still hardly chew it. Rich-Moor comes to the rescue with a freeze-dried diced chicken, not a match for "the real thing," but much more convenient for trail cooking.

Freeze-dried chicken is tender after only 10 minutes' cooking, needs no soaking, and has no additives. Saluting Rich-Moor for this coup, I gratefully spend $2.19 per 1¼-ounce package, which contains about ½ cup and will suffice, for example in Chicken à la King, to feed 4 to 6. *Note:* For a short haul in cool weather, leftover sliced chicken or turkey is excellent.

Freeze-dried beef Rich-Moor freeze-dried diced beef is also easy to cook and free of additives, when scarcity of time and fuel make cooking jerky impossible. Cost is $1.99 per 1-ounce package.

Ham Ham is easy to dry at home in the dryer, but it too needs to be soaked an hour to soften it before using. Most hams contain preservatives, and some are rather salty, and the flavors of whatever they are preserved in intensify upon drying. The freeze-dried product, again, is handy on the trail, as it needs no soaking when you cook it 10 minutes. Rich-Moor's freeze-dried ham costs $2.29 per 1¾ ounces.

Note: Write to Rich-Moor Corporation, P.O. Box 2728, Van Nuys, CA 91404, ask for a catalog, and tell them you want plain dried meats. They will write back to say you can only buy their things in stores and send you a list of retailers for your area; more correspondence will ensue. If enough of this goes on, hopefully retailers may begin to carry more of the useful plain meat items, as well as the whole dinners which presently crowd the plain foods off the shelves.

TESTING DRIED FOODS

Since different dried foods are bereft of differing degrees of moisture, they do not all exhibit the same characteristics, and the test that applies to one will not apply to another.

In general, however, here is what to look for:

vegetables—Rather than brittleness, aim generally for a leathery texture in sliced vegetables. "Whole" small vegetables like peas and corn should be hard, like pebbles. (See the chart on pages 36–7.)

purées and leathers—These darken slightly as they dry, and when they are dry enough, they pull easily off the pan. It is best to store them in the refrigerator.

meat—Jerky will be brittle and crack when broken; ground beef should be dry and crumbly; poultry should look dry and crumble into a powder around the edges when jostled.

stews with ground beef, and other make-ahead meals—Dry these until they are crumbly. Put them on paper towels to cool if they seem greasy after drying, and store them in the refrigerator.

fruits—In general, these will be still pliable when dried. If separate pieces do not stick to each other, they are probably dry enough. Berries should be brittle, like pebbles, as should banana chips and orange peel.

It is safer to over- than to underdry; but another way to ensure that the food will keep well is to store it in the refrigerator or the freezer. If you see any signs of spoiling in a batch of dried food (like mold) or if it smells funny, throw out the whole batch.

Generally, dried foods will keep up to six months in the refrigerator. They'll keep at least a month at room temperature if properly dried, and many will keep longer.

LABELING DRIED FOODS

Label each food with name and date—immediately. (Sometimes it's hard to identify a dried food.)

Add trail directions to make-ahead meals. For example, label a batch of pasta sauce like this:

> 1 cup meat sauce
> Add 1 cup water and cook 10 minutes.
> Serve with $\frac{1}{2}$ pound pasta, cooked 7 minutes.
> Serves 3 or 4.
> Date _____

Another way to label is simply to note the proportions of water you'll need to mix in. Do this when packing for a solo trip, or for any trip on which you would be repeatedly dipping nightly into the same batch of mix rather than making up a different dinner for each night. In this case, your directions might read:

> Shepherd's Pie (total 2 cups)
> Add an equal part of water and cook 10 minutes.
> $\frac{1}{3}$ cup mix plus $\frac{1}{3}$ cup water = 1 serving
> Serve with $\frac{1}{3}$ cup rice cooked 15 minutes in $\frac{2}{3}$ cup water—for 1 serving.
> Date _____

PACKAGING

Package dried vegetables, meats, and meals in plastic bags. Fruit leathers are best wrapped in clear plastic wrap. However, if you store food on shelves where mice or insects might get at it, put it into airtight jars and repackage it at trail time.

I like to store meats and meat-based things in the refrigerator, where I have set aside a special section just for dried things. One of the advantages of this part of the refrigerator is how good it looks to me at 6:30 at night after a particularly pressing day: backpacking food, luckily, can be as adaptable to the home kitchen as home food is to the wild one.

In order to keep a dried food indefinitely, store it in the freezer. Label it well, and don't forget it's there.

Note: A good way to keep track of the food you've dried is to keep a running list taped to the inside of a cupboard door—add and cross off items to keep it up-to-date.

DRIED FOODS YOU CAN BUY

ORIENTAL

Dried Oriental mushrooms   In contrast to the sliced pale mushrooms that you dry yourself, pretty as they are, the dried Oriental mushroom shouts, "I am a mushroom!" even when it comes in a plastic package.
It has a wonderful pungent flavor and will enhance any dish with its woodsy taste. For the cook who loves mushrooms but who approaches all wild ones with circumspect terror, dried Oriental mushrooms are ideal wilderness food. Soak them for half an hour until they are soft enough to cut or chew, and you should cut the tough stems off before cooking. Dried mushrooms are excellent in stir-fry dinners and as the base for a mushroom pasta sauce. Of course, they can be thrown into most soups and stews. (While the recipes refer to dried Oriental varieties, you can substitute any dried imported mushroom.)

Tree ears (mo-er)   Also called cloud or wood ears, black or tree fungus, or Szechuan mushrooms, this funny-looking dark gray fungus has achieved noteworthy status for its role in preventing heart disease. Although I'm sure backpacking does as much as anything to prevent heart disease, mo-er is a fine backpacking food. You wouldn't want to eat it by itself, but it is excellent in stir-fry recipes. After a 20-minute soaking, the tiny dark curled "flowerets" become quite floppy, and if you were at home, where cooking tends to be a shade more refined, you would cut the little hard nub out of their centers. There is a large and a small version: choose the small one unless you want to be dealing with a wet fungus big enough to wrap around a softball.

Miniature shrimp (shi-iame)   Shelled dried shrimp have much too strong a flavor to be eaten alone. A few of these little odoriferous critturs go a long way. Put a few into stir-fry dishes or soups, but limit their use to flavoring. I think even raccoons might shy away. "A very ancient and fishlike smell" as *The Tempest*'s Trinculo might describe it.

Tiger lily buds (golden needles)   Dried tiger lily buds look exactly as you'd expect they would, if you have ever glanced at these lovely flowers on the verge of blooming. As food, they are rather chewy and do not have a particularly distinct flavor, so they are a useful staple item in stir-fry dinners and soups.

Miso soup powder (miso-shiru)   This is a Japanese soup base made from soybeans flavored with extracts of seaweed, onions, and bonito (a fish). The contents of a tiny individual cellophane packet, combined with boiling water, make one cup of soup. This wins hands down, in my opinion, over Cup-a-Soup marketed via Madison Avenue, for flavor, heartiness, compact packaging, and, I suspect, nutritional value.

Hoisin sauce   Soybeans, garlic, sugar, vinegar, and chili peppers form the basis of this mahogany-colored Chinese sauce with the consistency of apple butter. Once opened, take it out of the can and put it into a jar to store in the refrigerator; carry it in a small leakproof plastic container on the trail.

It is an excellent dip for jerky, plain or grilled.

Sliced dried bean curds   In a rectangular package wrapped in lovely Chinese paper are 40 two-by-three-inch slices of dried bean curd. After a half hour's soaking, they are soft enough to cut into pieces—fancy triangles, if you are so inclined, and if you can avail yourself of a handy natural cutting board—and then stir-fry with other ingredients. Sliced bean curd is delicious with Oriental mushrooms, for instance.

Where to buy Chinese and other Oriental dried foods   See page 273 in the Appendix.

Dried foods you can buy in health-food stores and "ethnic"markets

pineapple	pears
papaya	apples
banana	chili peppers
apricots	special spices,
figs	such as curry mixtures

Look in the supermarket for these dried foods

raisins	onions
currants	chives
prunes	potatoes*
parsley	

Some of the more satisfying commercial soups are Knorr-Swiss, Yankee Trader (a Swiss mix distributed by Hickory Farms of Ohio), and Sunshine Valley Vegetable-Nut Soup Mix. The last is free of additives and can be bought through Walnut Acres (see page 272).

Two good Japanese soups are Kikkoman Instant Miso Soybean Soup Mix and Sapporo Ichiban Japanese-style Noodles and Soup Base.

For a list of places that mail-order dry foods, see page 271 in the Appendix.

---

*Use the dried sliced potatoes in commercial "au gratin" boxes or Potato Buds.

VALUABLE FOODS IN THE WILD KITCHEN

CHEESE

The myriad tastes, high protein content, and good keeping qualities of cheese make it wonderful traveling food. Cheese is not light, and it's not inexpensive, but there the drawbacks stop. A sprinkling of genuine Parmesan transforms a plate of desultory lentils and rice into a fine meal. The flavor of one of the unique cheeses, like Norwegian gjetost, a brown, nutty goat cheese, conjures up a scene of heather-covered hills leaning toward fjords misty with imminent rain. The very smell of cheese implies nothing less than well-being itself. There is clearly magic in cheese.

Not all cheeses keep well enough to pack, although certainly in very cool weather even a cream cheese will keep for a day or so. Generally speaking, the softer the cheese, the less well it keeps. Don't pack such cheeses as ricotta, cream or cottage cheese, or Brie; they're not only messy, they're extremely perishable.

But this leaves a vast, fascinating list of cheeses. Whether you buy only a great hunk of one kind, or branch out into several families of flavors, cheese can be an important component of your wilderness menu.

It is good on bread or crackers at lunch. When you add it to dinner stews, pasta, and whole grains, it contributes both flavor and protein. (Cheese has more protein per pound than beef, trout, chicken, eggs, most dried beans, buckwheat, or salami—excelled only by soybeans, peanuts, and peanut butter.)

Buy the best cheeses you can. The best way to learn what kinds please you most is to find a good cheese store whose proprietors are willing to let you taste their wares on the premises. Thus, you will be ensured not only of packing cheeses you like, but of expanding your knowledge of the spectacular range of cheese tastes, a pursuit which happily could go on for a lifetime.

The kind of cheese *not* to buy is exactly what some backpackers assume is right for wilderness travel—that awful orange stuff that goes under the name of "pasteurized processed cheese spread" in the supermarket. The assumption, I think, is that this garishly colored goo will keep better in all weathers than real food will. Such a misconception can be quickly cured by packing a few real cheeses on a trip and learning of their superior keeping as well as taste qualities. In fact, the flavor of good cheese tends to improve—in backpacking, in inverse proportion to its appearance. (It usually half melts into a shapeless, weird-looking blob.)

A note on how to pack cheese: a half-melted Havarti or cheddar will wreak havoc inside your pack if it's not properly wrapped. The best packing is made up of a layer or so of plastic wrap inside a Ziploc bag. Put all the individually wrapped lunch things together, including salami and bread or crackers, and then expect everything in this zipped capsule to partake of the aroma of salami.

The list of cheeses that follows represents only a modest foray into the delights of cheesedom.

Cheddars   These range from mild to sharp, and from white to yellow. The cheddars of Canada, Vermont, and New York are excellent; and Kraft's Coon Brand cheddar is quite good if you're too rushed to go beyond the supermarket.

Monterey jack   A white, smooth cheese with a flavor so mild children usually like it.

Havarti   A creamy brick cheese with a distinct but not strong flavor, also liked by children. It comes with or without caraway seeds.

Edam and Gouda   Mild Dutch cheeses whose red wax coverings distinguish them from other cheeses.

Parmesan   The august Italian cheese that is really best bought in a hunk, in a good cheese store, imported from Italy, and hang the cost. It would be good for lunch, but save it to cut into dinner dishes, especially with dried Oriental mushrooms, pasta and tomato sauce, and lentils. A supermarket brand (such as Stella) will be an inferior substitute but still better than none. Do *not* buy it grated in canisters.

Asiago   A lower-cost version of Parmesan, Asiago is made in this country, in Wisconsin and Michigan. It is delicious, both grated and in chunks.

Stilton   This English "blue" cheese is pungent and sharp, good with fresh apples or as a contrast to the milder cheeses you pack for everyday use. Taste it before you buy it, and don't try to keep it too long.

Swiss Emmenthal   With large holes, and *Gruyère*, with small, are the classic Swiss cheeses.

Gjetost   A golden-brown Norwegian goat cheese, with a nutty, sweet taste, unlike any other cheese. Most Norwegians have eaten it twice a day every day of their lives.

For further reading about cheese, *The World of Cheese* by Evan Jones is mouth-watering and informative.

FATS

It is important to carry some form of fat—oil, butter (clarified), or margarine. They make certain foods taste better; they add fat to the diet; and they're essential for frying, when your pans aren't Teflon, and still helpful when they are. They must be packed carefully, but they earn their keep. The choice of fats depends on your menu and gustatory requirements.

Butter   In hot weather, butter quickly becomes rancid. In that state it not only tastes terrible, it is bad for you. However, if you insist on carrying butter in order to avoid margarine, clarify it first and it will stay fresh.

When you clarify butter, you remove the milk solids. Melt the butter gently in a small pan. Then pour the pure yellow part, which is the clarified part, into a suitable trail container and let it cool; this is the part you take. (This is also the kind of butter I refer to whenever I mention it in a recipe.) The milky residue, though no good for cooking with its fat gone, is still good for flavoring foods at home.

Carry butter well contained. My first suggestion would be a margarine container, except obviously if you're looking for something to put clarified butter in for backpacking, you've probably never bought margarine in your life. A small screw-top container would be safe, although I'd make doubly sure it didn't leak into your pack by enclosing it in a Ziploc bag. The butter also packs nicely in a small Ziploc-style bag, available through Recreational Equipment, Inc. (see page 274).

Margarine   Although margarine is objectionable to some cooks, it has much to offer the backpacker. It keeps better than unclarified butter and will not get rancid even in the hottest weather. Margarine can be carried in the plastic tubs it comes in from the store, but enclose them carefully inside Ziploc bags. It can also be purchased, for super-convenience and safe carrying, in a plastic bottle, from which you squirt it at your food.

When you combine butter or margarine with oil for frying, the taste is enhanced (depending on your opinion of margarine), while the oil raises the burning point. We never bother to put butter on lunch bread, but it is sublime, of course, on hot biscuits. It improves the flavor of soups, stews, rice, and other grain dishes, including breakfast cereals.

(See page 176 for coating a frying pan with margarine and flour before "baking over the fire.")

Oil   Carry oil in a leakproof bottle for frying and salad dressings. Peanut oil is best for stir-frying, because it can be heated to very high temperatures without burning. Other frying, such as of fish, is done successfully in a mixture of oil and butter or margarine.

Except for stir-frying, the highly polyunsaturated safflower oil is a good all-purpose oil, while good imported olive oil is delicious both for frying and salad dressings. Any good oil will keep indefinitely in its pure state even in the hottest weather.

Butter Buds   A recent invention, Butter Buds are the dried taste parts of butter without the fat. Adding boiling water to them makes a melted-butter taste. (Being without fat, however, they cannot be used for frying.)

On a very food-light trip, when you don't want to carry even margarine, a few packets of Butter Buds are useful for adding flavor to stews, soups, rice, vegetables, or anything that you would put butter in. Butter Buds are excellent sprinkled on popcorn.

In preparing food before a trip, use Butter Buds in making up mixes and puréed vegetables to be dried, and that will save having to use margarine on the trail.

EGGS

Raw eggs, if fresh when bought, will keep for a few days even in hot weather, a fact that surprised me—I used to hardboil eggs before leaving until I discovered that they can go bad even faster than raw eggs do.

An efficient source of protein, eggs are useful when feeding people whose protein requirements are high, such as people with hypoglycemia.

Besides the obvious pleasure of eggs for breakfast, use a fresh egg in Spaghetti Carbonara, or to coat buckwheat before cooking.

Thanks to the clever plastic carriers to be found in backpacking equipment stores, raw eggs can be carried without breaking; lacking this contrivance, use the egg carton you bought them in.

One large egg weighs two ounces.

Dried eggs   Marshall Foods, Inc. (Egg Products Division, Marshall, Minnesota 56258) packages "E-Z Egg Mix," which is dried whole eggs, nonfat dry milk, soybean oil, and salt. Reconstituted with water, it can be scrambled (although no one will be fooled) and used in recipes for baking and pancakes. When I call for dry eggs or egg powder in my recipes, that's what I'm referring to.

DRY MILK

Since different brands of powdered milk vary considerably in taste, it's important to find one you like, not only to drink, but because, like wine, its flavor will affect everything it's put into for cooking (such as the white sauce mix and baking mixes in this book).

Having very unscientifically sampled several brands, I am satisfied with Alba instant nonfat dried milk, found in the supermarket, and I cling faithfully to it. Dried milk can be bought in quantity from co-ops and mail-order places (see page 272), but test a small amount first before ordering a large batch.

YOGURT

Yogurt and muesli are good together, and when you add fresh tiny blueberries, the combination is ambrosial, with the crunchy grains and nuts of the muesli stuck slightly together, the velvety, tangy yogurt, and the succulent tiny berries that burst sweetly in your mouth.

Yogurt keeps well on the trail unless the weather is very hot. It is easily made at home with milk and some plain yogurt as a starter. You can add flavorings according to your taste. I like to add a touch of sugar and a few drops of vanilla flavoring.

Directions for making yogurt   For 1 quart. Heat a quart of milk just to the boiling point for 1 minute. Let it cool to lukewarm. Stir in 2 tablespoons of fresh plain or vanilla yogurt, then put it either into one large bowl, several small ones, or individual 1-cup containers. Put these in a warm place (not over 110° F.)—the oven with the pilot light on, a warm spot next to a radiator or heat vent, even inside the food dryer with the light on—and let it sit until firm enough to hold together when you tilt the bowl, about 5 to 8 hours. Chill the yogurt for 3 hours in the refrigerator before using and store it there until you pack it.

Pack yogurt for the trail in a leakproof wide-mouth jar.

NUTS

Being a compact, delicious, and keepable protein, nuts have a valued spot on the camping menu. One starts with the basic use of the good old peanut in gorp and goes on to explore other varieties of nuts. Cashews, more expensive but more delicate and sweeter than peanuts, make gorp a little more elegant. Chopped hazelnuts in muesli, whole fresh almonds in stir-fry dinners, chopped walnuts, pecans, or pignoli in rice, all effect culinary transformations to please the wild palate.

Buy shelled nuts whole, and in quantity if you can, rather than in skimpy supermarket packages. Store them tightly enclosed in plastic in the freezer, where they will not get rancid.

Peanut butter   To some backpackers, peanut butter is a valuable and central staple in the hiking diet because of its high protein and fat (energy-giving) content. To others, like me, who have spread, smelled, and cleaned up peanut butter ever since their children were old enough to stand and ask for a piece of bread, peanut butter is *not* the ideal hiking food: I like to get away from it now and then.

However, when a British photographer, Peter Bird, decided to row his lonely way 8,500 miles across the Pacific Ocean in a 35-foot boat, he packed principally peanut butter. His spokesman said, "We figured he would need 4,000 calories a day and then we had to figure out how to cram 1,400,000 calories worth of food into a rowboat. We finally settled on peanut butter because it is the most dense in calories."

MEATS

With the exception of hard salami, smoked sausages, and Canadian bacon, which can each be carried a number of days without spoiling, meat that you pack should be dried, freeze-dried, or canned. Refer to the drying section for information about beef jerky, dried ground and pressed beefs, dried bacon, and freeze-dried meats (see pages 39–43).

The meats described here can be packed just as you buy them.

Hard salami   Good hard salami is excellent lunch food. It may seem heavy, overly aromatic, and expensive. But the best salami keeps indefinitely, and when you find one whose taste suits you, neither too spicy nor too bland, you'll be able to eat it day after day for lunch without tiring of it.

Such a food is worth looking for. Test salamis in delicatessens and markets, fancy or plain, until you've got one that pleases you. Buy it unsliced and carry it that way, in a hunk, very well wrapped in several layers of plastic wrap, and sealed inside a strong Ziploc bag. Although it seems expensive, a good salami is "cost effective" because of the qualities mentioned above, and it has a high protein content.

Smoked sausage   The difference between smoked and fresh sausage is significant for the backpacker. Whereas fresh sausage must be both browned and thoroughly cooked, a smoked sausage link is rendered edible after a few minutes in boiling water, long enough to heat it through (although it is much better to brown it). Slightly greasy water is not nearly as troublesome to discard in bear country as the real grease left after browning fresh sausages. Furthermore, fresh sausage is highly perishable, while smoked sausage can be carted around quite safely for a week, even in hot weather. Once, in a more ignorant day, I had to dispose of a half pound of fresh link sausages that had gone quite bad. Luckily this was in a relatively wild area along the Mattawa River in Canada. As I stood on Moose Island and guiltily sank the sausages that I hoped would decompose as "dead fish," I watched them sink all the way to the pebbly river bottom in that pure water and saw, with the clarity of poetry, the responsibility of carrying the right or wrong stuff into the woods.

Smoked link sausage is good not only for breakfast (try some in oatmeal), but it will enliven rice, lentil, bean, and pasta dishes.

Canadian bacon   Canadian bacon, which is all meat and no fat, even leaner than ham, is an efficient way of carrying meat. Although expensive and well-imbued with preservatives, it keeps well, cooks easily, and tastes good (except to purists objecting to the preservatives).

BEEF FLAVORINGS

Most kitchens have beef bouillon on hand, in cube or powder form. A few cooks keep what the British call "beef tea," Bovril, which can be bought in fancy grocery stores. All are invaluable in the making of trail gravy when you lack proper pan juices—the usual plight of the wilderness epicure.

Bovril, a thick, beef-smelling dark liquid, can be carried handily in a 35-mm film can, or other leakproof vessel. A little Bovril mixed into a paste with flour and water makes delicious gravy. Bouillon serves the same function; bouillon powder is slightly easier to work with on the trail than cubes, which sometimes have to be picked apart to help them dissolve.

The difference between a watery gruel and hearty gravy is three minutes, a fraction of an ounce, and a modicum of procedure. The procedure is as follows:

To make 1 cup gravy on the trail, using bouillon in cube or powder   To about 1 cup boiling liquid add 2 cubes beef bouillon, an oversize Knorr bouillon cube, or 1 package Herb Ox bouillon powder, and dissolve it. In a cup, make a thin paste of 1½ tablespoons flour in 2 or 3 tablespoons cold water, and stir this into the hot liquid. Cook slowly, stirring, for 2 to 3 minutes until the flour cooks and the gravy is thick.

To make gravy on the trail using Bovril   Make a paste of 2 tablespoons cold water, $1\frac{1}{2}$ tablespoons flour, and 1 teaspoon Bovril. Stir this into a cup or so of boiling liquid, and cook slowly, stirring, for 2 to 3 minutes until the flour cooks and the gravy is thick.

Adjust the amounts of beef extract and flour to the amount of liquid you intend to thicken: for example, double the amounts of beef extract and flour given above to make 2 cups gravy.

File somewhere in the back of your mind the information that $1\frac{1}{2}$ tablespoons flour thicken 1 cup liquid, and carry a little extra flour and bouillon. Watery stews or soups can be made hearty with gravy, and a ground beef dish can be stretched to feed more people when you increase its amount of gravy.

OTHER WAYS TO THICKEN COOKING LIQUIDS ARE

• Use part of a commercial cream-soup mix.
• Use a package of instant gravy.
• Use instant potatoes.
• Mix a little cornstarch or arrowroot with cold water to make a paste, and stir that into the liquid.

Three Basic Mixes

Tomato sauce, ground beef mix with gravy, and white sauce are basic to many dinner recipes in the book. Consider making and drying them in batches for easier packing of the dinners they belong in.

For instance, since tomato sauce is the same basic recipe as the one for home-dried pasta sauce, make a double recipe, then use extra sauce to pack with Beef Ragout, Arroz con Pollo, Erie Stew, or Jerky with Peppers (see pages 191–4). Or if you added to the Ground Beef Mix cheese and macaroni, extra gravy and mashed potatoes, or vegetables and biscuits, you'd produce three dinners different enough from each other to take on the same trip (see pages 195–8). White Sauce Mix is handy in many meals, from vegetable soup to creamed chipped beef.

Actually, once you have them on hand, these sauces are fun to experiment with in the spirit of the daring cuisine that backpackers are customarily up to. For example, combine ground beef mix with rice, and add a little cheese and your favorite flavoring; or use any of the sauces in combination with lentils and pasta, or a grain like bulgur. Toss in a few home-dried vegetables and presto! a new dinner, just awaiting a name.

Basic Tomato Sauce

Makes 1 six-ounce leather—about 1 cup—to feed 6 with pasta

⅓ onion, chopped very fine
2 cloves garlic, finely-minced
1 tablespoon olive oil and 1
    tablespoon margarine, or 2
    tablespoons of either
Two 6-ounce cans tomato paste

1 teaspoon salt
Pinch of sugar
2 teaspoons chopped parsley
Ground black pepper
Small pinch of basil
Small pinch of oregano

Sauté the onion and garlic together in the oil and/or margarine until they are soft and golden; stop before they begin to brown. Add the rest of the ingredients and cook slowly for about 10 minutes.

Spray a cookie sheet or other flat pan with a nonstick spray. Spread the mixture out in as thin a layer as possible—use 2 pans if necessary. Dry the sauce in the oven at 140° F. for about 6 hours with the door propped open a crack. Do not overdry or the reconstituted sauce will taste burned. Roll it up like a fruit leather and put it into a plastic bag, labeled "Tomato Sauce."

To reconstitute, add triple the amount of water to the dried sauce, bring to a boil, and simmer 5 minutes.

Basic Ground Beef Mix

Makes 1⅓ cups dried sauce, to feed 3 with pasta, potatoes, or rice

I never managed to convince myself that soy granules, in spite of their lightness and nutritive value, were really any fun either to cook or to eat. (To judge from the epithets other campers have given to this food, my attitude is not unique.) Finally, in exasperation, I browned, seasoned, floured, and dried a pound of hamburger to serve as a ground meat base for quick stews, to add to soup—to be used, basically, whenever there isn't time to cook jerky but one still wants *real* meat and gravy. The recipe can be doubled and tripled, and its own built-in gravy can be expanded.

1 pound lean ground beef	1½ packets instant beef bouillon, or
2 cloves garlic, finely minced	1½ beef bouillon cubes, or 1½
½ cup finely chopped onion	teaspoons Bovril
Ground pepper to taste	¼ teaspoon Worcestershire sauce
(optional) ¼ teaspoon rosemary	2 tablespoons flour
leaves	1 teaspoon salt

Brown the beef with the garlic and onion. Setting the pan slightly on a slant and pushing the meat to the higher side, let the fat collect and spoon it out. Add the rest of the ingredients, and cook over medium heat, scraping the flour off the bottom of the pan to brown it evenly.

Note: After browning ground meat, pour off whatever grease has collected. Although some fat ordinarily adds flavor to dishes made with ground meat, it will get rancid in dried foods if they are left for long at room temperature. It's best to store dried meals that might contain a little fat in the refrigerator or the freezer if you make them ahead of time.

Spread the mixture in a thin layer on a greased flat pan and dry it in a 140° F. oven with the door propped open, until it is crumbly, about 6 hours. After drying, spread it on paper towels to absorb any extra grease.

Store the dried sauce, labeled, in a plastic bag in the refrigerator. To reconstitute, add 1¾ cups water, bring to a boil, and simmer 5 minutes.

WHITE SAUCE

White sauce is the foundation of many familiar dishes. Clam chowder, cream soups, macaroni and cheese, other simple pasta dishes, Chicken à la King—all these have as their base this simple white sauce, known as *béchamel* in French cooking. It is easily made from butter, flour, and milk.

The classic method is to make a *roux* first by melting butter and adding flour. Cook this a moment, then stir in hot liquid (milk, usually), and cook, stirring, until the sauce thickens.

The traditional method of making white sauce with a *roux* can be done perfectly easily over a camp stove, if you don't have to keep your cooking super-streamlined because of weather or other reasons, and if you remember to hold the pot off the heat, when necessary, to avoid burning. All you need is to carry flour, dry milk, and butter or margarine separately as staples. This sauce made in the traditional way tastes better than the quick mix and has a nicer texture—but these refinements may escape you in arduous conditions.

If you want to make a quicker white sauce in camp, add water to a mix that you prepared at home out of Butter Buds, flour, and dry milk. I refer to this as white sauce mix.

The two methods are interchangeable in the recipes. If you plan to pack a single bag of mix to dip into for several meals, or to make the sauce from a *roux* more than once, carry your favorite spices in a little "traveling pantry." Don't forget salt and pepper—saltless white sauce rivals pablum for insipidity. And freely add cheese, when you can spare a little from the lunch supply, to create "sauce Mornay."

White Sauce Mix

Ingredients	3 servings	6–8	10–12	Big batch
Butter Buds	1 tablsp.	1 packet (8 teasps.)	2 packets ($\frac{1}{3}$ cup)	4 packets ($\frac{2}{3}$ cup)
Flour	$1\frac{1}{2}$ tablsp.	3 tablsp.	6 tablsp.	$\frac{3}{4}$ cup
Dry milk	2 tablsp.	$\frac{1}{2}$ cup	1 cup	2 cups
Salt*	pinch	$\frac{1}{4}$ teasp.	$\frac{1}{3}$ teasp.	$\frac{1}{2}$ teasp.
Water	1 cup	2 cups	4 cups	8 cups

Mix the ingredients together and put the mix into a container labeled "White Sauce Mix. Add 1 cup water to $\frac{1}{4}$ or $\frac{1}{3}$ cup mix for 3 servings." The proportion of $\frac{1}{3}$ cup mix to 1 cup water makes a medium-thick sauce.

The entire mix will make enough white sauce to feed 3 people about 10 times.

*If you use the white sauce mix for salty foods like clams or ham, add the salt on the trail.

Traditional White Sauce

Ingredients	1–2 servings	4	8–10	16
Butter or margarine	1½ tablsp.	3 tablsp.	6 tablsp.	½ cup
Flour	1½ tablsp.	3 tablsp.	6 tablsp.	½ cup
Dry milk	2 tablsp.	½ cup	1 cup	2 cups
Salt	pinch	¼ teasp.	⅓ teasp.	½ teasp.
Water	1 cup	2 cups	4 cups	8 cups

TRAIL DIRECTIONS:

Make up the milk in a cup or bowl with dry milk and water.
Melt the butter, add the flour, and cook slowly, 1 or 2 minutes.
Add the milk, stir until thick, for 4 or 5 minutes.

Stir-Fry Seasoning-Thickener

¼ cup dry sherry

¼ cup soy sauce

1 teaspoon sugar

4 teaspoons cornstarch

Mix the ingredients together and put into a labeled screw-top jar, inside a Ziploc bag for extra protection.

Before using on the trail, be sure to shake the mixture vigorously to dislodge the cornstarch from the bottom of the container, where it is sure to have settled. And measure out the amount of the mixture you want before you begin your stir-fry, to have it ready. For 2 people, use 1 tablespoon mix to 2 tablespoons water (that is, double the amount of water); keep the proportions the same for a larger stir-fry.

Salad dressings   It's best to carry separate ingredients for salad dressings and mix them on the trail. Oil and seasonings are likely to be part of your "traveling pantry," and you don't need to carry much vinegar.

Two basic salad dressings follow: mix them thoroughly just before you use them.

Sweet and Sour Salad Dressing

Enough for 1 cup dried sliced cabbage
that has been reconstituted

½ tablespoon sugar
½ tablespoon white vinegar
½ tablespoon oil
½ teaspoon salt

1½ tablespoons water
(optional) Minced fresh wild onion,
    or freeze-dried chives

French Dressing

Put on fresh foraged greens or on cucumber.

3 tablespoons oil
1 teaspoon wine vinegar
Pinch of salt
Pepper

(optional) Minced fresh wild onion,
    or freeze-dried chives; herbs (if
    you carry herbs): a pinch of
    tarragon, basil, or dill

Tomatoes   The simplest way to dry tomatoes is to slice them (through their equator, and so on), coat the slices lightly with oil, and dry them in the dryer or in the sun. If you start with home-grown tomatoes, you'll have an excellent dried product.

Tomato paste is condensed tomato purée, and you can dry a can of it to make a leather, which can be reconstituted for use in a pasta tomato sauce simply by adding water to it and cooking. Use hunks of it to flavor stews and soups, too. (Directions are on page 35.)

Tomato "flakes" can be obtained from Alpine-Aire Foods, Box 926, Nevada City, CA 95959.

Double-concentrate tomato paste comes in a tube and can be bought in specialty food stores.

Garlic   Fresh garlic is indispensable, especially in the spare wild kitchen. Having stubbornly packed garlic cloves, laboriously peeled and cut them, gotten my hands sticky, wrestled with that maddeningly clinging skin, exasperated family and friends, and earned for yet another cause epithets strongly hinting at lunacy, at last I discovered to my joy that there is an easy way to deal with fresh garlic on the trail. For this I am indebted to one Stanley Goldman, a mountain climber whose restaurant experience taught him many a culinary trick useful in the wild kitchen. Skiing along in the Bronx's Van Cortlandt golf course to condition himself for his next climb, he remarked casually, "Oh yeah, you smash the garlic clove with the flat of your knife blade. The skin pops off and you cut the clove how you want to." Eureka!

Fresh garlic transforms stir-fry dinners, pasta sauces, and mashed potatoes, to name a few beneficiaries, from "good" to "sublime." It certainly weighs little, won't spoil, melt, crumble, or smell until it's cut, and —to counteract its reputation—its smell and taste are quickly rendered gentle by even less than a minute's cooking.

Garlic is also good for you. I'm not sure whether a few cloves worn around the neck will deter either bears or colds, but consumed, it's reputed to ward off a range of diseases from viral infections to heart ailments. (Garlic powder and garlic salt are inadequate substitutes for fresh garlic and should not be used either at home or in the wild kitchen.)

Ginger   Buy whole (not ground) ginger in Oriental
stores, many vegetable stores, and sometimes in
the supermarket. It is a gnarled, knobby root. Peel
it, if necessary, and slice off thin slivers with a
sharp knife. Carry these in a film can or similar
small vessel. Ginger joins garlic to season the
beginning of many stir-fry meals.

Minced onions, dried onions, and leeks   The supermarket dried minced
onions that come in a jar tend to have a very strong flavor. They are convenient, but a little goes a long way. Typically, one tablespoon equals one
whole onion—that is concentrated!

In dishes where you don't want a particularly strong onion flavor, use
home-dried leeks or onions (see page 37) that have been sliced very thin.
Brown them in butter as they are, or after you have soaked them for 10
minutes and squeezed the water out.

Dried parsley and green pepper   Like dried onions and leeks, these are good
to have on hand at home when you are packing up meals. (See page 37.)

Spices and herbs   These will supply pleasure out of proportion to their
weight and are therefore a valuable part of your traveling pantry.

Besides the fresh garlic and ginger central to the success of stir-fry
meals, various ground and dried seasonings are invaluable to stews, soups,
and pasta meals, and especially to dishes with a white sauce base.

Rosemary is good with chicken and in stews; fragrant thyme and nutmeg enliven many white sauce meals; basil tastes good in many Italian
dishes, and chili powder, oregano, and cumin in Mexican ones. Spice combinations like curries are fun to experiment with when you are cooking
rice; and saffron, which you should buy in "threads" (they are the stigmas
of crocuses), does something truly wonderful to rice.

If you have a few favorite spices, consider carrying them in well-labeled
35-mm film cans, small emptied vitamin containers, or similar vials. It's
very convenient to have jars or bags of dried parsley, leeks or onions, and
green peppers on hand at home as you pack up meals.

(To pack fresh garlic and ginger, see pages 62 and 63.)

Sweeteners   There is no difference between white sugar, brown sugar, and honey in food value. Strictly speaking, they have no food value except for the energy they provide. So which you carry is a matter of personal preference.

Watch supermarket foods, however, for their sugar content. Sometimes it's much higher than you would expect. Tang, for instance, powdered orange drink, contains more sugar than any other ingredient. Mistrust instant foods marketed for the supposedly harried housekeeper—sugar is one ingredient added to commercial mixes to "improve" the real taste that ingredients without a long shelf life would have supplied. For some people, the body's quick burning of sugar leaves them hungrier than before, which implies that highly sugared hiking fare is the worst thing they can eat.

Pancake syrup   A little bit of pure maple syrup is a nice thing to carry to use lovingly and sparingly, as befits an elegant elixir.

Honey is good on pancakes, too.

To make your own syrup, mix brown sugar with water. Add water in a ratio of 2 parts water to 1 part sugar. The sugar will dissolve nicely even in icy water. One-quarter cup brown sugar (2 ounces) plus ½ cup water will make enough syrup to serve 3 people. If you want a butter flavor, add about 1 teaspoon Butter Buds to the syrup and warm it a little.

To improvise pancake syrup from molasses, which you might be carrying to make Indian Pudding, add ½ cup boiling water to 1 teaspoon molasses and 2 teaspoons sugar. The syrup may be watery but it is good.

And, wondrously, you can now reconstitute Vermont maple syrup by adding boiling water to a new product, "pure maple syrup granules." (The granules are also good as a general sweetener.) Write to Vermont Country Maple, Inc., Jericho Center, VT 05465 to learn where to obtain them locally, or send away for the Eddie Bauer Catalog (see page 274). (At the time of this printing, the product was so new it hadn't yet reached the backpacking catalogs.)

Camp breads   Besides your own homemade bread and crackers, you can make delicious pan breads in camp. The basic biscuit mix on page 174 is versatile enough to be used for biscuits, Bannock, dumplings, and Doughboys. (It is also the basis for pancakes.) I usually keep a batch of it in the refrigerator not only for impromptu camping trips but also in case the kids suddenly want pancakes for breakfast at home (it is so much better than a commercial mix).

Crackers   Crackers were invented for traveling. The Roman army marched through Europe munching on dry rusk, while for millennia sailors have plied the mighty seas fortified by tons of hard tack.

For backpacking purposes, look for sturdy, compact crackers that will not crumble and that will keep well after they are opened. Scandinavian flatbread packs well, for instance, as do many biscuits (Peak Freans sweet meal biscuits are delicious with a good Vermont cheddar) and modern versions of hard tack. Avoid saltines and gimmicky cocktail crackers. Supermarkets usually carry suitable traveling crackers, and the store where you buy your good cheese is likely to have an excellent assortment of crackers from many lands. Old-fashioned Scottish oat cakes, for instance, are wonderful to pack; they are tasty, with a crunchy texture due to the steel-cut oats from which they are made. (They are roughly comparable in price to Rich-Moor pilot biscuits.)

Tortillas   People from the Southwest will be familiar with a wider choice of tortillas than I. My favorite brand is Piñata, which is sold in the supermarket dairy or frozen-foods section. Flour tortillas, with a 10-inch diameter, do not crumble as readily as smaller (6½-inch) corn tortillas. Traditionally, flour tortillas are used for burritos and corn for tacos. You can heat tortillas simply under the lid of a small cookpot while warming the filling; or coat them with oil and grill them briefly; or heat them in a little oil in a frying pan.

GRAINS

Here are some grains that are good breakfast cereals and that are useful, too, in other ways. For other grains, see rice (page 224), Couscous (page 229), and the Whole Grain Cereal recipe (page 140).

Bulgur wheat   This is whole wheat which has been boiled, dried, and baked. It is used in Lebanese cooking to make kibbee and tabbouleh salad. It's a good trail cereal, it can substitute for rice in a lentil dinner, and you can make a tabbouleh salad mix out of it, which needs on the trail a 30-minute soak and some oil and lemon juice.

Like cracked oats, buckwheat, and rice, bulgur cooks in about 20 minutes, so it's not an item to pack when cooking time must be kept to a minimum.

Oats   Rolled or "quick" oats cook in 5 minutes. Since the process they undergo condenses rather than removes their nutritious kernels, oats are an excellent breakfast food. (Cracked oats are delicious, but remember that they take 20 minutes to cook.)

Buckwheat   This delicious grain can be eaten as a side dish or pilaf; buckwheat flour makes very good pancakes.

BEVERAGES

Good camp coffee and tea   In an old camping manual I found the following: "To have coffee in perfection the berry must be freshly roasted and freshly ground. This can be done with frying pan and pistol-butt; yet few but old-timers take the trouble."

From what I've seen of backpackers' coffee—a quick spoonful of instant coffee granules dissolved in boiling water in a camp cup—old-timers would be horrified. Rather than swallow this awful stuff, I suspect more backpackers than I have turned to tea, which can at least be made fairly decently in a cup when you pay attention.

Good steeped coffee and tea *are* possible on the trail in these modern times, though. Just follow these directions:

To brew fresh coffee on the trail   It is best to start with beans as freshly ground as possible. With a regular grinder (if not with pistol butt) grind the beans before leaving home and enclose them in an airtight bag.

To brew, use a clean pot or a can (see page 8). Put fresh-ground coffee—one heaping spoonful per cup and "one for the pot"—into the container. Add the requisite number of cups of cold water, then a pinch of salt, and cover. Bring this to a boil until the water just breaks through the crust, then stir, take it off the heat, sprinkle some cold water on it to settle the grounds, and let it stand for 5 minutes. (Never boil coffee!)
Note: Fresh eggs are generally too scarce for the backpacker to crush one, shell and all, into the grounds beforehand to make them settle, as oldtimers used to do.

Since the only responsible way to dispose of the grounds is to burn them, it's best not to brew fresh coffee when you're cooking only over a stove.

To make good tea on the trail   There are so many wonderful kinds of tea that it's fun to pick out a favorite kind to pack. Choose one you're familiar with, though—a hundred miles from nowhere is not the time to learn which teas *don't* appeal to you. Herb teas are caffeine-free and thus a pleasant evening drink.

To make tea in a pot   Tea is very sensitive to the containers you use, but since you probably won't be traveling with a teapot or a covered enameled pail preferred by the old-time woodsman, consider steeping tea in one of your fine backpacking cookpots. The important things, as with coffee, are to start with a clean container and not to let the tea boil; also, never let it steep more than 5 minutes unless you like the taste of sheep dip.

Boil water, then add tea leaves—about ½ teaspoon per cup. Take the pot off the heat, stir once to get the leaves to settle, cover, and let sit for 4 minutes *only*. Strain the tea through a small strainer into individual cups.

To make individual cups of tea   While tea bags are ideal for backpacking purposes, you can use loose tea and a tea ball, as well.

Start your cup of tea with freshly boiled water, if possible, and don't let the tea steep more than 5 minutes.

Don't try to burn a wet tea bag, nor should you scatter tea leaves around in an area where their slow decomposition would ruin the landscape. It's sometimes best to let used tea bags dry, then pack them out.

Hot Chocolate Mix

Here is a basic mix for about 20 cups hot chocolate:

4 cups dry milk*	½ teaspoon salt
1 cup unsweetened cocoa	(optional) 1 teaspoon instant
2 cups sugar	decaffeinated coffee

*One 3.2-ounce packet of Alba dry milk equals 1 cup.

Mix the ingredients and put them into a plastic container or double plastic bags. Label the mix "Hot Chocolate. Use ¼ cup per cup of boiling water."

Nancy Barker's
Very Rich Hot Chocolate Mix

Enough for about 24 cups hot chocolate (and especially rich, of course, with tiny marshmallows floating on top, half melted):

8 cups dry milk*
1 pound instant chocolate drink,
    like Swiss Miss or Nestlé's
    Quik

1 cup Cremora, Coffeemate, or
    Pream
4 heaping tablespoons powdered
    sugar

*One 3.2-ounce packet of Alba dry milk equals 1 cup.

Mix the ingredients and put them into a plastic container or double plastic bag. Label the mix "Rich Hot Chocolate. Add ½ cup of mix per cup of boiling water."

Instant Spiced Tea

A sweet hot drink.

2 cups powdered orange breakfast
    drink
1½ cups sugar
¾ cup instant tea

2 packages unsweetened lemonade
    mix
1 teaspoon ground cloves
1 teaspoon ground cinnamon

Mix the ingredients and put them into a plastic container or double plastic bag. Label the mix "Spiced Tea. Add 2 heaping teaspoons to 1 cup boiling water."

Water Important as food is to the backpacker, water is vital. Aside from the fact that no one can survive for long without water, even mild dehydration is simply not good for the body—or for the mind, either. Mental functioning can be seriously impaired in a state of extreme thirst.

Never chart a hiking course without being sure of your water supply. You must know ahead of time whether there will be water enroute, or if you must bring it with you. When you'll be hiking in a desert or another area of scarce water, plan with utmost care. In most cases, your map will tell you where to expect water; and many trails follow streams. Don't be misled by a map, however.

For instance, you could be hiking next to Georgian Bay, with gorgeous drinkable water in view at every turn of the Bruce Trail, but it's usually an arduous hour's climb down steep cliffs to get to it. Or, the spring shown on a desert map might have dried up or otherwise vanished. When you really are not sure that you'll find water on your planned route, carry enough to last you not only to a promised spring but also back to the last known water supply.

How pure is the water you find in the wilderness? It may not be as pure as it looks. For example, the water in Isle Royale, in the middle of some of the world's clearest water (Lake Superior), is unfit to drink because the parasites that inhabit the innards of the area's wolves and moose are reputed eager to include humans in their cycle, and water there must be boiled for ten minutes before it can be safely drunk. You should pay attention to what's upstream from the water you want to drink—towns? Other campers? Of course, you may get some answers about the fitness of an area's water supply simply by asking around.

Most parasites and other harmful microscopic water creatures can be killed by boiling the water, or by treating it with chemical water purification tablets of Halizone or chlorine. These can be bought from any wilderness outfitter and are obviously a sensible thing to carry. If you object to the slight chemical taste of treated water, let it sit for a few minutes before drinking it, or add powdered drinks like Kool-Aid to it to mask the taste of chemicals.

During winter camping, water supplies can be a problem. You might assume that melting snow is an easy source—until you find out how much snow, time, and fuel are required to do this, especially when the snow is powdery. If you do have to melt snow, begin with an inch or so of water in the bottom of the pot. But try to find even the tiniest source of running water, even if it's just a drip; rig up an outfit for the sun to do the melting, or simply carry water (and sleep with it to keep it from freezing during the night). Eating snow instead of drinking water to assuage winter thirst isn't a good idea, since the body then has to expend extra energy to warm itself from the resulting chill.

(For a detailed account of snow melting, and also for a set of instructions for building a solar still in the desert—instructions which might turn out to be invaluable—consult *The New Complete Walker*, by Colin Fletcher.)

The amount of water that each individual needs to drink per day varies. Hiking, in comparison to more sedentary activity, always increases your need for liquids; the standard "eight glasses per day" should therefore be increased to something that you are comfortable with, given the particular circumstances—the heat of the day, the arduousness of the hiking, the amount of water in the food you prepare (that counts). When planning menus for trip conditions when you can't afford to waste any water, choose meals that make good use of it in their preparation. Trail information preceding each recipe indicates how much water is used; in some instances, the recipe will offer an alternative method that is more economical in the use of water.

Salt   When you sweat heavily, your body loses salt, and you need to replace it. Either salt your trail food slightly more than at home, or swallow salt tablets, which can be bought at the drug store. The requirements for salt vary among people. So do symptoms of salt deficiency, though it typically shows up as exhaustion.

BAKE-AHEAD BREAD, CAKES, AND COOKIES

You are a fortunate hiker indeed if your pack contains home-baked provisions. Since the space inside your pack is precious, choose carefully among baked goods. You might combine a sturdy loaf of Whole-Wheat Bread and a golden pound cake, whose taste improves with each day you penetrate the wilderness. A batch of rich chocolate brownies may disappear far more quickly than the pita bread you bake to stuff with assorted nourishment. A loaf of Date-Nut Bread might replace fancy "energy bars" in your food plan but never the simple bread loaf that is the center of lunch and indeed of your very well-being.

Yeast breads

A backpacking cookbook might seem a funny place for a section on bread baking. To some backpackers, just the idea of taking a fresh homemade loaf of bread on a trip is impractical. But it's only impractical when you're making an extended and arduous hike in especially difficult terrain, or when you have to carry special extra gear or a great deal of water. In those conditions, forced to watch every ounce, you can substitute compact, dense crackers for good bread. But, even for a week's trip in total wilderness, you can pack either regular loaves or small loaves so that each hiker can carry his own supply.

The first time we packed homemade bread was accidental—home-baked bread is just not something I had thought of as wilderness fare. But there was a good whole-wheat loaf that would have gone to waste if we'd left it sitting at home—so we packed it. And, in one of our typical splendid lunches as close as we could get to the center of a mountain stream (sitting on rocks with the cold water rushing past us on both sides), the bread came into its own. A few days old, it had settled into itself, its flavors were mellow, and it had neither dried out nor crumbled to pieces in my pack. Its slightly nutty and "full" taste and texture gave our hard salami and soft, fragrant Havarti cheese a perfect complement. (Or was it the cheese and salami that complemented the bread?)

Later, after we had become accustomed to eating good bread in the middle of streams, I remembered picnics on islands among the fjords of Norway—we would pack a moist loaf of whole-wheat bread and slice it on site to accompany the sturdy brown Norwegian goat cheese, gjetost, and swallow light, sweet homemade wine with it—and realized what had guided my instinct in this "accidental" adding of good bread to our backpacking provisions.

You may wonder how a loaf of bread can remain intact inside a crowded pack. Locked in a plastic bag, pressed, jostled, and tossed in a week's worth of packings and unpackings, will it stay sliceable under the hungry gleam of a four-inch Swiss army knife?

That depends on the bread.

The bread recipes here are for breads with a rather high fat content, which makes them moist, and therefore they keep well—at least a week for most of them. They will be very tasty on their own account, and amenable to a range of cheese flavors from the sharpest cheddar to the mildest Muenster. They will be delicious! They will be so good that you'll calmly wedge a ¾-pound loaf into your pack under the incredulous eye of some nonbeliever who, if he is going to hike with you, is about to learn what a sublime lunch really is.

A few notes on how to make bread   Bread making has acquired a mystique, implying that it is difficult. There's a mystique all right—how could anything that transforms a regular house or apartment into a glowing haven of sweet domesticity by its smell alone not have a mystique? But the wonderful powers of bread, in the making or in the partaking, do not depend on difficult procedures.

First, the yeast. Yeast is a unicellular fungus whose enzymes convert sugar to carbon dioxide and alcohol. As the yeast "feeds on" the flour in the dough, the gases released make the bread rise. Because it is alive, yeast can be killed by overheating, so be sure not to put any scalded milk with it until you have cooled the milk to lukewarm. (A good method is to scald the milk, then add cut-up butter that needs to melt, then add cool liquids such as water and honey.)

Yeast cannot be rushed in its quiet feeding. But, if you are worried about being tied to the kitchen all day because you have bread in the making, it's good to know that the dough will go into a "holding pattern" at any stage of the recipe if you put it into the refrigerator, where it will wait—hours, if necessary—until you're ready to resume.

The more you knead the dough, the finer the texture of your bread will be. (Kneading dough is also very good for you, of course.) It's hard to describe how to knead without showing the motion—but kneading has a rhythm and it has a noise, if you like to thwump the dough on the counter, which is good for it.

A good bread recipe usually presents some leeway in the amount of flour. This is because the amount can vary wildly, depending on what the weather is like and probably on what kind of a mood you are in. You might use as much as a cup more (seldom less) of flour than the recipe calls for, but don't worry: the dough has its own quiet wisdom.

(Children love to knead, especially when you remember to get their little arms somewhat above the level of the counter to give them the proper leverage to keep from tiring. That is, stand them on a chair. And maybe divide the dough into two parts.)

Where does dough rise best? It needs warmth, but not really direct heat, and the degree of warmth will affect the rising time. Any place warmed by a pilot light, a radiator, or a water heater is a good place. (When you put the dough into a gas oven with a pilot light, don't turn the oven on.) Try a sunny window or a greenhouse, depending on your circumstances. Put a damp towel over the bowl, and note the size of the dough so that you'll have some notion of what "double in size" is going to look like.

The note on page 75 describes how to make individual rolls for each hiker's own personal bread supply, although on longer trips small rolls aren't as practical to carry, since they tend to dry out faster than a regular loaf. (Also the concept of the "individual hiker's bread supply" is quickly undone when you throw all the food into one heap at night before packing it to hang in a tree.) However, you do have this choice, at the point where you divide the dough into two equal parts before its second rising.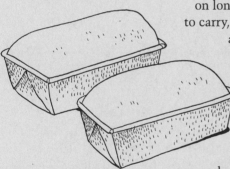

When the dough is rising the second time, be sure not to let it rise too much, or you will not have a compact loaf. (It continues to rise for a few moments when it goes into the hot oven.) If it gets more than a half inch above the rim of the pan, punch it down and let it rise over again. It won't be too tired.

Cool baked loaves outside of the pans, on racks. Bread freezes well, which is a good thing—it might be difficult otherwise to reserve enough loaves from hungry mouths for a backpacking supply. It's impossible to resist a thick slice of just-baked bread with butter melting on it while the incomparable fragrance of its baking still lingers, warming the air. Be cunning, and waft the second loaf out of sight if you want to taste it in the forest.

Note: Do not wrap bread or put it into plastic bags to freeze until it's completely cooled.

A note on bread flour   Some white flour is called for in all of these recipes, because the gluten in it gives the bread a better texture than all whole-wheat flour would and allows the bread to rise. All-purpose flour is fine to use, preferably unbleached.

If you have a blender, you can grind some flours yourself out of rolled or steel-cut oats or buckwheat. A variety of grains is available in food co-ops, health-food stores, and some good supermarkets. To send away for grains or for special flours, see the reference to Walnut Acres, page 272.

Whole-Wheat Bread

Makes two 8-inch loaves

Here is a dense, tasty whole-wheat bread that will travel well into the deepest wilderness. It is a good hiking bread: it slices easily, it keeps well, and it complements the finest cheeses, being flavorful enough to hold its own with stronger cheeses and delicate enough to allow milder ones their due.

Vary the basic recipe, if you want, by substituting molasses for honey. The taste of molasses provides a whiff of pioneer days, very fitting for wilderness travel. Other kinds of flour than whole wheat are good, too (see variations).

1 envelope dry yeast	$\frac{1}{2}$ cup honey or molasses
$\frac{1}{4}$ cup warm water	3 cups whole-wheat flour
1 cup milk	$3\frac{1}{2}$ to 4 cups white flour
3 tablespoons butter or margarine	(optional) $\frac{1}{2}$ cup raw sunflower
$\frac{3}{4}$ cup cold water	seeds or wheat germ
1 tablespoon salt	

Dissolve the yeast in $\frac{1}{4}$ cup warm water in a large bowl. Scald the milk in a saucepan. Turn off the heat, add the butter or margarine and let it melt;

then add ¾ cup cold water, the salt and honey, and let this sit until luke-warm.

Add the milk mixture to the dissolved yeast in the bowl. Add the whole-wheat flour and optional seeds and mix well. Add white flour until the dough is no longer sticky and you can knead it easily. Knead it for 10 minutes, adding more flour occasionally if necessary to keep it from sticking. Set the dough in a greased bowl, turning it so all of its surface gets coated. Cover with a damp towel and let rise in a warm place for an hour to an hour and a half, until double in size.

Punch the dough down, form it into 2 loaves, and place in 2 greased 8-inch loaf pans. Set these back in the warm place, covered, until the loaves rise no more than ½ inch above the rims of the pans. Bake at 375° F. for 35 to 40 minutes or until done. Take the loaves out of the pans and let them cool on racks.

Variations: Instead of whole-wheat flour, use oat flour (rolled oats ground in the blender), or a mixture of oat and rye flours (1½ cups and ½ cup, respectively), or a multi-grain flour, ground fine.

To make 14 individual rolls, about the size of hamburger buns: Divide the dough in half and divide each half into 7 equal parts. Form these into round shapes and flatten them to a one-inch height. Place them on greased cookie sheets. They can be close enough so that they almost touch, which they will when they bake. Bake them for 30 minutes or until nicely browned. Cool on racks and separate them after they are cool.

Finnegan Bread (White Bread)

Makes two 8-inch loaves

This is the indispensable white bread that my children love. It keeps very well, goes with everything, and has the proper sturdy texture for the trail.

1 envelope dry yeast
¼ cup warm water
1 cup milk
3 tablespoons butter or margarine

1 cup cold water
5 tablespoons sugar
2 teaspoons salt
About 6½ cups white flour

Dissolve the yeast in ¼ cup warm water in a large bowl. Scald the milk in a saucepan. Turn off the heat, add the butter and let it melt. Add 1 cup cold water, the sugar, and salt, and let the mixture cool to lukewarm. Add the milk mixture to the dissolved yeast, then add flour until the dough can be kneaded easily. Knead the dough for 10 minutes. Place it in a greased bowl, turning to coat all its surfaces. Cover with a damp towel and set it to rise in a warm place until double in volume.

Punch the dough down and knead it for a few minutes. Shape it into two loaves and put these in two greased 8-inch loaf pans and let rise again until nearly double. Bake at 450° F. for 10 minutes; reduce the heat to 350° and continue to bake for 35 to 40 minutes, or until done.

Oatmeal Bread

Makes two 8-inch loaves

1 cup oats, rolled or steel cut
2 cups boiling water
3 tablespoons butter or margarine
1 envelope dry yeast
¼ cup warm water
½ cup molasses or honey
2 teaspoons salt
1 cup whole-wheat flour
4½ cups white flour
(optional) ¼ cup sunflower seeds
(optional) ¼ cup cracked wheat

Pour 2 cups boiling water over the oats in a large bowl. Let them sit for 15 to 20 minutes, adding the butter about halfway along. Dissolve the yeast in ¼ cup warm water. When you are sure the oats are lukewarm, add the molasses, salt, and dissolved yeast. Mix in the whole-wheat flour and the optional ingredients. Add the white flour, working with your hands until the dough is easy to handle. Knead it for 10 minutes or until smooth and elastic. Put the dough into a greased bowl, turning to coat all surfaces. Cover with a damp cloth, and put in a warm place to rise until double in volume.

Punch the dough down, shape it into 2 loaves, and set in 2 greased 8-inch loaf pans to rise until nearly double. Bake at 375° F. for 40 to 45 minutes, or until done, and cool on racks.

Seven-Grain Cereal Bread

Makes two 8-inch loaves

The crunchiness and good taste of this bread are due to seven things: cracked wheat, oats, triticale, millet, soybeans, buckwheat, and yellow corn (at least in the seven-grain cereal I found—I don't know if this is a standard combination of grains, but it's delicious; I found it in a natural-foods store).

1½ cups boiling water
1 cup seven-grain cereal
1 envelope dry yeast
½ cup warm water
½ cup honey
⅓ cup oil
2 teaspoons salt
2 eggs
3 cups whole-wheat flour
2½ to 3 cups white flour

Pour 1½ cups boiling water over the seven-grain cereal in a large bowl. Let this cool to lukewarm. Dissolve the yeast in warm water. Add the yeast and all the ingredients except the white flour to the cooled seven-grain cereal and mix well. Work in the white flour and knead 5 minutes, adding more flour if the dough is too sticky. Put the dough into a greased bowl, turning to coat all its surfaces. Cover it with a damp towel, and let it rise in a warm place until double in volume.

Punch the dough down, shape it into 2 loaves, and set these in 2 greased 8-inch loaf pans to rise until nearly double. Bake at 375° F. for 40 to 45 minutes and cool the loaves on racks.

Swedish Limpa Bread

Makes 2 round loaves

I first tasted this bread *after* a backpacking trip, at a "reunion" celebrating our survival of seven days of bushwhacking in the wilds of Canada. It was good in civilization and it's good in the backcountry.

2 envelopes dry yeast
½ cup warm water
1½ cups milk
2 tablespoons butter or margarine
2 teaspoons caraway seeds
½ teaspoon fennel seeds

½ cup packed brown sugar
2 tablespoons molasses
Grated peel from 1 orange
About 4 cups white flour
2½ cups rye flour

Dissolve the yeast in ½ cup warm water in a large bowl. Scald the milk. Add the butter and stir until it melts, and let mixture cool until lukewarm. Add it, plus the seeds, sugar, molasses, and orange peel, to the yeast in the bowl. Add 2½ cups of the white flour and mix thoroughly. Add the rye flour and stir in white flour until the dough is stiff enough to knead. Knead it for 10 minutes, then put it into a greased bowl, turning to coat its surfaces. Cover with a damp towel and let rise until double.

Punch the dough down, divide it in half, and let it rest for 10 minutes. Form it into 2 round loaves. Put these on greased cookie sheets and let them rise until double. Bake at 375° F. for 30 minutes and cool on racks.

Russian Black Bread

Makes 2 round loaves

1 square unsweetened chocolate
2 cups water
1 cup bran flakes
1 cup cornmeal
2 envelopes dry yeast
½ cup warm water
¼ cup oil
½ cup molasses
2 tablespoons brown sugar

1 tablespoon salt
1 tablespoon instant coffee
1 teaspoon crushed fennel seed
  (optional)
2½ to 3 cups white flour
2 cups rye flour
1 cup whole-wheat flour
Glaze: 1 egg white mixed with 1
  tablespoon water

Melt the chocolate in 2 cups water and pour this over the bran and corn-meal in a large bowl. Let cool. Meanwhile, dissolve the yeast in ½ cup warm water. To the cooled bran and cornmeal, add the oil, molasses, yeast, brown sugar, salt, coffee, fennel, if desired, and $2\frac{1}{2}$ cups of white flour. Mix well. Add the rye and whole-wheat flours, then add more white flour until you can knead the dough. (It will be sticky.) Knead it for 5 minutes, adding more flour if necessary, then put it into a greased bowl, turn, and cover with a damp towel. Let it rise until double.

Punch the dough down. Divide it in half and form each half into a ball. Set these on greased cookie sheets, cover, and let rise until nearly double, about 30 minutes. Brush the loaves with a mixture of egg white and water. Bake at 375° F. for 50 to 60 minutes, until the loaf sounds hollow when tapped—the crust should be very dark. Cool on racks.

Note: In very hot, humid weather, this bread will not keep more than 3 or 4 days.

Buckwheat Bread

Makes two 8-inch loaves

The distinct flavor of buckwheat permeates this bread—a pungent, sort of promising smell. If you haven't eaten buckwheat yet as a grain, the bread is a nice introduction to a new taste.

$1\frac{1}{4}$ cups boiling water
1 cup medium buckwheat groats
   (kasha)
1 envelope yeast
$\frac{3}{4}$ cup warm water
1 tablespoon brown sugar

1 cup plain or vanilla yogurt
1 tablespoon salt
$\frac{1}{4}$ cup oil
1 cup buckwheat* or whole-wheat
   flour
$4\frac{1}{2}$ to 5 cups white flour

*You can make buckwheat flour by grinding buckwheat groats in the blender.

Pour $1\frac{1}{4}$ cups boiling water on the buckwheat groats in a large bowl and let them sit for 20 minutes. Dissolve the yeast in $\frac{3}{4}$ cup warm water. When the buckwheat mixture is lukewarm, add the dissolved yeast, the sugar, yogurt, salt, and oil. Mix in the buckwheat or whole-wheat flour and a few cups white flour, and mix until smooth. Add enough more white flour to make a stiff dough. Knead the dough until smooth and elastic, for about 10 minutes. Put the dough into a greased bowl, turn, cover with a damp towel, and let rise until double in volume.

Punch it down, put it into 2 greased 8-inch loaf pans, cover, and let rise until nearly double. Bake at 375° F. for 30 to 35 minues or until done.

Pita

Makes 12 pita

Pita bread is fun to make, since it puffs up in the hot oven, like popovers do, and emerges with a hollow inside. That makes it fun to eat, too, since its pocket invites a variety of delicious fillings—perfect for trail sandwiches. (See page 244 for stuffing ideas.) Judith Jones has shared her delicious recipe for a whole-wheat pita, and here's my version.

1 envelope dry yeast
$\frac{1}{8}$ teaspoon sugar
$1\frac{1}{2}$ cups warm water
2 teaspoons salt

1 tablespoon olive oil
1 cup whole-wheat flour
$2\frac{1}{2}$ to $3\frac{1}{2}$ cups white flour

In a large bowl dissolve the yeast and sugar in $\frac{1}{2}$ cup of the warm water. Stir in remaining warm water, salt, and olive oil. Mix well, then stir in the whole-wheat flour and $2\frac{1}{2}$ cups white flour.

Turn the dough out onto a floured surface and knead for about 10 minutes, adding more flour as necessary to make a firm, elastic dough. Clean out the bowl and rub with additional oil, put the dough in, turning to coat, and cover with a damp towel. Let rise in a warm place until double in volume—about $1\frac{1}{2}$ hours.

Put the dough on a large lightly floured surface and roll into a long cylinder; then cut off 12 equal sections. Form each section into a ball: Stretch the dough with the palms of your hands, gently pulling the sides down, and pinch the ends carefully together where they meet underneath. As each ball is formed, set it on a floured surface and cover with a towel. Let them rest about 5 minutes, then flatten each one with a rolling pin to a 6-inch disk. Lift the disks onto a floured surface and cover while forming the others. Let them rest for 20 minutes while you heat the oven to 500° F.

On the middle rack should be placed two or three 6-inch unglazed clay tiles, a baking stone, or a large, heavy baking sheet.

Carefully transfer the pita shapes to the hot oven with a paddle or a large spatula or by gently picking up the disks and tossing them onto the hot surface. Work quickly to retain the heat in the oven; shut the door and only peek in after a minute or so, to see that the rounds have puffed up like balloons. Continue baking for 2 to 4 minutes, then remove one by one with a spatula, resting the cooked pita on a cool surface while you bake your remaining disks. Gradually they will deflate as they cool.

Stack the cooled pita and put them in a plastic bag, pressing them further to make them compact for traveling. If you are not going to use them right away, store them in the freezer, as they'll keep for only a few days.

Nut loaves and other rich loaves

There are other sweeter breads welcome on trips where weight isn't crucial. The apple, date-nut, and banana loaves are heavy—about a pound each—but that chewy pound is packed with nutrients and a panoply of good tastes.

Apple Bread

Makes one 8-inch loaf

¼ cup butter or shortening
⅔ cup sugar
2 eggs, well beaten
2 cups sifted flour
1 teaspoon baking powder
1 teaspoon baking soda

1 teaspoon salt
2 cups apples, peeled and coarsely grated
1 teaspoon grated lemon peel
⅔ cup chopped nuts

Preheat the oven to 350° F. Prepare an 8-inch loaf pan by lining the bottom with waxed paper; then grease pan and paper. Cream together the butter, sugar, and eggs. Sift the dry ingredients together and add these alternately with the apples to the creamed mixture. Stir in the lemon peel and nuts.

Bake 1 hour or until done. Cool in the pan for 10 minutes, then turn out of the pan and cool on a rack. Do not slice until completely cool.

Note: This bread will keep less than 1 week in very hot weather.

Date-Nut Bread

Makes one 8-inch loaf

1 cup boiling water	1 egg
1 cup dates, cut up	1 teaspoon vanilla
1 teaspoon baking soda	1½ cups flour
1 tablespoon butter	1 cup chopped nuts
1 cup sugar	

Preheat the oven to 325° F. Grease an 8-inch loaf pan. Pour the boiling water over the dates, add the baking soda, and let cool. Combine the remaining ingredients with the date mixture.

Bake for 1½ hours or until done. Remove from the pan and cool on a rack.

Note: Since this loaf weighs 2 pounds, you might want to carry only part of it. Freeze the other part for another trip.

Banana Bread

Makes two 8-inch loaves

½ cup boiling water	3 very ripe bananas, crushed
¼ cup steel-cut oats, cracked wheat, or wheat germ	¼ cup chopped nuts
½ cup butter or shortening	2 cups flour
1 cup sugar	1 teaspoon salt
2 eggs	1 teaspoon baking soda

Preheat the oven to 350° F. and grease two 8-inch loaf pans. Pour the boiling water over the oats or wheat and let sit for 10 minutes. Cream the butter and sugar together. Add the eggs, one at a time, beating after each one. Add the bananas, nuts, and grain. Add the flour, salt, and baking soda, and mix well.

Bake 45 to 50 minutes, and cool on racks.

English Muffins

Makes two 8-inch loaves or 12 individual muffins

English muffins are delicious when toasted over the fire and used under Eggs McHugh (a camping version of Eggs Benedict) or creamed chipped beef. The dough can also be formed into two 8-inch loaves, which do not dry out as quickly as their prototype and can be sliced like bread. We have enjoyed the muffins untoasted, too, in unexpectedly fireless situations.

Omit the dusting of cornmeal to make them tidier to pack.

2 cups milk	1 tablespoon sugar
1 envelope dry yeast	2 teaspoons salt
½ cup warm water	¼ teaspoon baking soda
6 cups white flour	Cornmeal

Scald the milk and let it cool. Dissolve the yeast in the warm water in a mixing bowl. Add 3 cups flour, the sugar, salt, baking soda, and cooled milk to the dissolved yeast. Add the rest of the flour to make a stiff batter.

To make individual muffins: Set the dough to rise in a greased bowl, covered with a damp towel, until double in size. Punch the dough down and separate it into two parts; pat each half out onto a flour surface until ½ inch high. Cut these each into 6 or 7 round forms. Set them onto a cookie sheet that has been greased and dusted with cornmeal. Dust the tops of the muffins with cornmeal. Let rise ½ hour, then bake for 20 minutes at 400° F. or until lightly golden. Cool on racks.

Or put into two 8-inch loaf pans that have been greased and dusted with cornmeal. Let them rise until just above the rims of the pans. Bake at 400° F. for 25 minutes.

Irish Soda Bread

Makes one 8-inch loaf

You can slice this bread paper-thin for tea at home, and the same denseness makes it ideal for the trail, where it is no less elegant. Serve it with or without butter. It comes in three versions, plain, fancy, and whole wheat. For the recipe I am indebted to my neighbor Maureen Keating and her Irish ancestors.

Plain white bread

4 cups white flour
1 tablespoon sugar
½ teaspoon salt

¾ teaspoon baking powder
¾ teaspoon baking soda
1½ to 2 cups buttermilk

Mix the dry ingredients very well. Then add buttermilk to make a soft dough, like biscuit dough. Knead on a lightly floured board for 2 to 3 minutes, until the dough is quite smooth and velvety-looking. Form it into a round cake and place it on a well-buttered 8-inch cake pan or a cookie sheet. Cut a cross on top with a floured sharp knife. Bake at 375° F. for about 45 minutes or until the loaf turns a nice brown and sounds hollow when you tap it with your knuckles.

Fancy white bread

Add to the above ingredients:

1 tablespoon sugar
1 tablespoon caraway seeds
½ cup golden raisins or currants,
    which you flour lightly and stir
    into the batter at the last
    minute

Whole-wheat bread

Vary the basic recipe by using 2 cups whole-wheat flour and 2 cups white flour. The whole-wheat version uses 1 very level teaspoon baking soda.

Cakes

The standards for trail cakes are high: they must be moist enough not to crumble, they must stay fresh for many days, and they must be exquisitely good, to earn their keep.

Numerous recipes do not follow, but the ones that do have survived our screening process and are truly well trail-tested.

Pound Cake

Makes two 8-inch loaves

Whatever the first sign of a backpacking trip is in the usual household—packs lined up against the wall, tent spread out in the living room, the rustling of topographical maps—in our house, the harbinger is frequently the baking of this truly splendid pound cake.

Its worth as a wilderness dessert has been tested thoroughly, including one moonlit ingestion by a New Hampshire raccoon that dug past even gorp to feast on it in my inadequately watched pack.

½ pound butter
3 cups flour
2 cups sugar
4 eggs
1 cup milk

1½ teaspoons baking powder
Grated peel of 1 lemon and 1
    orange*-
1 teaspoon vanilla

*Avoid using the white part of the rind, which is bitter. Chop the grated peel into tiny pieces with a large sharp knife.

Preheat the oven to 350° F., and butter and flour two 8-inch loaf pans.

Soften the butter. (You can cut it into a bowl and let it sit on top of the stove while the oven heats.) Sift the flour into a bowl.

Cream the butter with the sugar, and beat in the eggs. Then add 2 cups sifted flour alternately with the milk. Stir the baking powder into the remaining flour and add to the batter, stirring only until smooth. Add the grated lemon and orange rinds and the vanilla. Pour into the pans and bake for 1 hour or until done: the cake will spring back when you press it with your finger, and it will pull slightly away from the sides of the pans.

This is one recipe where sifting the flour is important: it gives the cake a texture firm enough to withstand the vigorous buffetings it will get inside your pack. (If you sifted the flour before measuring, as is more common, the amount would then be off. It's a weird recipe, but it works.)

Brownies

These dark, moist, rich brownies earn every ounce of their "keep." And they keep well, in case they happen to last beyond the first day. After finding them to be the best brownies I'd ever eaten, I asked Luanne Sukenik for her recipe, which she said came from two neighboring spinster ladies who made them when she was a child:

4 squares unsweetened chocolate
1 cup (½ pound) margarine or
    butter
2 cups sugar
¼ teaspoon salt

4 eggs
1¼ cups flour
1 teaspoon vanilla
1½ cups walnuts, chopped

Grease and flour a 9-by-13-inch pan, and preheat the oven to 375° F.

Melt the chocolate and butter together in a saucepan over low heat. Put the mixture into a bowl and let it cool somewhat. Stir in the sugar and salt. Add the eggs one at a time, mixing thoroughly after each one, but do not beat—this would make the brownies dry and tough. Add the flour, stirring only until mixed. Add the vanilla and the nuts.

Bake for 20 to 25 minutes. Take the brownies out at the appointed time even if they seem slightly underdone, rather than relying on a "toothpick test"—they should be quite moist.

Blueberry Cake

Makes one 8-by-8-inch cake

Blueberry cake is an old-fashioned New England muffin that I learned how to make from my stepmother, who learned it from her Quaker family in New Bedford, Massachusetts. It has fed many a whaler, she said. Sweet, dense, and imbued with the taste of fresh blueberries, it's good for hikers, too, since it is moist enough to hold together inside their packs.

4 tablespoons butter ("butter the
    size of an egg")
1 cup milk
2 cups flour

1½ cups sugar
1½ tablespoons baking powder
Pinch of salt
1 cup fresh blueberries, floured

Preheat the oven to 400° F. and grease and flour an 8-by-8-inch pan, or prepare a muffin tin with papers.

Soften the butter by putting it into a Pyrex measuring cup with ½ cup of the milk and setting the cup in the oven for about 10 minutes while it preheats. (The butter will melt or nearly melt. Use potholder to remove.)

Mix together the flour, sugar, baking powder, and salt. Make a well in the dry ingredients and add the butter, milk, and the other ½ cup of milk. Do not beat or stir hard, but rather stir just enough to get the flour wet. Add the blueberries, remembering not to stir hard.

Turn into the prepared pan or muffin tin and bake 40 minutes in the flat pan or about 30 minutes for muffins.

Lizzie Smith's Shortbread

Makes two 8-inch cakes

2 cups flour
½ pound (1 cup) butter
½ cup sugar

⅛ teaspoon salt
½ cup cornstarch

Mix the ingredients into a lump with your hands. Divide the mixture in half and press each half into an 8-inch cake pan using the palm of your hand. With a fork, prick the tops and flute the edges of the cakes. Take a knife and make sections (as you cut a pie), to make the pieces easier to break when the cakes are done. Or use a 9 x 13-inch pan.

Bake at 300° F. for approximately 1 hour. Cook only until the cakes are lightly browned.

Note: The key to good shortbread is in the consistency of the butter. It should be soft enough to mix by hand, but should still have a slight chill from the refrigerator.

Cookies

The best backpacking cookies have a chewy texture. Other kinds will get stale or be reduced to powder in a crowded pack, whichever comes first. Luckily, four delicious cookie "classics"—old-fashioned sugar cookies, chocolate-chip, peanut-butter, and oatmeal—have the perfect texture for a trip: they are moist, yet have nice crunchy edges.

In order to allow these cookies to achieve their promised chewy-crunchy texture, pay attention to a few things. While they are baking, watch them carefully as they near their shortest suggested cooking time, and take them out of the oven just as their edges have turned brown.

Be sure to remove them from the cookie sheet to cooling racks immediately after they come out of the oven, so that they do not stick to the cookie sheet. For chewiest textures, put cookies into an airtight container after only ten minutes or so of cooling, before they have a chance really to dry out.

Peanut-Butter Cookies

Makes about 50 cookies

½ cup (¼ pound) butter
½ cup peanut butter
½ cup sugar
⅓ cup brown sugar
2 tablespoons molasses
1 egg

½ teaspoon vanilla
1¼ cups flour
½ teaspoon baking soda
½ teaspoon salt
(optional) ½ cup coconut, or ½ cup chopped nuts

Preheat the oven to 350° F. and grease some cookie sheets.

Cream together the butter and peanut butter. Beat in the sugars and molasses, the egg and vanilla. Mix together the flour, baking soda, and salt and add to the first mixture. Add the optional ingredients.

Drop the batter by teaspoonfuls onto greased cookie sheets. Flatten with the tines of a fork. Bake for 7 to 10 minutes. Remove to a rack.

Sugar Cookies

Makes about 30 cookies

½ cup (¼ pound) butter
1 cup sugar
1 egg or 2 yolks, beaten well
1 tablespoon milk
½ teaspoon vanilla

1½ cups sifted flour
1 teaspoon baking powder
¼ teaspoon salt
Sugar

Cream the butter. Beat in the sugar, egg, milk, and vanilla. Resift the flour together with the baking powder and salt, and add them to the first mixture. Refrigerate the dough 3 to 4 hours, until it is firm.

Preheat the oven to 375° F. and grease some' cookie sheets. Roll the dough into small balls about ¾ inch in diameter and place 2 inches apart on cookie sheets. Flatten the tops with the bottom of a glass that you have dipped in sugar. (Wet the glass first to get the sugar to stick.)

Bake the cookies 8 to 10 minutes, until they are lightly browned. Watch them carefully! so they don't get too brown. Transfer them to cooling racks right away, or they will stick to the cookie sheets. For a special finish, brush them with melted butter and dust with confectioners' sugar.

Oatmeal Cookies

Makes about 50 cookies

¾ cup butter
1 cup firmly packed brown sugar
½ cup white sugar
1 egg
¼ cup water
1 teaspoon vanilla

1 cup flour
3 cups quick (rolled) oats
1 teaspoon salt
½ teaspoon baking soda
½ cup golden raisins
½ cup shredded coconut

Preheat the oven to 350° F. and grease some cookie sheets.

Cream together the butter and the two sugars. Beat in the egg, water, and vanilla. Combine the flour, oats, salt, and soda, and add to the batter. Add the raisins and coconut. Drop by rounded teaspoonfuls onto greased cookie sheets and bake for 12 to 15 minutes.

With a spatula, remove the cookies immediately from the cookie sheet and cool on racks for about 10 minutes. For very chewy cookies, put them into an airtight container even before they are quite cool.

Chocolate-Chip Cookies

Makes about 50 cookies

1 cup (½ pound) butter or
     margarine
½ cup white sugar
1 cup brown sugar
1 teaspoon vanilla

2 eggs
2¼ cups flour
1 teaspoon baking soda
1 teaspoon salt
12-ounce package chocolate chips

Preheat the oven to 375° F.

Cream the butter with the sugars, then add the vanilla. Beat in the eggs. Stir in the flour, baking soda, and salt, and add the chocolate chips.

Drop the batter by teaspoonfuls onto ungreased cookie sheets, and bake for 10 to 12 minutes—don't let the cookies get too brown, or they will be too dry to pack well.

3

MENU PLANNING

The long trip/The group trip/
Children/The winter trip/Nutrition/
Packing/The solo hiker/Planning for
nature's gifts

. . . Taste is perhaps the most wildly idiosyncratic corner of the idiosyncratic backpacking field; and attitudes toward meal-making run it a close second.

COLIN FLETCHER
The New Complete Walker

As I have indicated in the previous chapter, provisions that you've dried or collected ahead of time look good when it's time to pack hiking food, especially when the sudden urge to lope into the hills overtakes you on Thursday afternoon and you want to depart after work on Friday. You can usually combine such foods with what you raid from the refrigerator to save yourself a trip to the store, since the food supply for such short trips is rarely complicated—it doesn't even have to be particularly light.

For slightly longer trips that involve some planning, say a trip of four or five days, you'll appreciate having dried foods on hand, too. From a supply of your home-dried vegetables and jerky, for instance, you might make up four such dinners as Jerky Stew, Super Soup, Beef Ragout, and a hearty pilaf. If the dried food you keep on hand tends to be Oriental, it's easy to assemble stir-fry dinners. Lentils, split peas, barley, buckwheat, or rice lend themselves to nutritious meal plans, especially when combined with your home-dried ground meats or vegetables. Precooked meals that you've dried (Ground Beef Mix, pasta sauces, and "refried beans" for soups or burritos) are nice to have on hand; you can easily put together the dry mixes for biscuits, white sauce, or other things to accompany them to create easy "instant" trail meals of your own making.

The food for a more extended outing (like a long trip or one involving a large group) really will consist mostly of dried foods, so the more you have on hand, or the more you can start preparing ahead, the freer you'll be from commercially prepared foods.

These trips require, as well, a written menu; some kind of an intermediate list from which to tally ingredients to buy, cook, or dry; and possibly even a total provisions list, where you can add up amounts, weights, calories, and costs.

The three sample menu plans that follow use one possible system of keeping track of all the food packed for an extended trip. Although this method may not fit your needs or personal way of doing things, it might be helpful as an example. Each plan is prefaced by a short description of the imagined trip and its food requirements, with an accompanying list of suitable dinners for that type of trip. To the right of each menu is a list of what will be needed for those dishes specifically (excluding kitchen staples). The final provision list can be used as the final shopping-checklist; while my provisions lists show the amounts and total weights of all the foods, you might also use such a list to record things like calories and costs, if necessary.

Some kind of a menu plan is essential to keep from forgetting anything or—heaven forbid—from carrying too much food. Keep in mind the goals you want for your hiking fare (lest details come to obscure them). I've usually got in mind food that is tasty, light, easy to fix, and geared, the best I can manage it, to my companions' appetites, to the conditions of landscape and weather, and to the specific apparatus of my wild kitchen. And, last but not least, remember that hiking fare is fuel. Note: My sample menus, geared to medium appetites, may call for less food than you would pack for your group. But the final tally of weights on pages 105, 112, and 118 (which do not include cooking gear), are well below 2½ pounds per person per day, so there's room for expansion. The figures are on the low side, too, because much of the food is home-dried—that's a further recommendation for it!

First, a few general comments on choosing meals.

As you think about what meals you'd like to enjoy, keep in mind the expected trail conditions. You can check the trail information at the beginning of each recipe to find out the cooking time, amount of water, and equipment necessary.

In high altitudes, for example, water takes longer to boil, so it's best to keep the cooking time short. Or, if you have to carry your water supply, you should choose recipes in which the water requirements are low. Gear your meals, too, to your source of cooking heat—for instance, a tiny cartridge stove won't cook Jerky Stew for you, but a Peak I will.

For more efficient packing of food, there are ways to save time. Check the recipes to see how you might use a dried sauce more than once, and make a large batch of it. Jerky is always useful; it is a real staple. Use it in recipes as a snack, and for extra protein in light breakfasts or lunches. A collection of certain dried vegetables can be useful in more than one recipe, and the best thing to do with surplus dried vegetables is to pack them into a bag, which will weigh practically nothing, and add them to instant soups.

As you fill in the meal chart, remember to put first the recipes whose ingredients may not keep well or that are relatively heavy, like canned foods.

When your trip extends to several weeks, pack provisions for the weeks after the first one either to be dropped to you in the wilderness (as, for instance, an air drop into northern Canada) or to mail to yourself if you plan to surface in towns. (Consult your local post office about details.)

The menu given here for the second week assumes an air drop, but if you arrange to pick up provisions in a town on your itinerary, you'll be able to shop for items like baked goods, sausage, yogurt, fruit, and eggs. Then you could simply repeat the first week's breakfasts and lunches.

The provisions list grows out of the menu chart. It is a shopping list, a checklist, and a way to keep track of what everything costs.

Although you must guess how much of some foods to take, you can use a format that looks something like this to list all ingredients so you don't forget anything. The foods listed first are figured rather exactly according to their use in specific recipes, while the foods appearing in the second part of the list are general provisions, to be estimated as best you can. Consult the chart on page 124 for a list of suggested amounts of certain foods to pack, whether you're making an elaborate menu plan or simply improvising your meals.

THE LONG TRIP

Imagine a long hike, of a week or more, with a small number of participants—say between one and four. After covering a lot of ground in one day, these hikers will be tired and ravenous. Their food should be as light as possible and simplicity itself to prepare. It should require only a modicum of equipment, uncomplicated culinary techniques, and, of course, a minimum of time. The supply of fuel or water might be limited, too.

These hikers should get together and reach a consensus about certain matters. For example, which meals can be repeated? (You might want to repeat meals in order to simplify your menu-planning, packing, and trail preparation. Using identical gear and following a similar procedure are a help when you're tired and darkness is falling.) Which "fat" should they carry—clarified butter, margarine, or oil? Which kind of sweetener? Is peanut butter an important staple? Is anyone a vegetarian? And so on.

SUITABLE DINNERS FOR A LONG TRIP WITH A FEW HIKERS

1. Dried ingredients obtained without a food dryer

Spaghetti Carbonara
Lentils with Rice or Mashed Potatoes
Spaghetti and White Clam Sauce
Rice with Dried Oriental Mushrooms
Macaroni and Cheese
Salmon, Peas, and Noodles
Pasta and Tomato Sauce
Knockwurst and Hot Potato Salad
Dried Oriental Mushrooms in Cream Sauce with Pasta
Stuffed Pita Bread
Arroz con Pollo
Beef Hash with Gravy
Creamed Chipped Beef and Mashed Potatoes
Spaetzle with Cheese and Croutons
Pasta with Ham, Peas, and Mushroom Sauce

Wild Rice with Peas and Chicken

Lentil Soup

Clam Chowder

Split Pea Soup

Chicken à la King

Polenta and Sausages

Rice with Potato and Bacon

2. Ingredients (most) are cooked, then dried in the oven (all of these meals are quick to prepare on the trail)

Erie Stew

Pasta and Home-Dried Meat Sauce

Mock Shepherd's Pie

Quick "Baked" Beans

Burritos

Meat Tacos

Huron Stew

Black Beans and Rice

Pasta and Tomato Sauce

Squash Soup

Black Bean Soup

3. Ingredients are dried in a food dryer (or good hot sun)

Lentils with Eggplant and Noodles

Zucchini and Pasta

Super Soup

Cream of Vegetable Soup

Beef and Vegetable Stir-Fry

Chicken and Vegetable Stir-Fry

Shrimp or Tuna and Barley Pilaf

Barley Soup

Vegetable and Ground Beef Stew

Jerky Stew with Dumplings*

Jerky with Peppers*

Beef Ragout*

Erie Stew

East Meets West Stew*

*Long cooking time (more than ½ hour)

Menus and What to Pack for a Two-Week Hike for Three Hikers

Menu		What Will Be Needed*
Day 1		
LUNCH	Whole-wheat pita, crackers, cheese, salami, peanut butter, jam, brownies	See the provisions list on page 101 for amounts.
DINNER	Instant soup Beef and Vegetable Stir-Fry Rice	Instant soup mix; 3 oz. beef jerky; selection of dried parsnips, carrots, zucchini, Oriental mushrooms; 1 cup rice Camp staples: peanut oil, soy sauce, garlic cloves
SNACKS	Gorp	See the provisions list for amount.
DRINKS	Tea, coffee, Hot Chocolate Mix, dry milk, Koolaid, orange juice crystals	See the provisions list for amounts.
Day 2		
BREAKFAST	Dried fruit Scrambled eggs Biscuits	Dried fruit; fresh eggs; 1 cup Biscuit Mix Camp staples: butter
LUNCH	See Day 1.	
DINNER	Instant soup Chicken à la King	Instant soup mix; ½ pkg. each freeze-dried chicken and freeze-dried peas; 5 oz. pasta; ⅓ cup White Sauce Mix Camp staples: none

*Listed here are the main ingredients from the recipes. Kitchen staples like bouillon cubes and flour aren't included.

Menus and What to Pack: Two-Week Hike, Three Hikers (continued)

Menu	What Will Be Needed
Day 3	
BREAKFAST Cream of wheat with dates Canadian bacon	½ cup cream of wheat; dates; Canadian bacon Camp staples: milk, brown sugar, butter
LUNCH See Day 1.	
DINNER Mushroom Soup Spaghetti Carbonara	Dried mushrooms; 6 oz. pasta, bacon pieces; 1 cup grated Parmesan Camp staples: butter, flour, milk, oil, garlic cloves
Day 4	
BREAKFAST Muesli and yogurt Canadian bacon	1–1½ cups Muesli; yogurt; Canadian bacon Camp staples: none
LUNCH See Day 1.	
DINNER Instant soup Beef and Vegetable Stir-Fry Rice Camp Cake	Instant soup mix; 3 oz. jerky; vegetables—see Day 1 dinner; 1 cup rice; ½ recipe Camp Cake Camp staples: peanut oil, soy sauce, garlic cloves
Day 5	
BREAKFAST Dried fruit Cream of wheat Smoked link sausages	Dried fruit; ½ cup cream of wheat; smoked link sausages Camp staples: milk, brown sugar, butter
LUNCH See Day 1.	
DINNER Lentil Soup with dumplings Carrot and Raisin Salad Chocolate Pudding	1 recipe Lentil Soup; 1 cup Biscuit Mix; carrots, raisins; ½ recipe Chocolate Pudding Camp staples: milk, brown sugar, butter
Day 6	
BREAKFAST Buckwheat Cakes Smoked link sausages	½ recipe Buckwheat Cakes; smoked link sausages Camp staples: brown sugar, butter

LUNCH	See Day 1.	
DINNER	Instant soup Pasta with Ham, Peas, and Mushroom Sauce Mixed Fruit with Brandy	Instant soup mix; $\frac{1}{2}$ pkg. each freeze-dried ham and freeze-dried peas; dried mushrooms; 6 or more oz. pasta; $\frac{1}{3}$ cup White Sauce Mix; dried fruit and brandy. Camp staples: none

Day 7

BREAKFAST	Dried fruit Muesli	Dried fruit; $1\frac{1}{2}$ cups Muesli Camp staples: milk
LUNCH	See Day 1.	
DINNER	Instant soup Jerky with Peppers Rice	Instant soup mix; 4 oz. jerky, dried green pepper, mushrooms; tomato leather; 1 cup rice Camp staples: none

Day 8

BREAKFAST	Buckwheat cereal	$\frac{2}{3}$ cup buckwheat Camp staples: milk, sugar, butter
LUNCH*	Pilot biscuits, oat cakes, crackers, salami, cheese, peanut butter, jam, cookies, Lizzie Smith's Shortbread	See provisions list for amounts.
SNACKS	Fruit leathers, Gorp	See provisions list for amounts.
DRINKS	Repeat Week I.	See provisions list for amounts.
DINNER	Barley Soup with dumplings Chocolate Pudding	$\frac{1}{2}$ recipe Barley Soup; 1 cup Biscuit Mix; $\frac{1}{2}$ recipe Chocolate Pudding Camp staples: none

Day 9

BREAKFAST	Dried fruit Bannock with jam or honey	Dried fruit; 1 cup Biscuit Mix Camp staples: butter, flour, jam, honey
LUNCH	See Day 8.	
DINNER	Instant soup Dried Oriental Mushrooms in Cream Sauce with Pasta Freeze-dried peas	Instant soup mix; 6 or more oz. pasta; Oriental mushrooms; $\frac{1}{2}$ pkg. freeze-dried peas Camp staples: none

*Food for the second week has been delivered to hikers.

Menus and What to Pack: Two-Week Hike, Three Hikers (continued)

Menu	*What Will Be Needed*
Day 10	
BREAKFAST Cream of wheat Dates	$\frac{1}{2}$ cup cream of wheat; dates Camp staples: milk, brown sugar, butter
LUNCH See Day 8.	
DINNER Instant soup Mock Shepherd's Pie Carrot salad Surprise dessert	Instant soup mix; 1 recipe Ground Beef Mix; $\frac{3}{4}$ cup Potato Buds; $\frac{1}{2}$ cup grated Parmesan (or cheese from lunch supply); dried carrots; surprise dessert Camp staples: vinegar, oil, sugar
Day 11	
BREAKFAST Muesli	$1\frac{1}{2}$ cups Muesli Camp staples: milk
LUNCH See Day 8.	
DINNER Instant soup Wild Rice with Peas and Chicken Indian Pudding	Instant soup mix; 3 oz. wild rice; $\frac{1}{2}$ pkg. each freeze-dried chicken and freeze-dried peas; $\frac{1}{2}$ recipe Indian Pudding Camp staples: butter, molasses
Day 12	
BREAKFAST Buckwheat Cakes	$\frac{1}{2}$ recipe Buckwheat Cakes Camp staples: butter, brown sugar
LUNCH See Day 8.	
DINNER Instant soup Black Beans and Rice Zucchini and cheese	Instant soup mix; $\frac{1}{3}$ master bean recipe; 1 cup rice; $\frac{1}{2}$ cup grated Parmesan (or cheese from lunch supply); fresh zucchini Camp staples: garlic cloves
Day 13	
BREAKFAST Muesli	$1\frac{1}{2}$ cups Muesli Camp staples: milk
LUNCH See Day 8.	

DINNER	Instant soup	Instant soup mix; 1 recipe Ground
	Huron Stew	Beef Mix; 6 oz. pasta; tomato
	Popcorn	leather; $\frac{1}{2}$ cup grated Parmesan
		(or cheese from lunch supply); $\frac{1}{4}$
		cup popcorn
		Camp staples: $\frac{1}{3}$ cup oil, Butter
		Buds

Day 14

BREAKFAST	Cream of wheat with dates	$\frac{1}{2}$ cup cream of wheat; dates; what-
	Jerky	ever jerky is left over
		Camp staples: milk, brown sugar,
		butter

Note: Breakfasts for Days 7–14 have milk as their only protein. Add an ounce or so of jerky to each person's breakfast to provide more protein, if wanted, to this important meal.

Provisions List: Two-Week Hike, Three Hikers

FOODS USED IN SPECIFIC RECIPES

Item	Times used		Amount		Total Amount	Weight
	Week 1	Week 2	Week 1	Week 2		
CEREALS, GRAINS, PASTA, DRY MIXES, AND SOUP						
Buckwheat Cakes mix	1	1	2 c.	2 c.	4 c.	1 lb., 8 oz.
Buckwheat		1		$\frac{2}{3}$ c.	$\frac{2}{3}$ c.	4 oz.
Cream of wheat	2	2	1 c.	1 c.	14-oz. box	14 oz.
Muesli	2	2	3 c.	3 c.	6 c. (36 oz.)	2 lbs., 4 oz.
Rice	3	1	3 c.	1 c.	4 c.	2 lbs.
Wild rice		1		3 oz.	3 oz.	3 oz.
Pasta	3	2	1 lb.	12 oz.		1 lb., 12 oz.
Biscuit Mix	2	2	2 c.	2 c.	4 c.	1 lb., 8 oz.

Provisions List: Two-Week Hike, Three Hikers
Foods Used in Specific Recipes (continued)

Item	Times used		Amount		Total Amount	Weight
	Week 1	Week 2	Week 1	Week 2		
Mashed potatoes (Potato Buds)		1	¾ c. (2 oz.)		¾ c.	2 oz.
White Sauce Mix	2		⅔ c.		⅔ c.	4 oz.
Instant soups			5 pkgs. (8 oz.)	5 pkgs. (8 oz.)	10 pkgs.	1 lb.
Home-made soup mixes Barley		1		½ rec.	½ rec.	2 oz.
Lentil	1		1 rec.	1 rec.		5 oz.
MIXES, HOME-COOKED						
Ground Beef Mix		2		2 rec. (2⅔ c.)	2 rec.	14 oz.
Refried beans				⅓ rec.	⅓ rec. (from 5 oz. dried beans)	5 oz.
DRIED MEATS						
Jerky (stir-fry dinners, snack; eat with breakfast, Week 2)	3		7 oz.	9 oz.	16 oz. from 4 lbs. beef chuck	1 lb.
Freeze-dried chicken	1	1	11¼-oz. pkg.		1 pkg.	1 oz.
Freeze-dried ham	1		11¼-oz. pkg.		1 pkg.	1 oz.
DRIED VEGETABLES AND FRUITS; LEATHERS						
Fruits (mixed)	3	2	1 lb.	1 lb.		2 lbs.
Dates	1	2	2 oz.	4 oz.		6 oz.
Fruit leathers		7				8 oz.

					Weight
Parsnips, carrots, zucchini, mushrooms, green peppers					6 oz.
1 bag of extra vegetables for soups	1	1 bag	2 bags		4 oz.
Freeze-dried peas	2	2		2 pkgs.	5 oz.
Dried Oriental mushrooms	2	1		1 1-oz. pkg. shii-take	1 oz.

DESSERTS (DINNER)

					Weight
Cake mix	1		½ rec.		½ rec.	9 oz.
Indian Pudding		2		1 rec.	1 rec.	4 oz.
Chocolate Pudding mix	1	1	½ rec.	1 rec.		12 oz.
Popcorn		2	½ c.			4 oz.
Butter Buds						1 oz.

FRESH FOODS

					Weight
Eggs			6		6	12 oz.
Canadian bacon	2		12 oz.			12 oz.
Smoked sausage links	2		1 pkg.		1 pkg.	8 oz.
Parmesan cheese, grated	2	3	1 c.	1 c.	2 c.	8 oz.

FOODS USED FROM GENERAL PROVISIONS—ESTIMATED

Item	Amount		Total Amount	Weight
	Week 1	Week 2		
Salami (2 ⅓ oz. per person per day)	3 lbs.	3 lbs.	6 lbs.	6 lbs.
Cheese (3 oz. per person per day)	4 lbs.	4 lbs.		8 lbs.
Peanut butter	1 lb.	1 lb.		2 lbs.
Jam	8 oz.	8 oz.		1 lb.
Bread				
Whole wheat	2 loaves		2 loaves	3 lbs.
pita	6 pita		6 pita	12 oz.

Provisions List: Two-Week Hike, Three Hikers
Foods Used from General Provisions (continued)

Item	Times used Week 1	Times used Week 2	Amount Week 1	Amount Week 2	Total Amount	Weight
Crackers						
Whole wheat			2 boxes	2 boxes	4 9-oz. boxes.	2 lbs., 4 oz.
Oat cakes				1 pkg.		12 oz.
Pilot biscuits				4 7½-oz. pkgs.	2 lbs.	
Brownies			½ rec.		½ rec.	1 lb., 4 oz.
Shortbread				1 rec.	1 rec.	1 lb., 5 oz.
Gorp (1 lb. per person per week)			3 lbs.	3 lbs.	6 lbs.	6 lbs.
Yogurt			1 c.		1 c.	8 oz.
Brown sugar			1½ c.	1½ c.	3 c.	1 lb., 8 oz.
White sugar			½ c.	½ c.	1 c.	8 oz.
Flour			3 tablsp.	3 tablsp.	⅔ c.	4 oz.
Butter or margarine			2 lbs.	2 lbs.	4 lbs.	4 lbs.
Oil (olive)			1 tablsp.		1 tablsp.	—
Oil (peanut) (for stir fry and popcorn)			¾ c.	¼ c.	1 c.	8 oz.
Lemon juice			1 lemon		1 lemon	3 oz.
Soy sauce			¾ c.		¾ c.	6 oz.
Garlic cloves			10 cloves	2 cloves	12 cloves	1 oz.
Ginger, fresh						—
Salt			1 oz.	1 oz.	2 oz.	2 oz.
Pepper						1 oz.
Molasses				⅓ c.	⅓ c.	3 oz.
Teabags			21	21	42	4 oz.
Coffee, ground (3 cups a day)						8 oz.
Hot Chocolate Mix (50 cups)			1 rec.	1 rec.	2 rec.	4 lbs.
Milk, dry (4 qts.)			2 c.	2 c.	4 c.	13 oz.
Koolaid (4 qts.)			1 c.	1 c.	2 c.	5 oz.

Orange juice powder	15-oz. pkg.	15-oz. pkg.	2 pkgs.	10 oz.
Dessert brandy	2 oz.		2 oz.	2 oz.

	52 lbs., 314 oz.
Total weight	= 72 lbs.
Total weight per week	= 36 lbs.
Total weight per person per week	= 12 lbs.
per day	= 1.7 lbs.

THE GROUP TRIP

The menu for a large group of people is different in several ways. Decisions are usually made by the trip "leader," rather than by the consensus of a few. The participants of a large group, who may all be relative strangers, will expect a varied menu, but the larger work force will make greater variety possible. Not knowing the group's hiking ability, the leader is likely to plan for a shorter hiking day, thus allowing more time to cook. More pots and a bigger stove encourage fancier cuisine; dinners can regularly include vegetables (or salad) and dessert, while breakfasts may be elaborate enough for such delicacies as sourdough pancakes.

SUITABLE DINNERS FOR A LARGE GROUP (MORE THAN SIX)

1. Dried ingredients obtained without a food dryer

Pasta and Tomato Sauce

Lentils with Rice or Mashed Potatoes

Macaroni and Cheese

Salmon, Peas, and Noodles

Dried Oriental Mushrooms in Cream Sauce with Pasta

Arroz con Pollo
Beef Hash with Gravy
Creamed Chipped Beef and Mashed Potatoes
Chicken à la King
Polenta and Sausages

2. Ingredients (most) are cooked, then dried in the oven (all of these meals are quick to prepare on the trail)

Pasta and Home-Dried Meat Sauce
Mock Shepherd's Pie
Pasta and Home-Dried Tomato Sauce
Quick Chili
Erie Stew
Black Beans and Rice

3. Ingredients are dried in a food dryer (or good hot sun)

Beef and Vegetable Stir-Fry
Jerky Stew with Dumplings*
Lentils with Eggplant and Noodles
East Meets West Stew*
Super Soup
Jerky with Peppers*
Beef Ragout*
Shrimp or Tuna and Barley Pilaf

*Long cooking time (more than ½ hour)

Menus and What to Pack for a One-Week Hike for Ten Hikers

Menu		*What Will Be Needed**

Day 1

LUNCH	Bread, crackers, cheese, salami, peanut butter, jam, cookies, Pound Cake	See the provisions list on page 109 for amounts.
DINNER	Instant soup Chicken à la King Pound Cake	Instant soup mix: 1 pkg. each freeze-dried chicken and freeze-dried peas; 1 lb. pasta; 1 cup White Sauce Mix; Pound Cake Camp staples: none
SNACKS	Gorp	See the provisions list for amount.
DRINKS	Tea, coffee, Hot Chocolate Mix, dry milk, orange juice crystals, Kool-aid	See the provisions list for amounts.

Day 2

BREAKFAST	Dried fruit Western Omelet	Dried fruit; 1 dozen eggs; $\frac{1}{2}$ pkg. freeze-dried ham; selection of dried leeks, green peppers, mushrooms Camp staples: butter
LUNCH	See Day 1.	
DINNER	Instant soup Beef and Vegetables Stir-Fry Rice Raisin spice Camp Cake	Instant soup mix; 10 oz. beef jerky; selection of dried carrots, parsnips, zucchini, Oriental mushrooms; $2\frac{1}{4}$ cups rice; 1 recipe Camp Cake Camp staples: peanut oil, soy sauce, garlic cloves

Day 3

BREAKFAST	Oatmeal Canadian bacon	3 cups oatmeal; Canadian bacon Camp staples: milk, brown sugar

*Listed here are the main ingredients from the recipes. Kitchen staples like bouillon cubes and flour aren't included.

Menus and What to Pack: One-Week Hike, Ten Hikers (continued)

Menu		What Will Be Needed
LUNCH	See Day 1.	
DINNER	Fred's Potato Soup Shrimp and Barley Pilaf Popcorn	A double recipe of Fred's Potato Soup using 2 cups Potato Buds; 1 cup barley; 2 cans shrimp; selection of dried green peppers, mushrooms, leek; ½ cup popcorn Camp staples: ⅓ cup oil, Butter Buds

Day 4

BREAKFAST	Creamed Chipped Beef and Mashed Potatoes	3 pkgs. pressed beef; 1 cup potato powder; 1 cup White Sauce Mix Camp staples: none
LUNCH	See Day 1.	
DINNER	Instant soup Pasta and Home-Dried Meat Sauce Fresh cucumber Lizzie Smith's Shortbread	Instant soup mix; 1½ lbs. or more pasta; 2 recipes Home-Dried Meat Sauce; 1 cup grated Parmesan; cucumber; shortbread Camp staples: none

Day 5

BREAKFAST	Dried fruit Granola Smoked link sausages	Dried fruit; 1 recipe granola; smoked link sausages Camp staples: milk
LUNCH	See Day 1.	
DINNER	Instant soup Jerky Stew with Dumplings Mixed Fruit with Brandy	Instant soup mix; 8 oz. beef jerky; selection of dried carrots, parsnips, mushrooms; 1 recipe Biscuit Mix; 2 pkgs. gravy mix; dried fruit; brandy Camp staples: none

Day 6

BREAKFAST	Dried fruit Granola Smoked link sausages	Dried fruit; 1 recipe granola; smoked link sausages Camp staples: milk
LUNCH	See Day 1.	

DINNER	Instant soup Mock Shepherd's Pie Tabouleh Salad Chocolate Pudding	Instant soup mix; 3 recipes Ground Beef Mix; 1 cup potato powder; 1 cup grated Parmesan; 1 cup bulgur wheat; selection of dried parsley, leeks, tomatoes; 2 recipes Chocolate Pudding Camp staples: olive oil, lemon

Day 7

BREAKFAST	Oatmeal Johnnycakes	3 cups oatmeal; 1 recipe Cornbread mix Camp staples: milk, brown sugar, butter

Provisions List: One-Week Hike, Ten Hikers

FOODS USED IN SPECIFIC RECIPES

Item	Times used	Total amount	Weight
CEREALS, GRAINS, PASTA, DRY MIXES, AND SOUPS			
Oatmeal	2	6 c.	13 oz.
Granola	1	6 c.	1 lb., 8 oz.
Bulgur (Tabbouleh Salad)	1	1 c.	
Rice (with stir fry)	1	2¼ c.	1 lb., 2 oz.
Barley (in pilaf)	1	1 c.	8 oz.
Pasta	2		2½ lbs.
Mashed potatoes (powder)	2	2c. (23.2-oz. pkgs.)	7 oz.
Pancake mix	1	1 rec. (2½ c.)	1 lb.
White Sauce Mix	2	2 c.	12 oz.
Cornbread	1	1 rec. (2¼ c.)	14 oz.
Gravy mix	1	2 pkgs.	2 oz.
Soups	5	10 pkgs.	1 lb.

Provisions List: One-Week Hike, Ten Hikers

Foods Used in Specific Recipes (continued)

Item	Times used	Total amount	Weight
MIXES, HOME-COOKED			
Ground Beef Mix	1	3 rec.	1 lb., 5 oz.
Meat sauce for pasta	1	2 rec.	1 lb.
DRIED MEATS			
Beef, pressed, dried in oven	1	3 pkgs.	1 oz.
Freeze-dried chicken	1	1 pkg.	1 oz.
Freeze-dried ham		½ pkg.	1 oz.
Jerky (from 4 pounds beef chuck)	2		1 lb., 4 oz.
Cans of shrimp	1	2 cans	13 oz.
DRIED VEGETABLES AND FRUIT			
Fruit, mixed	4		5 oz.
Oriental mushrooms	1		0.5 oz.
Leek, green pepper, mushrooms, carrots, zucchini, parsnips, parsley, tomatoes, 1 bag extra vegetables for soup	5		5 oz.
DESSERTS (DINNER)			
Chocolate Pudding mix	2	2 rec. (4½ c.)	1 lb., 8 oz.
Popcorn	2	1 c.	10 oz.
Butter Buds		1 packet	1 oz.
Camp Cake		1 rec.	1 lb., 2 oz.
Cheesecake (2 pkgs.)	1		1 lb., 5 oz.
Pound Cake		28-in. cakes	3 lbs.
Indian Pudding	2	1 rec.	4 oz.
FRESH FOODS			
Eggs	1	1 dozen	1 lb., 8 oz.
Canadian bacon	2		2 lbs.

Smoked sausage links	2	2 pkgs.	1 lb.,	8 oz.
Parmesan cheese, grated (with dinner)	2			8 oz.
Extra cheese (cheddar)	5		1 lb.	

FOODS USED FROM GENERAL PROVISIONS—ESTIMATED

Item	Amount	Weight
Salami (1⅓ oz. per person per day)		6 lbs.
Cheese (1⅓ oz. per person per day)		6 lbs.
Peanut butter (½ oz. per person per day)		2 lbs., 4 oz.
Jelly (¼ oz. per person per day)		1 lb.
Bread	4 loaves	6 lbs.
Crackers	6 8-oz. boxes	3 lbs.
Cookies	5 1-lb. boxes	5 lbs.
Shortbread	1 rec.	1 lb., 5 oz.
Cucumber	1	10 oz.
Onions	2	5 oz.
Gorp (1 lb. per person per week)		10 lbs.
White sugar	2 c.	1 lb.
Brown sugar	2 c.	1 lb.
Flour	½ c.	4 oz.
Margarine		2 lbs.
Salt		4 oz.
Pepper		2 oz.
Honey	2 c.	1 lb.
Oil (peanut)	2 c.	1 lb.
Oil (olive)	1 tablsp.	1 oz.
Lemon juice	1 lemon	3 oz.
Maple syrup granules	1 c.	8 oz.
Soy sauce or seasoning-thickener	1 c.	8 oz.
Teabags	48	4 oz.

Provisions List: One-Week Hike, Ten Hikers

Foods Used from General Provisions (continued)

Item	Times used	Total amount	Weight
Coffee, instant (for 60 cups)			6 oz.
Hot Chocolate Mix (for 70 cups)	3 rec.	6 lbs.	
Milk, dry (for 8 qts.)	8 cups	2 lbs.,	8 oz.
Orange juice powder	6 5-oz. packets	1 lb.,	14 oz.
Koolaid (for 7 qts.)		1 lb.,	6 oz.
Brandy (in dessert)			4 oz.
		81 lbs.,	265 oz.

Total weight	= 98 lbs.
Total weight per person per week	= 9.8 lbs.
per day	= 1.5 lbs.

CHILDREN

Children's appetites undergo a marvelous transformation on backpacking trips. For one thing, they get very hungry. And if they help with the cooking, their sense of participation joins with a general feeling of the adventure of eating "out," so they're willing to try foods they refuse to eat at home. (Of course, the lack of choice is of considerable moment in this metamorphosis.)

A canny parent strikes a middle ground between "old favorites" like macaroni and cheese or tacos and new dishes. For instance, children are fascinated by the various parts of a stir-fry and enjoy its whole nuts, jerky, and crisp vegetables, and the mysterious taste of soy sauce. On the other hand, a big serving of plain rice will please the fussiest small person. Other things children seem to enjoy are Jerky Stew with Dumplings, Beef Ragout, hash with gravy, all the ground beef recipes, Spaetzle with Cheese and Croutons, anything with sausage in it, fancy breakfasts—especially Eggs McHugh and Creamed Chipped Beef—and of course Doughboys, popcorn, and desserts.

Anyone who has backpacked with small children knows that provisions must be kept as light as possible. A young soul just attached to sleeping bag and pad, water bottle, a set of extra clothes, and a bag of gorp will notify you wordlessly that a single extra peanut added to his/her burden will weigh a lot more than a millstone.

Use the list of recipes suitable for a large group (see pages 105–6) to make up a menu for a group of children such as scouts.

THE WINTER TRIP

Winter camping is another category that requires a somewhat special menu. Your body must burn more calories in cold weather simply to keep warm. Some campers estimate caloric need to be double that of the normal requirement.

"Pad" winter meals with extra calories by adding extra butter, margarine, or oil; more cheese, chocolate, dry milk, wheat germ, barley and other grains, extra mashed potatoes, soybean powder—anything you can think of. Take a snack to bed with you. Drink lots of soup and hot chocolate. Do not eat snow, which reduces the body's core temperature.

Winter menus should feature cooking procedures that are as uncomplicated as possible, for obvious reasons. And water is not to be wasted! Because melting snow is difficult.

SUITABLE DINNERS FOR A WINTER TRIP

1. Dried ingredients obtained without a food dryer

Pasta with Ham, Peas, and Mushroom Sauce

Creamed Chipped Beef and Mashed Potatoes

Arroz con Pollo (without the saffron)

Chicken à la King

Polenta and Sausages

Macaroni and Cheese

Split Pea Soup

Lentil Soup

Barley Soup

Lentils with Rice or Mashed Potatoes

Pasta and Tomato Sauce

2. Ingredients (most) are cooked, then dried in the oven (all of these meals are quick to prepare on the trail)

Huron Stew

Erie Stew

Quick Chili

Pasta and Home-Dried Meat Sauce

Burritos

Black Bean Soup

3. Ingredients are dried in a food dryer (or good hot sun)

Super Soup

Vegetable and Ground Beef Stew

Zucchini and Pasta

Menus and What to Pack for a One-Week Winter Hike for Three Hikers

Menu		What Will Be Needed*

Day 1

LUNCH	Instant soup, bread, cheese, salami, brownies	See the provisions list on page 117 for amounts.
DINNER	Super Soup with cheese Crackers Chocolate Pudding	½ recipe Super Soup, using a selection of dried mushrooms, carrots, eggplant, parsnips, corn, cabbage; crackers; ½ recipe Chocolate Pudding Camp staples: milk, butter
SNACKS	Gorp, pemmican, chocolate bars	See the provisions list for amounts.
DRINKS	Tea, Hot Chocolate Mix, dry milk	See the provisions list for amounts.

Day 2

BREAKFAST	Dried fruit Oatmeal Smoked link sausages	Dried fruit; 1 cup oatmeal; smoked link sausages Camp staples: milk, brown sugar, butter
LUNCH	See Day 1.	
DINNER	Macaroni and Cheese Cookies Hot Chocolate Mix	6 oz. pasta; 1 cup White Sauce Mix; cheese; cookies Camp staples: hot chocolate mix

Day 3

BREAKFAST	Dried fruit Cream of wheat Jerky	Dried fruit; ½ cup cream of wheat Camp staples: milk, brown sugar, butter
LUNCH	See Day 1.	
DINNER	Huron Stew Indian Pudding with cream	1 recipe Ground Beef Mix; 6 oz. pasta; tomato leather; ½ recipe Indian Pudding Camp staples: Cream, molasses

*Listed here are main ingredients from the recipes. Kitchen staples like bouillon cubes and flour aren't included.

Menus and What to Pack: One-Week Winter Hike, Three Hikers   (continued)

Menu	What Will Be Needed

Day 4

BREAKFAST	Buckwheat Cakes Canadian bacon	$\frac{1}{2}$ recipe Buckwheat Cakes; Canadian bacon Camp staples: maple syrup granules, butter
LUNCH	See Day 1.	
DINNER	"Quick" Chili Crackers Brownies	1 recipe home-dried chili; crackers; Brownies Camp staples: none

Day 5

BREAKFAST	Creamed Chipped Beef and Mashed Potatoes	1 2-oz. pkg. pressed beef; $\frac{1}{3}$ cup White Sauce Mix; $\frac{3}{4}$ cup Potato Buds Camp staples: none
LUNCH	See Day 1.	
DINNER	Polenta and Sausages with Cheese Indian Pudding	$\frac{1}{4}$ cup cornmeal; smoked link sausages; $\frac{1}{2}$ recipe Indian Pudding Camp staples: butter, cream, molasses

Day 6

BREAKFAST	Oatmeal Canadian bacon	1 cup oatmeal; Canadian bacon Camp staples: milk, brown sugar, butter
LUNCH	See Day 1.	
DINNER	Super Soup with dumplings Chocolate Pudding	$\frac{1}{2}$ recipe Super Soup; 1 cup Biscuit Mix; $\frac{1}{2}$ recipe Chocolate Pudding Camp staples: none

Day 7

BREAKFAST	Dried fruit Oatmeal Smoked link sausages	Dried fruit; 1 cup oatmeal; smoked link sausages Camp staples: milk, brown sugar

Provisions List: One-Week Winter Trip, Three Hikers

FOODS USED IN SPECIFIC RECIPES

Item	Times Used	Total amount	Weight
CEREALS, GRAINS, PASTA, DRY MIXES, AND SOUPS			
Oatmeal	3	3 c.	7 oz.
Cream of wheat (packed with ¼ teaspoon salt)	1	½ c.	3 oz.
Cornmeal (Polenta)	1	¼ c.	2 oz.
Pasta	2		12 oz.
Mashed potatoes (Potato Buds packed with 1 tablsp. dry milk)	1	¾ c.	2 oz.
Biscuit Mix	1	1 c.	6 oz.
White Sauce Mix	2	⅔ c.	4 oz.
Buckwheat Cakes mix	1	2 c.	12 oz.
Instant soups (lunch)	7	7 pkgs.	12 oz.
Super Soup	2	1 rec.	8 oz.
MIXES, HOME-COOKED			
Ground Beef Mix	2	2 rec.	14 oz.
Chili	1	1 rec.	8 oz.
DRIED MEATS			
Jerky (snack)		Dry 2 lbs. beef chuck	8 oz.
DRIED VEGETABLES AND FRUIT			
Dates (in cream of wheat, as snack)	1		4 oz.
Tomato leather	1		5 oz.
Mushrooms, carrots, eggplant, parsnips (in Super Soup)			3 oz.
1 bag extra vegetables for soups			2 oz.

Provisions List: One-Week Winter Hike, Three Hikers (continued)

FOODS USED FROM GENERAL PROVISIONS—ESTIMATED

Item	Amount	Weight
Salami (2½ oz. per person per day)		3 lbs., 8 oz.
Cheese (3 oz. per person per day)		4 lbs.
Bread	2 loaves	3 lbs.
Crackers	3 8 oz. pkgs.	1 lb., 8 oz.
Cookies	2 pkgs.	2 lbs.
Brownies	1 rec.	2 lbs., 8 oz.
Pemmican	½ rec.	1 lb., 2 oz.
Gorp (1 lb. per person per week)		3 lbs.
Chocolate bars		3 lbs.
Brown sugar	2 c.	1 lb.
Molasses (for Indian Pudding)	⅓ c.	3 oz.
Maple syrup granules	½ c.	4 oz.
Salt		2 oz.
Pepper		1 oz.
Butter/margarine		3 lbs.
Hot Chocolate Mix (for 24 cups)	2 rec.	4 lbs.
Tea (loose, for 6 c. per day)	½ c.	2 oz.
Milk, dry (for 6 qts.)	6 c.	1 lb., 1 oz.
Heavy cream (for Indian Pudding)	1 c.	8 oz.
		31 lbs., 56 oz.
Total weight		= 41 lbs.
Total weight per person per week per day		= 13.7 lbs. = 2 lbs.

NUTRITION

Because there is so much unkown in the study of nutrition, I will maintain a respectful distance, except to report what I think are standard truths that relate to backpackers. It's unlikely that you'd do much harm to yourself nutritionally in the week or so that you backpack, anyway. But you do need energy from your food. Energy comes from each of the three kinds of food—carbohydrates, fats, and protein.

CARBOHYDRATES

Your body easily breaks down carbohydrates into glucose, *the* fuel of the body. Growing evidence indicates that a diet high in carbohydrates supplies the best energy (and general health). Runners who fuel up on carbohydrates before races perform well; rats whose diets are higher in carbohydrates than protein are more cheerful and spunky than rats fed mostly protein. The grand "spark plug" in the body's energy-burning system, carbohydrates are found in grains, vegetables, pasta, bread, cereal, and dried fruit.

Sugar, the simplest form of carbohydrate, is the "quick-energy" food, but it's unwise to eat much sugar except for that specific purpose. You can get energy from all good foods, and most have nutritional value as well. Besides, eating great amounts of sugar leaves some people hungrier, in an hour or so, than they were to begin with.

FATS

These are a more concentrated source of calories than either carbohydrates or protein, with about double the amount of calories per ounce. Include more fats in your menu plan when caloric need is higher, as in cold-weather camping.

The body needs fats to function properly, though Americans tend to eat far more than they need. To a spare hiking diet, however, you should add them in the form of butter, margarine or oil, cheese, peanut butter, and sausage.

PROTEIN

The body burns protein for energy when its supply of ready energy—carbohydrates—has run out. Stored as fat after its primary purpose of building cells has been accomplished, protein therefore is eventually perfectly useful as fuel. The adult minimum daily requirement for protein has been estimated at around 50 grams—or what you'd get in two glasses of milk and four ounces of meat (which is one ounce of jerky).

Foods that are high in protein are lean meat (backpacking meats tend to be lean), nuts, peanut butter, cheese, eggs, milk, certain dried beans, legumes, and grains—notably soybeans, lentils, buckwheat, and bulgur.

Individual nutritional needs vary according to physical makeup, eating habits as babies, specific hormonal output of the moment, etc., and—I'm sure—one's mental state. And, of course, new, not always trustworthy, nutritional theories pop up daily.

The best way to eat well, until someone proves otherwise (and from the looks of things, this will take a while), is to eat a variety of foods. Actually, it would be difficult for a backpacker who took his food the least bit seriously not to eat right, because the typical backpacking foods—dried meats, vegetables and fruit, grains, nuts, peanut butter, cheese, pasta, rice, bread, and hard salami—are excellent foods. It makes sense to include mostly carbohydrates and some protein and fat in each meal. Eating a good breakfast sets up the day's metabolism to work well. Regular exercise tends to make the body more efficient at burning fuels, so realize that your appetite will vary, and not always as you'd expect.

With all the variations in individual metabolism, experiment a little to see what suits you best. Pay attention to what you eat, and see how much energy it seems to give you as you hike; note how soon you're hungry after eating certain foods or combinations of them; and simply notice how *good* you feel after eating one meal or another. These are more important clues to nutritional wisdom, it seems to me, than the fanciest theories.

PACKING

KEEPING TRACK OF OUNCES

The weight of food to pack for each hiker varies from 1 to $2\frac{1}{2}$ pounds per day. The figure depends on such factors as the size and appetite of the hiker, the amount of fuel and water that must be included in the provisions, any special equipment that must be carried, the coldness of the weather, and the degree of fancy gastronomy wished.

10 WAYS TO CUT DOWN ON THE WEIGHT OF PROVISIONS

1. Substitute fruit leathers for gorp, Potato Buds for rice, pasta for rice, Butter Buds for butter or margarine.
2. Eat less.
3. Use recipes with only the shortest cooking times to cut down on fuel.
4. Pack made-ahead meals to save cooking time.
5. Eat heavy meals first, like canned goods, fresh eggs, and rice.
6. Pack only one-pot meals.
7. Use dried soups and dumplings for dinner.
8. Keep strictly to the pounds-per-person limit that you decide on.
9. Save fuel by undercooking foods slightly and letting them sit for a few moments, covered, to finish cooking.
10. Save water—Use the one-pot method in trail directions if it's offered as an alternate method.

LABELING MEALS

Labeling packages of food is important on all but the simplest trips.
    It's best to use ink.
    Record the following information:

> name of the food
> number of servings (if needed)
> which meal, which day

Dinners that have several parts—for example, soup, a main dish with pasta, salad, and dessert—are best packed by first assembling each part in its own bag, then packing everything into a single larger bag that holds them all; and finally labeling the result something like "Dinner 4—Spaghetti and Meat Sauce."

Include the trail directions. These can be crucial, unless you are very familiar with your recipes and do all your own trail cooking. Even a very economical set of instructions, which specifies the amount of water needed, cooking times, and the order of events, can be very helpful. (The recipes in this book repeat such things as the directions for smashing a clove of garlic, but it would be silly to write this over and over.)

Xeroxing the recipes you'll need is a possible way to duplicate trail directions.

THE SOLO HIKER

Rather than make up a menu chart, solo hikers are inclined to pack their food and cook it in as simple a manner as possible.

Excellent meals can be made by packing basic ingredients in separate bags. For example, by using the chart on page 124, you could measure out your total supplies for the trip (of pasta, rice, etc.); put them into bags in which you include notes for water amounts and cooking times; and then, in accompanying bags, put grated cheese, dried sauces or beans, or white sauce mix. Into other bags you could pack things like nuts, seeds, and seasonings.

The simple, nourishing meals that would result typically require only one pot (which doubles as a dish) and 20 minutes or less cooking time:

Pasta and Cheese

Cook 2 ounces pasta in ½ pot water. Drain. While hot, add a tablespoon or so of grated cheese, 1 teaspoon butter or margarine (they'll melt), and a little salt. Embellish, if you want, by retaining some of the water and stirring in a teaspoon or so of white sauce mix and by adding a pinch of parsley or an herb you like.

Pasta and Meat Sauce

Boil 4 cups of water (about ¾ potful).

Extract ½ cup and add it to ½ cup dried meat sauce to soak in a second pot.

In the first pot, cook the pasta in the remaining water for about 5 minutes, until almost done, and take this off the heat.

Cook the sauce in the second pot for 5 minutes, adding more water if necessary.

Drain the pasta and serve with the sauce.

Tea, Cereal, and Sausage for Breakfast

Boil 2 cups of water.

Extract 1 cup for tea.

Cook 1 sausage link for 3 minutes.

Add ⅓ cup oatmeal to the pot, boil, cover, and cook 1 minute.

IMPROVISING

Rather than making up a detailed menu plan like those at the beginning of the chapter, you may prefer to improvise when you're out in the wilderness. If so, when you're packing, use the chart that follows to figure out how much food to take.

I've based my estimates for most of these foods on what I consider to be normal serving sizes. Amounts of some foods are fairly standard, like oatmeal or rice. Others are more open to more personal tastes, like salami and cheese. My figures for these foods are calculated for appetites that I'm used to—neither gigantic nor timid. Increase or decrease your own amounts according to your and your companions' preferences—for small groups you'll be able to get together to consult about such matters. With foods like honey, sugar, or peanut butter, it's very good to find out ahead of time how many people will want them. With flour, I usually simply fill an old vitamin bottle, label it, and carry it just in case I'll find I want to thicken a watery stew or roll a fish in flour before frying it.

Multiply the amounts given in the chart by the number of days of the trip, or by the number of times you'll eat that particular food.

Amounts Per Meal to Pack of Important Foods

Item	1 person		3 persons		10 persons	
	Amount	Weight	Amount	Weight	Amount	Weight
CEREALS, GRAINS, PASTA, DRY MIXES						
Cream of wheat	¼ c.	1½ oz.	½ c.	3 oz.	1 c.	6 oz.
Rolled oats	⅓ c.	1 oz.	1 c.	2 oz.	3 c.	6 oz.
Whole grains	¼ c.	2½ oz.	⅔ c.	4 oz.	2½ c.	1 lb.
Cornmeal	2 tablsp.	1¾ oz.	¼ c.	2 oz.	1¾ c.	14 oz.
Rice	¼ to ⅓ c.	3 oz.	1 c.	8 oz.	2¼ c.	1 lbs., 2 oz.
Pasta		2–4 oz.		6–12 oz.		1½– 2½ lbs.
Spaetzle	1¾ c.	5 oz.	2 c.	12 oz.	6 c.	2 lbs., 3 oz.
Mashed potatoes	¼ c.	—	¾ c.	2 oz.	2¼ c.	7 oz.
(packed with 1 teasp. Butter Buds and 2 tablsp. dry milk, per 3-person serving)						
Potato Buds Instant powder	1½ tablsp.	—	⅓ c.	2.2 oz.	1¾– 1 c.	7 oz.
Biscuit Mix	⅓ c.	2 oz.	1 c.	6 oz.	2½ c.	15 oz.
Pancake mix	⅓ c.	2 oz.	1 c.	6 oz.	3 c.	1 lb.
Cornbread mix	¼ c.	1 oz.	⅔ c.	4 oz.	2 c.	13 oz.
Muesli	½ c.	3 oz.	1½ c.	9 oz.	6 c.	1 lb., 8 oz.
Granola						
Super Soup	½ c. mix	3 oz.	1 c. mix	6 oz.	2 c. mix	12 oz.

White Sauce Mix	1½ tablsp.	—	⅓ c.	2 oz.	1 c.		6 oz.
HOME-COOKED MIXES	Consult recipes						
DRIED MEATS							
Jerky	¼ c.	1 oz.	½ c.	3 oz.	1½ c.		10 oz.
Dried hamburger	½ c.	2 oz.	1 c.	5 oz.	3 c.	1 lb.	
Freeze-dried chicken, ham or beef	¼ c. (½ pkg.)	—	½ c. (1 pkg.)	1 oz.	1½ c.		3 oz.
Crumbled, dried pressed beef	¼ c.	—	½ c.	—	¾ c.		1 oz.
DRIED VEGETABLES AND FRUIT							
Dried fruit	½ c.	4 oz.	1 c.	8 oz.	2 c.	1 lb.	
Freeze-dried peas or other vegetables	½ c.	—	1 c.	1 oz.	3 c.		3 oz.
Home-dried mixed vegetables	½ c.	—	1 c.	1 oz.	3 c.		3 oz.
DESSERTS							
Chocolate Pudding mix	⅓ c.	2 oz.	1 c.	6 oz.	2¼ c.		12 oz.
Cake mix			½ rec.	9 oz.	1 rec.	1 lb.,	2 oz.
Popcorn	2 tablsp.	1 oz.	¼ c.	2½ oz.	½ c.		5 oz.
Oil to go with popcorn	1 tablsp.	—	2 tablsp.	1 oz.	⅓ c.		3 oz.
FRESH FOODS, LUNCH AND SNACK FOODS							
Canadian bacon		2–3 oz.		4–6 oz.		1 lb.	

Amounts Per Meal to Pack of Important Foods (continued)

Item	1 person		3 persons		10 persons	
	Amount	*Weight*	*Amount*	*Weight*	*Amount*	*Weight*
Smoked sausage links		1½ oz.		4 oz.		12 oz.
Cheese, grated (to add to dinners, soups, etc.)	⅓ c.	1½ oz.	½ c.	2 oz.	1 c.	4 oz.
Salami		2 oz.		6 oz.		1 lb., 4 oz.
Cheese		2½ oz.		7½ oz.		1 lb., 8 oz.
Peanut butter		1 oz.		3 oz.		10 oz.
Jelly		1 oz.		3 oz.		10 oz.
Bread		2 oz.		6 oz.		1 lb., 4 oz.
Crackers		2 oz.		6 oz.		1 lb., 4 oz.
Gorp (1 lb. per person per week)		2⅓ oz.		7 oz.		1 lb., 7 oz.
Hot Chocolate Mix	¼ c.	1 oz.	1 c.	4½ oz.	3½ c.	1 lb.
Coffee						
ground	2 tablsp.	—	⅔ c. for 6 c.	2 oz.	1 generous c. (for 10 c.)	3 oz.
instant	1 teaspoon	—	1 tablsp.	—	¼ c.	1 oz.
Tea, loose	½ teaspoon	—	1½ teaspoon (for 3 c.)	—	1½ tablsp. (for 10 c.)	—
Teabags	Count them out					
Koolaid	2 tablsp.	½ oz.	¼ c. (for 1 pint)	1 oz.	½ c. (for 1 quart)	2 oz.
Milk, dry	¼ c. (for 1 c.)	1¾ oz.	½ c. (for 1 pint)	1½ oz.	1 c. (for 1 quart)	3 oz.

GENERAL STAPLES

Butter or margarine		½–1 oz.		2–3 oz.		4–5 oz.

Flour	Depends on the recipes.					
Sugar, white or brown	½–1 oz.			2–3 oz.		4–5 oz.
Honey						
Maple syrup	2 tablsp.	1 oz.	⅓ c.	3 oz.	1 c.	8 oz.
Maple syrup granules	2 tablsp.	1 oz.	⅓ c.	3 oz.	1 c.	8 oz.
Salt						
Pepper						
Soy sauce	2 tablsp.	1 oz.	¼ c.	2 oz.	1 c.	8 oz.
Peanut oil for a stir fry	1 tablsp.	½ oz.	3 tablsp.	1½ oz.	⅓ c.	3 oz.
Stir-fry season-ing/thickener	1 tablsp.	—	2 tablsp.	1 oz.	½ c.	4 oz.

PACKING THE EQUIPMENT FOR COOKING

Assemble and pack your cookpots and other equipment only after you've made the final menu choices. That way, you'll be sure to bring only the equipment you need; and you won't forget anything.

A FINAL NOTE ON PACKING FOOD

After attending with utmost care to the many details of a menu plan, you might forget that your real goal is simply to eat well—after a long day's hike, you'll feel that you deserve the best!

And so, before you get totally bogged down in considerations of pounds, ounces, and calories, keep in mind certain other basic facts, to wit: that jerky is good eaten plain, but spectacular when grilled and dipped in Hoisin sauce; that leftover pancakes are delicious; that homemade bread tastes marvelous in the out-of-doors; that a surprising variety of fresh foods packs very well and earns its keep when you spring them on unsuspecting palates along about day four; that packing other "surprise" treats should be de rigeur; that backpacking children are not the picky eaters they are at home; that you can't go on a trip without inventing at least one clever cooking technique; and that wilderness dining is truly exquisite, whether you're feasting on linguini with clam sauce redolent of garlic and subtle herbs or happily gulping a makeshift supper of instant soup while the rain drips steadily, with a sweet, fresh smell, in front of your tent door.

PLANNING FOR NATURE'S GIFTS

Another pleasure of eating outdoors is the addition of wild foods to your menu. Although you can't count on them, a fresh fish for breakfast or a handful of raspberries adds delight to the week's menu that nothing you've brought with you seems to match.

Pack a few extra provisions like extra flour and butter on the chance that you may be cooking some wild foods you're lucky enough to pluck from Nature's bounty.

FORAGING

I am not a practiced forager by any stretch of the imagination, but that doesn't mean that I can't be easily tempted by tiny wild blueberries growing close to the ground along the shore of Lake Superior, or by wild strawberries that beckon fragrantly from a sunny field. Tiny in comparison with their cultivated cousins, these taste incomparably better and would encourage the most jaded palate among us to leave the fat, domesticated varieties to crowded stores and *nouvelle cuisine.* No sane backpacker leaves unnibbled wild raspberries, black or red; watercress, mint, and wild chives are also easily recognizable, delicious wild fare. Depending on where we roam, most of us eat some wild foods.

But intensive foraging, when one plans to make wild foods the mainstay of one's diet, is quite another matter. Foraging and backpacking don't really mix.

A forager is an expert—he's either a botanist or he's learned at the knee of one how to identify precisely each leafy handful he plucks from

Nature's bounty. A good place to learn expert foraging is at a botanical garden, where you can sign up for food-forage classes. This is better than trusting books. I attended two such forages on the Bronx's Wave Hill estate with botanist-savant-cook Helen Russell. Demonstrating with hand-held examples, encouraging us to nibble the while, she said that the best way to learn is to go slowly, to start with things you know for sure, like dandelion leaves, and to add new plants little by little. That is the way to avoid making a mistake that could be fatal, she admonished, waving a branch of hemlock at us.

There are other reasons why backpacking and intensive foraging don't mix. To bring the rakes, shovels, shears, knives, and pails necessary to unearth plants like *Sagittaria* or cattails is hardly the way for the back-packer to travel. And the pots and pans and extra ingredients such as fresh eggs, tomato sauce, fresh potatoes, ground beef, and ham hocks necessary to render burdock and mugwort delicious are decidedly cumbersome.

Besides, when you backpack, you are trying to get somewhere, to see the things you want to see before your time is up. Serious foraging, requiring more than a little wandering, will interfere with your itinerary.

Some recipes in this book do incorporate wild food, however, either from the accomplished forager's point of view or from the novice's. An accomplished forager would quickly recognize an edible plant and would know whether to pluck it. If a recipe says, "Fresh greens would add a nice touch," the practiced forager might be able to provide fresh greens from among the lamb's-quarters and purslane he knows how to identify. Meanwhile, for novices like myself, I have included recipes for watercress soup and berry cobbler. It's lovely to be able to put fresh mint into your tabbouleh salad or blueberries into muesli, and the more plants you can certainly identify, the more fortunate you are. Finding ways to fit flora into your brought foods is one of the special pleasures of wilderness cuisine.

But your brought menu should be complete without them.

I do not mention wild mushrooms in any recipe, except to note once or twice that they terrify me. Not that they're not wonderful—but I like to procure mushrooms in stores, where I can think of them as delicacies rather than pale question marks. If you are a mushroom expert, you are fortunate. (If you want to become a mushroom expert, there is most likely a mycological association nearby that you can link up with. Do not *ever* try wild mushrooms on your own!)

A few easily identifiable edible wild plants:

Blueberries (also called huckleberries) In late summer
and early fall, you'll find wild blueberries on variously
sized plants—growing very low to the ground, on foot-
high bushes, or even on high bushes. They grow where
they can get both sunlight and the acid from decaying
plant materials, so they'll be in places like the edges
of woods. If you don't eat them all on the spot, combine your harvest with
cereal, granola, or pancakes; or cook them with biscuit mix for a sump-
tuous dessert. Blueberries grow all over the northern U.S. and in Canada
and Alaska.

Strawberries Wild strawberries are tiny and much
more flavorful than their domestic counterparts.
They grow close to the ground in sunny places, like
open fields, all over North and South America. If
you've found a delicious crop of wild strawberries, you don't
need any advice on how to eat them.

Raspberries, red and black These berries grow in prickly
bushes, but a few scratches are a small price to pay.
They crush easily, so if you are lucky enough to find a
pint or so, eat them up. Use them as a topping for pancakes
or eat them with cereal; or make a quick "flummery" by
adding half again as much sugar, a little water, and boiling
for 5 minutes.

Mint The leaves grow opposite each other on a
square stem. These characteristics, plus mint's
easily recognizable smell, let you identify it
readily, even though there are about 10 different
kinds of mint growing in the U.S. Cut the
leaves into salads, especially Tabbouleh Salad;
crumble a little into almost any stew;
flavor biscuits with crumbled bits of the leaves.
Mint tea is made by steeping the dried leaves in
boiling water for about 4 minutes.

Watercress   Watercress grows through North America partly submerged in marshes or slow-moving parts of streams. It is harvestable from spring to fall. Use only what's above water. You'll recognize it easily if you've bought it in markets, as it is the same plant. Its fresh, slightly peppery taste makes it good for salad; and you can make a cream soup out of it, too (page 172).

Wild onions   These are easy to recognize—just use your nose. If the plant doesn't have an oniony smell, don't eat it. The onion family members that grow wild are onion, leeks, garlic, and chives. They grow all over North America and can be eaten spring through fall. In case you are digging up the root part of these plants, be sure to leave some in the ground for next year's crop. Cut the root or leaf parts into stews and soups; use chives and leek tops in salads.

Purslane   You've probably seen this small, ground-hugging succulent growing in your garden and taken it for a weed. A relative of portulaca, it has fleshy leaves and stems that add a slightly gelatinous texture to stews and soups, thickening them slightly. You can pinch off the end leaves and use them raw in salad; or add some yogurt along with a cut-up clove of garlic. Wash purslane well to get rid of the dirt or sand.

Further reading   Gibbons, Euell, *Stalking the Wild Asparagus*, New York, David McKay Company, 1962. Mr. Gibbons can certainly tell a good story. His book is informative, entertaining, and full of recipes. But anybody who urges you to raid wild honeybee hives, or to catch snapping turtles at night with your bare hands, should be read warily. (I have read two accounts of catching snapping turtles, Lillian Hellman's and Mr. Gibbons's, and of the two I trust Miss Hellman's. She related that one such irate reptile was completely determined to snap off a limb of hers or of Mr. Hammett's, causing them both to regard it with the utmost caution.) In the case of wild plants, there is such a thing as too much enthusiasm.

Russell, Helen Ross, *Foraging for Dinner,* Nashville, Thomas Nelson, 1975. Her way with the uninitiated is relaxed and easy, and she is also something of a raconteur. She has taken some care to organize the book with good food as well as plant identification in mind, and the result is a useful, and very good, cookbook as well as a field guide. (She does not mention turtles of any kind.)

Just as you can't guarantee finding blueberries or watercress, you may not be able to include freshly caught fish—that finest of foods—in your menu. But if, like many backpackers, you do pack fishing gear and hope for success, remember to take a few cooking items. Consult the basic fish recipes (pages 134–6) after you decide how you'd want to cook your fish, pack ahead the basic ingredients you will need.

The following directions for the care and cleaning of fish may be helpful. Trout does not need to be scaled.

Cleaning Fish   After you catch a fish, kill it right away—knock its head on something like a log or a rock to break its neck, if you can. And clean it as soon as possible, too. If you keep a fish alive underwater for a while, be sure to put the line through its mouth rather than its gills, as the latter torments the fish and makes it ill. And keep your cleaned fish dry, cool, and ventilated until you cook it.

To clean a trout:

1

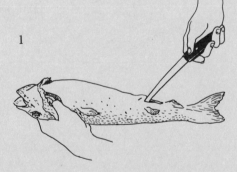

1. Hold the trout, anchoring your thumb in the gills, and slit the belly from the anal vent to the gills.

2. Cut the skin that attaches the gills to the jaw.

2

3

3. You will be able to pull the gills away from the head by putting your thumb in the cavity between them and pulling toward the tail. As you do this, you'll find that all the entrails, attached, will come away too, very neatly. If you find that the gills and entrails don't come out together, just remove them in separate stages.

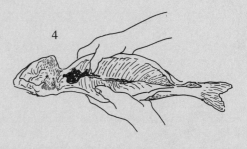

4

4. Scrape with your thumbnail back along the spine toward the head to dislodge the remaining blood vessel.

Wash the fish. It can now be cooked without scaling, preferably with the head on.

Note. If the fish isn't a trout but some other similarly shaped fish, you probably need to scale it. Do this before cleaning. Holding your knife at an angle, scrape backward along the skin from tail to head. Then cut off the fins, if they are big.

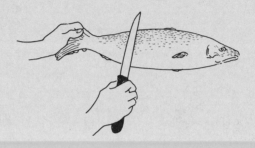

To Grill Fresh Fish   This is the simplest and, as many fishermen feel, the best way to cook fish—as long as you have a wood fire. Fry the fish over your stove if you don't.

Grease the grill and lay the fish on it over a bed of red-hot coals (not a flame). If you don't have a grill, skewer the fish lengthwise on a sharp stick, turning it to cook all sides. The old-timer would hold over the fish a piece of bacon on another stick to baste it. Be sure not to overcook: a 12-inch trout, for instance, should take no more than 10 minutes in all, and a larger fish proportionately longer.

Put a little butter on the fish after it is cooked, and use salt and pepper to taste.

To Fry Fresh Fish   Make sure the cleaned fish is dry. Small fish can be fried with heads and tails on.

For your source of heat, use either a wood fire or a stove. You'll need a frying pan, a spatula, possibly a little flour to roll the fish in before frying, and some oil, or a combination of oil and butter or margarine.

Roll the fish in the flour, if used.

Heat a frying pan, then add oil, or a mixture of oil and butter, to a depth of $\frac{1}{4}$ inch. Only when the oil is hot add the fish. Just as with other frying procedures, don't try to crowd too much into the pan; fry several fish a few at a time rather than filling the pan, which wouldn't allow the oil to stay hot and would contribute to soggy fish. (The idea is to seal the juices inside the flesh by quickly cooking the outside of the fish.)

Cook only until done, which is about 5 or 6 minutes per side in the case of small trout. The fish is cooked when the meat close to the backbone is white and you can pull it gently away from the bone.

Cooked trout can be easily filleted by first making a long cut along the backbone going from the head to the tail. Then with fork and knife pull the meat away from the ribs, going from spine down. The meat will usually come off in one big piece. Do the same to the meat on the other side.

Fresh Fish Cooked in Foil   For this method of cooking a fresh fish, you need hot coals. The foil seals in both the juices and the flavors. The fish can be whole or filleted.

Spread out a sheet of aluminum foil big enough to fold over and wrap the fish in. With your fingers, spread a little butter or margarine on the foil and lay the fish on it skin side down. On top of the fish lay such things as pieces of fresh onion, sliced almonds, parsley, more butter, and a little black pepper (no salt—it pulls out moisture). Fold the foil carefully lengthwise over the fish, turning the edges to make a seal; fold each end similarly.

Lay the wrapped fish on the grill or on a bed of hot coals to cook for 15 to 20 minutes. Do not overcook it! It's done when the meat has turned white.

To pack a foil-fish cooking kit for those fish you are sure you'll catch, put the nuts, onion—either whole fresh or dried—parsley, or spices together in a small plastic bag to use when needed. (Avoid carrying a *cut* fresh onion; use small ones.) Label this outfit "For fish," and add it to cooking rice in case the fish are, after all, uncooperative.

Boiled Fish, Indian Style   The Pacific Indians dried much of their enormous catches of salmon, and then they boiled the dried fish in baskets. If you're wondering how anyone could boil anything in a basket, here is their method, as reported by William Clark (of Lewis and Clark) in an October 1805 entry in his journal. The fish was delicious, he said.

Collect firewood and break it into small pieces. (The Indian who cooked Mr. Clark's salmon used a big piece of pine driftwood, which he split with an elkhorn wedge and a "curioesly carved" stone mallet.) Make a brisk fire, and lay a number of good-sized round stones, about 6 inches across, in the fire. Have a tightly woven basket or cookpot of water ready with the fish in it. When the stones are hot, put them in with the dried fish, and boil until done. Serve "on a platter of rushes neetly made," if you have one, or on a camp plate.

Note: While you may not be interested in cooking a dried fish or in using a basket, it might be helpful to know that hot stones will, when put into a pot, cook the contents.

4

SMALL MEALS

Breakfast/Lunch/Snacks

So we went over to where the canoe was, and
while he built a fire in a grassy open place
amongst the trees, I fetched meal and bacon
and coffee, and coffee-pot and frying pan, and
sugar and tin cups. . . . I catched a good big cat-
fish, too, and Jim cleaned him with his knife,
and fried him.
When breakfast was ready, we lolled on the
grass and eat it smoking hot.

MARK TWAIN,
Huckleberry Finn

BREAKFAST

My favorite place on a camping morning is halfway to the bottom of my sleeping bag, craftily feigning sleep, while someone else's labors send the first sudden whiffs of wood smoke and the fragrance of crisply browning sausages to my inquisitive nose.

An unmistakably somnolent morning personality, I nevertheless cling stubbornly to the concept of the Good Breakfast, even when I have to get up and cook it. I can think of several notables who enjoyed hearty outdoor breakfasts—Paul Bunyan putting away mountains of Hot Biscuit Slim's pancakes, Nick Adams serving up buckwheat cakes for his adoring kid sister when they ran away to the last good country in Michigan, Huckleberry Finn and Jim feasting on big fried Mississippi catfish.

Of course, backpacking cuts down on the scope of these classic outdoor breakfasts. Although some hikers lope off down the trail after a gulp of hot tea and a swallow of gorp, I think even the breakfast stripped to its bare bones should provide a modicum of taste, energy, and nourishment.

At "energy," the hiker pricks up his ears. There should be both protein, the food that the body takes longest to burn and thus the most sustaining, and carbohydrates, the spark plug of the body's energy-burning fund. Fats and sugars are present in some form in most breakfasts, although it is good to keep the proportion of sugar down; it hasn't any sustaining power. (Neither does tea, but that is irrelevant in view of the crucial contribution to wakefulness this valuable liquid makes.)

When there *is* time for a repast—for pancakes and sausage, for trail Eggs "Benedict," for a fancy Western Omelet using fresh eggs, or, best of all, fried fish caught by the dawn angler, and when you can build the fire to cook it on—even non–breakfast-eaters are wooed. An egg fried over the fire, its edges crunchy and brown, its yolk broken clumsily by some barely ambulatory chef and cooked half solid, transforms my son from the finickiest of kid eaters into a contented, beaming gastronome.

But the quick breakfast of cereal, augmented with protein—milk, a sausage or two thrown in with oatmeal, or a simply cooked egg—is excellent. Most of the time you do simply want to be off, doing what you came for—walking.

Granola

Makes 6 cups (1½ pounds)

3 cups rolled oats
1 cup shredded coconut
1 cup coarsely chopped nuts
¼ cup honey

¼ cup melted butter
1½ teaspoons cinnamon
½ teaspoon salt
1 cup raisins

Combine all the ingredients except the raisins in a mixing bowl. Spread in a greased 9-by-13-inch pan and bake for 25 to 30 minutes at 325° F. until very lightly browned, stirring about every 10 minutes.

Cool the granola in the pan, add the raisins, and store in plastic bags.

Eat granola for breakfast with milk or yogurt on it, or plain. It also makes a good snack.

Muesli

Makes about 11 cups (2½ pounds)

Muesli is fancy granola, and like its plainer cousin can be eaten plain or with milk or yogurt, for breakfast or as a snack. It is sensational eaten with yogurt and fresh fruit, like wild blueberries.

1 cup dry-roasted soybeans
¾ cup sunflower seeds
4-ounce package chopped almonds, or 1 cup hand-chopped almonds
1 cup chopped hazelnuts (filberts)
¾ cup sliced or shredded coconut
4 cups rolled oats

½ cup honey
½ cup peanut or safflower oil
¼ teaspoon salt
About 2 cups combined dried fruits for example:
1 cup crushed sweet banana chips or chopped dried apple
1 cup raisins

Mix together the soybeans, sunflower seeds, nuts, coconut, and oats. Add the honey and oil, and mix together with your hands. Spread the mixture onto 2 shallow pans that are large enough so that the mixture is no more than ½ inch deep.

Bake at 275° F. for about 45 minutes, stirring occasionally. Be sure it doesn't get too brown.

Let the mixture cool in the pans, and it will dry and separate as it cools. Add the chopped dry fruits in the proportions you prefer.

Whole-Grain Cereal

TRAIL INFORMATION

TIME	15 to 20 minutes
WATER	1¼ to 1½ cups
EQUIPMENT	1 pot
SERVINGS	2 to 3

The cereal can be soaked overnight to shorten the cooking time unless the weather is very hot (it doesn't keep well). (In fact, you should store whole grains in the refrigerator or freezer at home if you're going to have them around for a while.)

PREPARE AHEAD

Ingredients

½ cup bulgur, number 3 (or cracked oats, buckwheat groats [kasha], or a combination of grains like seven-grain cereal)

⅛ teaspoon salt
1 teaspoon butter or margarine
2 teaspoons dry milk
Brown sugar to taste

Packing the food

Put into a small bag with the trail directions: bulgur and salt.

Carry in general provisions: butter or margarine, dry milk, brown sugar.

TRAIL DIRECTIONS—WHOLE-GRAIN CEREAL

1. Put ½ cup cereal into a pot with 1¼ cups water. Bring to a boil, then simmer for 10 to 15 minutes, covered. Stir once or twice.

2. Add 1 teaspoon butter and let the cereal sit off the heat for 5 minutes. Add 2 teaspoons dry milk, and brown sugar to taste, mix well, then mix in a little water. Optional: An egg can be poached on top of the cooking cereal during the last 5 minutes.

Pancakes

The basis for pancake mix is biscuit mix; just add dry egg and extra dry milk in the proportions given below.

You can do this on the trail, too, if you suddenly decide you want pancakes for breakfast and you've got an extra batch of biscuit mix on hand: Add 1 tablespoon each dry milk and dry egg per cup of biscuit mix for 6 pancakes. A fresh egg is even better; and don't worry: a whole egg won't overwhelm just one cup of biscuit mix—on the contrary, it will make outstanding pancakes.

TRAIL INFORMATION

TIME	15 minutes
WATER	2¼ cups, approximately
EQUIPMENT	1 bowl, 1 frying pan
SERVINGS	6

PREPARE AHEAD

Ingredients: to make one batch of pancake mix for 18 pancakes

1 biscuit mix recipe:
  2 cups flour
  ½ teaspoon salt
  1 tablespoon baking powder

1 tablespoon sugar
2 tablespoons dry milk
½ cup shortening
1 teaspoon butter or oil

Preparing and packing the mix

Combine the ingredients for biscuit mix as given above, except the shortening. Add 3 more tablespoons of dry milk, and 3 tablespoons dry egg. Cut in the shortening with two knives.

    Package the mix with the trail directions.

Carry in general provisions: butter or oil.

TRAIL DIRECTIONS—PANCAKES

    1. For 18 pancakes, add 2¼ cups of water to 3 cups pancake mix. Stir until mixed, but don't try to get all the lumps out.

    2. Heat a teaspoon or so of butter or oil in a frying pan. When the pan is hot enough to cook a drop of batter, ladle out spoonfuls of the pancake batter and brown the cakes on both sides. The first side is done when you can see bubbles forming in the batter and the edges browning.

Note: Use up all the batter; it is much more pleasant to eat leftover pancakes than to contemplate disposing of unwanted batter. Cold pancakes make a good lunch dessert when you spread them with butter or a little honey or with whatever seems tasty, including granola or gorp. They are quite good plain, too.

To make 6 pancakes: Add ⅔ cup water to 1 cup of pancake mix.

    There are ideas for pancake syrup on page 64.

Jim Hewins's Sourdough Pancakes

Most backpacking schedules don't allow time to make sourdough batter, which needs to ferment all night and another half hour in the morning. But for a layover day or a leisurely morning, especially in a large group, these camp sourdough pancakes are a light, golden treat, with a flavor very distinct from regular baking-powder pancakes.

TRAIL INFORMATION

TIME	See above
WATER	3 cups
EQUIPMENT	Large pot with lid, frying pan, spatula
SERVINGS	10 to 12

PREPARE AHEAD

Ingredients

3 cups flour	1 or 2 eggs, or 2 to 4 tablespoons
1 envelope dry yeast	dry egg
1 teaspoon salt	1 tablespoon oil
1 teaspoon baking soda	Butter
1 tablespoon brown sugar	Syrup (see page 64)

Packing the food

Put into 3 separate bags, then package with the trail directions: 1. flour; 2. yeast; 3. salt, baking soda, sugar, and dry egg, if used.

Carry in general provisions: oil; fresh eggs, if used; butter; and syrup.

TRAIL DIRECTIONS—SOURDOUGH PANCAKES

1. The night before, put the flour and yeast into a large pot and stir in 3 cups warm water. Cover and let sit all night.
2. In the morning, add 1 tablespoon oil, the salt, soda, sugar, and dry egg (or 1 or 2 fresh eggs) to the batter. Froth it up, as the woodsman says, and let it sit for ½ hour.
3. Lightly oil a skillet. Fry the pancakes as directed on page 89 and serve them with butter and syrup.

Note: For a smaller group (5 to 6 people), make half the recipe at a time.

Buckwheat Cakes Nick Adams

Here is that famous camper's buckwheat cake method:

> Rapidly he mixed some buckwheat flour with water and stirred it smooth, one cup of flour, one cup of water. . . . On the smoking skillet he poured smoothly the buckwheat batter. It spread like lava, the grease spitting sharply. Around the edges the buckwheat cake began to firm, then brown, then crisp. The surface was bubbling slowly to porousness. Nick pushed under the browned undersurface with a fresh pine chip. He shook the skillet sideways and the cake was loose on the surface. I won't try to flop it, he thought. He slid the chip of clean wood all the way under the cake, and flopped it over onto its face. It sputtered in the pan.
>
> ERNEST HEMINGWAY,
> *"Big Two-Hearted River"*

Nick knew what he was doing; it's an excellent pancake.

Now, if your taste runs to fancier pancakes—maybe you want yours to rise, to have a hint of egg and milk in them—make a "prepared flour":

PREPARE AHEAD

Ingredients

2 cups buckwheat flour*   4 tablespoons dry milk
½ teaspoon salt   2 tablespoons dry egg
4 teaspoons baking powder   1 teaspoon butter or oil

*If you don't have buckwheat flour, grind buckwheat groats in the blender to a fine powder.

Packing the food

Mix all ingredients and put into a bag labeled "Buckwheat Pancakes—add ¾ cup water to 1 cup mix."

Carry in general provisions: butter or oil.

TRAIL DIRECTIONS—BUCKWHEAT CAKES NICK ADAMS

1. For 6 pancakes, add ¾ cup water to 1 cup mix. Stir but don't try to get the lumps out.
2. Heat 1 teaspoon butter or oil in a frying pan. Cook the pancakes until done on the first side (bubbles will form in the batter), then flip and cook second side.

Eggs McHugh

This hearty breakfast dish requires a wood fire and a relaxed schedule.

TRAIL INFORMATION

TIME	20 to 30 minutes
WATER	None
EQUIPMENT	Grill
	Frying pan and spatula
SERVINGS	6

PREPARE AHEAD

Ingredients

6 English muffins
6 slices Canadian bacon
¼ pound mild cheese, like
    Monterey jack

6 eggs
Butter or margarine

Packing the food

Package individually, then put into a larger bag with the trail directions: English muffins, Canadian bacon, and cheese (or carry in general provisions).

Carry in general provisions: eggs and butter or margarine.

TRAIL DIRECTIONS—EGGS McHUGH

1. Split the muffins and grill them, cut side down, over the fire. Butter them and keep them warm if possible.
2. Fry the slices of Canadian bacon in a little butter. Cut the cheese into 6 portions.
3. Put a piece of bacon on one side of each muffin to keep it warm. Fry the eggs and put them on the bacon. Put the cheese on and close the muffins.

Eggs Desperate

This recipe was born one morning following a Lake Superior storm of the dimensions that crack freighters. Since the storm had left both us and the landscape soaked and tired, we didn't build a fire to fry the eggs and sausages that we had to eat before they spoiled, but rather used our stove to boil them in the following improvisation.

TRAIL INFORMATION

TIME	10 to 15 minutes
WATER	4 cups
EQUIPMENT	1 pot
SERVINGS	4

PREPARE AHEAD

Ingredients

4 eggs
6 to 8 smoked link sausages

1 teaspoon butter or margarine
(optional) 4 slices bread

Packing the food

Carry all in general provisions.

TRAIL DIRECTIONS—EGGS DESPERATE (BOILED EGGS AND SAUSAGES)

1. Put the unshelled eggs and the sausages in a pot and cover them with water; bring to a boil and cook for almost 3 minutes. Pour the water off and take out the eggs, which you do not shell just yet so they'll stay warm.

2. Add 1 teaspoon butter to the sausages in the pot and brown them. Then shell the eggs to serve with the sausages, and give a piece of bread to each person.

Western Omelet, with Fresh Eggs

This isn't a *classic* omelet, of course—the pan's not the right kind, the heat source may have a mind of its own, etc. I'm not sure what makes it so good—the crunchy, aromatic green pepper; the dusky mushroom flavor; the fact that the light dry things give you more volume than the eggs alone; the fresh eggs themselves. (Don't try to do this with dried eggs, because somehow the additions totally disintegrate the already questionable texture of reconstituted dry eggs.)

TRAIL INFORMATION

TIME   30 minutes soaking, 5 to 10 minutes cooking
WATER   ½ cup
EQUIPMENT   1 bowl, 1 frying pan
SERVINGS   3

PREPARE AHEAD

Ingredients

2 tablespoons dried sliced green pepper°
2 tablespoons dried sliced onion,° or 1 teaspoon dried minced onion
2 tablespoons freeze-dried ham, or bacon pieces°

2 tablespoons dried sliced mushrooms, or 1 large dried Oriental mushroom
(optional) 2 slices dried tomato
2 tablespoons butter or margarine
3 fresh eggs
(optional) 1 ounce cheese

Packing the food

Put into 2 bags with the trail directions: 1. green pepper, onion, meat, mushrooms, and tomato; 2. cheese (or carry in general provisions).

Carry in general provisions: butter or margarine and eggs.

TRAIL DIRECTIONS—WESTERN OMELET

1. Soak the dry things in water to cover for 30 minutes. Cut off and discard the stem of the Oriental mushroom, if used, and cut the mushroom into pieces. Squeeze the water out of everything.

2. Melt 2 tablespoons butter in a frying pan. Cook the soaked things gently for a few minutes, then add 3 eggs and scramble them. Cook over low heat, adding a little cut-up cheese if you want, until firm.

°Indicates items that can be dried at home. See pages 28–45.

LUNCH

The best way to pack lunch is to go out and buy a big hunk of the best hard salami you can find. Then, since you must have a good background for this salami, you bake bread. And nothing better balances the two of them than very good cheese. (See pages 48–50 on cheese, page 54 for salami.)

Some hikers, on the other hand, find lunch the time to experiment, and they make gastronomical forays into weird sandwiches, yet-unexplored ethnic foods, new nuts, dried fruits, and highly touted nutritional elixirs that their families would never tolerate on the table at home.

Peanut butter is a great favorite for its high protein and energy content (although I consider the hiking lunch the perfect excuse to escape the stuff).

Like breakfast, lunch should have proteins, carbohydrates, and fats. In cold weather, a cup of hot soup warms chilled bones and fires the resolve. Several instant soups, such as Knorr's, are quite good.

For something to drink, cold stream water is unexcelled.

Lunch dessert is mostly pound cake or brownies, or a little gorp, or an apple someone has snuck into his pack.

The way to pack lunch is to put your favorite luncheon materials into a separate plastic package, which becomes a kind of daily smorgasbord. Don't worry much about the variety or lack of it. A backpacker doesn't get bored at lunch.

SNACKS

With all the dazzling individuality that our hiking diets display, we backpackers do share one dietary habit—we snack prodigiously. Considering the 250 to 300 calories burned in an hour of vigorous walking, the extra energy provided by snacks is a vital part of the hiker's diet. In fact, some backpackers prefer to think of the day's menu as one long series of snacks, feeding themselves, like birds, practically on the wing.

The "gorp bag" is the hiker's universal snack fund, easy to throw together and infinitely variable. Energy bars, easily made at home, can be filled with delicious nutrients. The American Indians' pemmican, which Lewis and Clark described as "Buffa meat dried or jerked pounded & mixed with grease raw," is the basis for another snack, higher in protein; the original can be vastly improved by adding dried fruits, nuts, and raisins and by replacing grease with peanut butter and honey.

Whatever snack food you prefer, give it careful attention. Make your own snacks to save money—then fill them with good vitamin-rich food, instead of "empty" sugar calories that supermarket snacks often contain. Pack enough snack food to last the whole trip, and give each person his own ration to mete out as he will—this has its own special pleasure, which children, as you might expect, learn from.

In winter, snacks gain more dietary importance because the body needs many more calories to keep warm as well as travel efficiently. In very cold weather, even after you've padded meals with calories by adding fats, cheese, extra dry milk, dry soups, barley, etc., a 260-calorie candy bar has far more significance than it does displayed in the lobby of the building where you sit at your desk all day. It's even a good idea to take a snack to bed with you on a winter trip in case you wake up, chilled, in the middle of the night.

Note: It's always nice to pack a "surprise treat" to pull out of your pack when people are least expecting it, to present either as a snack or a surprise dessert. While our taste runs to fancy foods that we otherwise never buy except for presents, like elaborately coated nuts, Macadamia nuts, halvah, excellent licorice, maple sugar candy, very good dried fruit, a Droste chocolate apple, Swedish "fish" (well, *this* list could go on quite a bit longer)— you'll have your own idea of a special treat.

Gorp, like pemmican, is snack food. The word is an acronym for "good old raisins and peanuts." I wonder if I'm the only person who has ever thought of renaming it; but I fear that to dislodge from the hiker's vocabulary a word that names the very kernel of the backpacking diet is a task beyond even the most determined etymologist.

With a higher sugar content than pemmican, gorp's function is to give quick energy. Its ingredients vary endlessly according to personal taste, on a basic theme of nuts, M & M's, and raisins. Each hiker, including each little kid, should have his own plastic bag filled with gorp, to use at his own rate.

Two recipes for gorp follow.

Classic G.O.R.P.

M & M's   Peanuts, cashews, or mixed nuts
Raisins

If the nuts are salted, put them into a mixing bowl and shake them up to dislodge some of the salt. Take the nuts out with your hands, and, starting with another bowl or using the same one after you've discarded the extra salt, add the other ingredients. Mix them all with your hands. Pack a bag of gorp for each person and fasten with a twist tie. It is not a good idea to use Ziploc bags for gorp because they will not outlast the endless openings and shuttings to which they will be subjected.

Note: There is another side to this salt business. If you do not use much salt in cooking, the extra salt on the nuts will be important, especially in hot weather, for the body's salt requirement. (See page 70 for more on salt.)

G.O.R.P. II

Peanuts, cashews, or mixed nuts
Sweet banana chips

Chopped, sugared dates

Mix the ingredients in a bowl with your hands, after shaking off any excess salt, per the recipe above. Pack the mixture into evenly divided portions for each hiker, using plastic bags with twists.

Pemmican

The Indians made pemmican from their stores of dried foods. It is good traveling fare as it is full of protein and keeps indefinitely. The rather strong flavor of pemmican can be varied according to the requirements of your palate. Apricots are stronger in flavor, for instance, than other dried fruits, and the cayenne can be omitted.

Two 2½-ounce packages pressed, cooked beef, dried and crushed*
1½ cups raisins
1½ cups chopped nuts—peanuts, cashews, pecans, etc.

1 cup chopped dried fruit—apples, peaches, dates, apricots, etc.
2 tablespoons honey
2 tablespoons peanut butter
(optional) Dash of cayenne pepper

Put the crushed dried beef in a mixing bowl. Add the raisins, nuts, and fruits, and mix.

In a saucepan, gently heat the honey and peanut butter until they melt. Blend them into the dry ingredients. Add cayenne to taste.

Pack the pemmican into one large bag or several small ones.

*Buy this in the lunchmeat section of the supermarket. To dry, see page 30.

Jerky with Dip

Jerky is a fine snack, whether you have dried it simply seasoned with salt and pepper or marinated. (See pages 39–41.)

For a delicious appetizer, or a meat accompaniment to a pilaf or other meatless dish, eat jerky the way it comes, or grill it over the fire.

A dip of spicy-sweet Hoisin sauce (see page 46) is good. Or make a special dip before you leave home by combining 4 tablespoons Hoisin sauce with 1 tablespoon each peanut butter and Chinese sesame oil.

Peanut-Butter–Honey Bars

Makes twenty-four 1-by-2-inch bars

1 cup peanut butter
½ cup honey
½ cup wheat germ

½ cup coconut
½ cup quick oats
Powdered sugar

Put the peanut butter and honey in a small bowl, and set it on top of the stove while the oven preheats to 250° F.

Mix the wheat germ, coconut, and oats. Then add the peanut butter and honey and mix well.

Sprinkle some powdered sugar on your counter top. Press the mixture out on it to make a rectangle about 6 by 10 inches. Sprinkle powdered sugar over the top of the rectangle. Then cross-cut into 24 bars.

Bake for 30 minutes at 250° F. on an ungreased cookie sheet, and cool on racks. Put the bars in a plastic bag to carry.

Note: Vary the "dry" ingredients with such things as chopped dates, nuts, and other dried fruits. Remember to maintain a general approximation of proportions: 1 cup peanut butter and $\frac{1}{2}$ cup honey to $1\frac{1}{2}$ cups other things.

Cheese Squares

Makes twenty-four $1\frac{1}{2}$-inch squares

I must warn you of two drawbacks of these wonderful little mouthfuls: they're so delicious hot that you'll have a hard time getting them as far as your pack; and they are of such a delicate texture that they won't last long before they turn to crumbs. But enjoy the crumbs.

$\frac{1}{4}$ pound ($\frac{1}{2}$ cup) butter
1 cup grated cheddar cheese, about
    6 ounces

$\frac{3}{4}$ cup flour
$\frac{1}{4}$ teaspoon salt

Preheat the oven to 400° F.

Soften the butter and mix well with the grated cheese, flour, and salt.

Press out onto a cookie sheet in a rectangular shape and smooth the edges. (The mixture will spread, so be sure your pan has rims or that the cheese dough doesn't come within a few inches of the edge.)

Bake for 20 minutes, until just golden brown. As soon as you remove them from the oven, cut into 24 squares or rectangles with a sharp knife, and transfer these to cooling racks.

Stack the squares inside a small plastic bag with a tie, and protect from getting smashed in your pack, possibly by putting in a cookpot.

5

THE MEAL AT THE
END OF THE DAY

*Soup/Camp breads/Main dishes/
Grains as side dishes/Salads and
vegetables/Camp desserts*

*I can remember picnics at the beach or in the
woods when the salty tang of the sea breeze or
the fresh sharp scent of the pines seemed like
nature's spice for the food we were eating.*

JAMES BEARD,
Beard on Food

Good food and beautiful surroundings go together. But it's more than that. It's that you walked to your dinner spot, independent, self-reliant, self-contained. And it's more than that, too—there is a magic in the combination of the beauty or the power of Nature (depending) and the way you feel. After you have left all the rattleclaptrap of civilization a few days behind you, your automatic screening-out of its din and dirt finally winds down. You realize, startled, the extent of the constant energy you have had to expend in that necessary self-protection. Now your senses are eagerly (vulnerably, as you learn on re-entry) open to every sight and sound and smell— the sudden lift of a startled bird ahead of you, the pattern of sunlight that reaches the forest floor, the sound of the wind in branches, the cool, sweet taste of mountain water, the music it makes falling over rocks, the smell of moss and of fir and even of sweet, reedy sand. No wonder you're ready to appreciate good food.

Reward—celebration—warmth—conviviality—exhilaration—dinner means all these things to the backpacker.

The preparation for dinner is part of the ritual of pleasant domestic chores called "setting up camp"—locating water, finding a level spot (very gratefully), donning camp slippers, pitching the tent, fluffing out the sleeping bag, rummaging in the pack for dinner supplies. All this proceeds in fairly predictable order.

The fisherman interrupts this ritual before the last step, seizes his fishing gear, and retires for an hour to the dappled shade of the stream. The forager, sniffing wild onion, vanishes to investigate. The hiker with a stir-fry repast in mind pauses long enough before putting up his tent to cover with water a handful of jerky, Oriental mushrooms, tiger lily buds, sliced vegetables, and tiny shrimp. According to his timing, by the time his tent is pitched, and his sleeping bag beginning to fluff to its promised loft, the mushrooms will have attained theirs and be ready for the skillet, whereupon he will measure rice into a cookpot and add twice the water, light his stove, and so begin a familiar, delicious dinner.

Or the wilderness menu might begin with a revitalizing hot soup, focus on a hearty stew to which camp breads in some form are a vital addition, continue with a crunchy salad, and end with a rich chocolate dessert.

The circumstances of the campsite influence the culinary output from your brought provisions, of course. Pudding won't cool without a cold stream; fish, historically, aren't always cooperative; and jerky stew has to wait for another night if it's raining, and you choose to eat soup with dumplings for dinner instead.

When you consult the trail information at the beginning of the recipes, you'll see that preparation time on the trail varies between 10 minutes and an hour. Integrate soaking time into your camp activities, which is usually no problem when soaking time is only 30 minutes.

Some dinners are unsuitable for large groups, while others would be impractical for the solo hiker. For instance, enough Spaghetti and White Clam Sauce for 10 people requires 3 to 4 cans of clams, while the solo hiker would think it a little silly to carry 1 can of clams to eat up all by himself at one meal—and clams don't keep. But the dish is elegant for 2. A stir-fry is perfect for 1 to 5 people but gets a little unwieldy for 10. Two people might not want to putter over jerky stew for an hour, but it's a splendid meal for a medium-size or large group. Shrimp-barley pilaf easily feeds a mob, but for one it's ridiculous. And so on. However, you may see possibilities in a dish that I don't, or have appetites to feed that far exceed the norm, or think of ways to stretch a recipe with extra ingredients. On balance, it's probably better to bring too little than too much, not only because no one wants to carry superfluous weight, but because any *cooked* extra food is heavy to carry out and wrong to throw away.

Within this chapter are descriptions of a few basic cooking techniques that unfetter you from expensive, dull supermarket "quickies" and freeze-dried dinners.

Pasta is wonderful wilderness fare—delicious, light, and easy to make quick sauces for. Learn to cook pasta properly, to dress it with a range of simple sauces, and accord it the elegant place on the trail menu it deserves.

Chinese stir-fry methods are perfectly adaptable to the wild kitchen. It's hard to resist making stir-fry meals the principal wilderness meals— once you know how easy and how rewarding it is to cook with garlic and ginger (that is, fresh cloves and root, not dehydrated varieties) and with other fresh ingredients that Madison Avenue hasn't brainwashed you into thinking are inconvenient to cook with. In addition, Chinese dried foods are fascinating, delicious, and not hard to obtain.

Since fillings for Mexican tacos and Burritos can be made and dried at home and tortillas can be easily warmed, Mexican meals are among the simplest to make on the trail.

Learn how to cook plain rice and fancy rice (pilafs), and extend the knowledge to delicious whole grains, lovingly appreciated by vegetarians and by people in much of the rest of the world.

Making gravy out of bouillon and basic white sauce, *béchamel*, out of butter, flour, and milk are so easy that every hiker should know how to thicken a watery sauce, extend a dish to feed more people, or simply make it tastier. Gravy and white sauce allow you to turn jerky, dried hamburger, and freeze-dried meats into good dinners.

The biscuit mix you make at home yields a fluffy product even when cooked over a backpacking stove. You can easily make dumplings instead, when pans are scarce, by floating the same batter on top of a hearty stew or soup.

Adding even an ounce or two of cheese to the top of a dinner is a good way to increase protein and fat, and it can do wonders for the taste of many dishes. Butter, margarine, and oil are good additions; and dried bacon pieces, freeze-dried meat, and smoked sausages are tasty ways to add protein.

The processes described in Chapter 2 for cooking, drying, and packing at home help you prepare for camp cooking that requires minimal complexity and water (for instance, winter camping). Recipes for make-ahead meals using Basic Ground Beef Mix and refried beans are the wilderness epicure's homemade answer to commercial instant meals.

Other ways to shorten camp cooking time and to carry less weight are to incorporate Butter Buds into meals rather than adding butter or margarine; use a White Sauce Mix rather than making white sauce from scratch; choose the 1-pot method for dishes like pasta, to save water as well as time. (See page 121 for a list of ways to save weight.)

Soups are a boon to the menu planner, whether they are the instant soup you buy for a quick first course or a more elaborate home-packed soup hearty enough to plan *as* dinner. To some soups, as you can see when exploring the soup section that follows, the addition of dumplings makes a truly delicious meal, as do other accompaniments—even bread and cheese borrowed from lunch. Under extreme duress caused by weather, longer hiking than you expected, or an unforeseen insect attack, a soup meant to be predinner can fill in as the main dish. Predinner soups are perfectly useful when used as planned; in addition to the wonderful lift they give to weary bones, they diminish the appetite so portions of dinner can be smaller, allowing you to cut down on food weight if necessary when packing.

You'll find main dish ideas in several places in the book. For example, check the potato recipes (pages 251–4) and the ideas for stuffing pita (page 244).

When adding salad, soup, or vegetable to dinner, think about how it might complement the main dish. Balance an all-white pasta dish with a crunchy green vegetable. Precede hearty Huron Stew with Mushroom Soup. Rice with Potato and Bacon asks for something spicy like Cole Slaw with a sweet-sour dressing. Tabbouleh Salad, with its fresh flavors and crunchy texture, joins nicely with any stew. It's not the same palette of colors and textures you have at home to choose from, but in the wild you appreciate, undistracted, small things—the wonderful aromatic crunch of almonds in a stir-fry, the creamy mushroom sauce on properly cooked pasta, or the surprising tart-dusky combination of good Parmesan with lentils.

Desserts aren't as important to the solo hiker as they are to the family group or the congenial epicurean party who may be "hiking to eat." One of the nicest things about dessert is its surprise value: turning over a home-made cake mix to the culinary putterer to fool with long after everyone else has sated himself will yield a sybaritic reward just when you thought you'd never be hungry again.

Black Bean Soup

It is possible to use other beans, like navy or pinto, to make this soup.

TRAIL INFORMATION

TIME	10 minutes
WATER	4 cups
EQUIPMENT	1 pot
SERVINGS	4

PREPARE AHEAD

Ingredients

2 cups dried cooked black beans*
2 beef bouillon cubes
1 tablespoon dried minced onion°
½ teaspoon dry mustard
2 cloves garlic

(optional) 2 tablespoons each dried
    green pepper and parsley°
(optional) ⅔ cup grated cheese
1 tablespoon butter or oil

*From two 16-ounce cans or ⅔ pound dried beans; see pages 36 and 237.

Packing the food

Put into 2 small bags, then package with the trail directions: 1. beans, bouillon, onion, mustard, garlic, optional green pepper and parsley; 2. cheese (or carry in general provisions, ungrated).

Carry in general provisions: butter or oil.

TRAIL DIRECTIONS—BLACK BEAN SOUP

1. Smash the garlic cloves with the flat of your knife to remove their skins. Cut into bits and cook for a few minutes in 1 tablespoon butter or oil in a pot.

2. Add the remaining contents of the bean bag and 4 cups water, and cook 10 minutes. Add grated cheese or cut in a few tablespoons of cheese from the lunch supply.

Squash Soup

This is a thick, tasty soup that you can make quickly in camp in one step. The base is dried puréed squash; since that's good enough to eat as is, the soup follows suit and is delicious.

Other soups you can make from puréed vegetables, following the same basic directions, include cream of parsnip, carrot, broccoli, celery, beans, or a mixture of vegetables (for instance, the purée of potato, turnip, carrot, onion, and celery on the next page).

TRAIL INFORMATION

TIME	10 minutes
WATER	2 cups
EQUIPMENT	1 pot
SERVINGS	2 to 4

PREPARE AHEAD

Ingredients

½ cup dried puréed squash (see page 35)
2 tablespoons White Sauce Mix (see page 60)

Small pinch of ginger and of nutmeg
½ teaspoon dried minced onion°
Salt to taste

Packing the food

Pack all the ingredients together with the trail directions.

TRAIL DIRECTIONS—SQUASH SOUP

Add 2 cups water to the dried ingredients, stir well, as you heat them to boiling. Simmer for a few minutes; add more salt to taste.

°Indicates items that can be dried at home. See pages 28–45.

Puréed Vegetable Soup

Try this delicious puréed soup made of five vegetables for a speedy and fine trail soup.

It is important neither to overcook nor to overdry the soup, in order to preserve its delicate flavors.

TRAIL INFORMATION

TIME	10 minutes
WATER	About 4 cups
EQUIPMENT	1 pot; a small whisk helps
SERVINGS	4 to 8

PREPARE AHEAD

Making and drying the soup

2 teaspoons butter
1 tablespoon oil
1 large onion, chopped fine
1 medium potato, peeled and
    chopped fine
2 carrots, peeled and chopped fine

2 ribs celery, chopped fine
2 turnips or parsnips, chopped fine
Freshly ground pepper and nutmeg
2 chicken bouillon cubes
(optional) ½ cup dry milk
Salt to taste

Heat the butter and oil in a large saucepan, and cook the onion over low heat about 5 minutes, until soft. Add the rest of the vegetables and just enough water to cover them, about 1½ cups. Grind in some pepper and some fresh nutmeg, add the bouillon, and bring to a boil. Then simmer, covered, for 30 minutes but no longer. Add optional milk and salt to taste.

Purée the soup in the blender, about a cup at a time. Spray cookie sheets or other flat pans with nonstick spray, then spread the soup out and dry it in the oven at 140° F. for 6 hours or until you can pull it away from the baking sheet.

Note: You will have 2 cups dried soup, which needs approximately double the amount of water to reconstitute. If you consider using part at a time, remember that ½ cup dried soup makes 1 generous or 2 small servings.

Packing the food

Put the dried soup in a plastic bag with the trail directions.

TRAIL DIRECTIONS

Put the soup in a cookpot. Add 4 cups water. Bring to a boil, stirring, then cover and simmer for a few minutes. If you've got a wire whisk, it will help to get the lumps out.

Fred's Potato Soup

TRAIL INFORMATION

TIME	10 minutes
WATER	4 cups
EQUIPMENT	1 pot
SERVINGS	4 to 6

PREPARE AHEAD

Ingredients

1 cup Potato Buds
½ cup dried milk
2 envelopes instant beef bouillon
    (about 1 tablespoon)

1 tablespoon dried parsley°
Pinch of thyme

Packing the food

Package all ingredients together with the trail directions.

TRAIL DIRECTIONS—FRED'S POTATO SOUP

    1. In a pot, boil 4 cups water.
    2. Add the dry ingredients, bring back to a boil, and simmer for a moment.

Lentil Soup

TRAIL INFORMATION

TIME	30 minutes
WATER	3 cups
EQUIPMENT	1 pot
SERVINGS	2 to 3

PREPARE AHEAD

Ingredients

½ cup lentils
1 teaspoon dried carrot flakes°
1 teaspoon dried minced onion°
¼ to ½ teaspoon salt
¼ cup Potato Buds
(optional) 1 teaspoon butter or
    margarine, or 2 tablespoons
    Parmesan cheese

(optional) 1 cup biscuit mix for
    dumplings (see page 174),
    packed in its own bag and
    carried with the soup

Packing the food

Put into 3 small bags, then package with the trail directions:

Lentils, carrot, onion,
    and salt

Potato Buds
Biscuit mix

Carry in general provisions: optional butter or cheese

TRAIL DIRECTIONS—LENTIL SOUP

1. Add 3 cups water to the lentil mixture in a pot. Cover and bring to a boil; then take the pot off the heat to sit for 15 minutes.

2. Boil again, simmer for 15 minutes. Add Potato Buds and cook a few more minutes. Add 1 teaspoon butter or margarine or cut some Parmesan cheese into the soup.

3. To make dumplings: Add ¼ cup water to 1 cup biscuit mix and make a stiff batter. Form into small balls about the size of ping-pong balls and float them on top of the soup. Cover so they steam and cook until done during the last 20 minutes, cooking time.

Split Pea Soup

This is a good soup, certainly hearty enough for dinner, when you make camp early enough to allow an hour to soak the peas before cooking. Dumplings turn the soup into a feast to satisfy the hungriest appetite.

TRAIL INFORMATION

TIME	1 hour soaking, 30 minutes cooking
WATER	4½ to 5 cups
EQUIPMENT	1 pot
SERVINGS	6

PREPARE AHEAD

Ingredients

¾ cup (½ pound) split peas
2 tablespoons dried diced ham°
1 tablespoon dried minced onion°
¼ cup carrot flakes or vegetable flakes°
(optional) ¼ cup White Sauce Mix (see page 59) or Potato Buds

(optional) 1 cup biscuit mix (see page 174), packed in its own bag and carried with the soup
½ teaspoon salt
Pepper to taste

Packing the food

Put into 3 small bags, then package with the trail directions: 1. peas, ham, and vegetables; 2. White Sauce Mix or Potato Buds; 3. biscuit mix.

Carry in general provisions: salt and pepper.

TRAIL DIRECTIONS—SPLIT PEA SOUP

1. Empty the contents of the pea bag into a pot and add 2½ cups water. Cover, bring to a boil, and simmer for 2 minutes. Turn the heat off and let sit for 1 hour.

2. Add 2 more cups water and ½ teaspoon salt and some pepper. Bring to a boil and simmer for 30 minutes.

3. Add ¼ cup White Sauce Mix or Potato Buds, stir, and cook a few more minutes. Add more water if the soup is too thick.

4. To make dumplings: Add ¼ cup water to 1 cup biscuit mix and make a stiff batter. Form into small balls about the size of ping-pong balls and float them on top of the soup. Cover so they steam and cook until done during the last 20 minutes' cooking time.

A note on adding White Sauce Mix: When you dump White Sauce Mix into a hot soup, it will make lumps, which most backpackers ignore under arduous conditions. Under refined conditions (for instance, in daylight, in temperatures above freezing, in air not aswarm with insects), you can take the trouble to avoid the lumps: Add enough cold water to the mix in a separate cup to make a thin paste, then stir that into the soup. Using a whisk helps, too.

Barley Soup

This is a hearty soup full of good flavors.

TRAIL INFORMATION

TIME	30 minutes
WATER	3 to 4 cups
EQUIPMENT	1 pot
SERVINGS	6 to 10

PREPARE AHEAD

Ingredients

2 beef bouillon cubes, or 1 Knorr's double beef bouillon cube
¼ cup barley
2 tablespoons dried sliced green pepper, broken°

¼ cup dried sliced mushrooms, broken°
1 tablespoon dried minced onion°
1 teaspoon dried carrot flakes°
½ tablespoon dried parsley°

(optional) Few pieces of jerky, broken (see page 39)
2 tablespoons flour
¼ teaspoon salt
2 to 3 tablespoons butter or

margarine
(optional) 1 cup biscuit mix (see page 174), packed in its own bag and carried with the soup

Packing the food

Take the bouillon cubes out of their wrappers and package everything except the butter with the trail directions.

Carry the butter or margarine in general provisions.

TRAIL DIRECTIONS—BARLEY SOUP

1. Melt 2 to 3 tablespoons butter in a pot. Add the dry ingredients and stir a few minutes until the flour is absorbed.
2. Add 3 to 4 cups water, cover, and cook 20 to 30 minutes.
3. To make dumplings: Add ¼ cup water to 1 cup biscuit mix and make a stiff batter. Form into small balls about the size of ping-pong balls and float them on top of the soup. Cover so they steam and cook until done during the last 20 minutes' cooking time.

Mushroom Soup

The extra step of soaking, then browning the mushrooms results in an excellent soup.

TRAIL INFORMATION

TIME	10 minutes soaking, 10 minutes cooking
WATER	4 cups
EQUIPMENT	1 cookpot, 1 dish for soaking the mushrooms
SERVINGS	4 to 6

PREPARE AHEAD

Ingredients

1 cup dried sliced mushrooms°
   (about 10 ounces fresh
   mushrooms)
3 tablespoons dried minced onion°

½ cup dry milk
1 chicken bouillon cube
4 tablespoons butter or margarine
4 tablespoons flour

Packing the food

Put into 2 small bags, then package with the trail directions: 1. mushrooms and onion; 2. dry milk and bouillon cube (unwrapped).

Carry in general provisions: butter or margarine and flour.

TRAIL DIRECTIONS—MUSHROOM SOUP

1. Soak the mushrooms and onion for 10 minutes. Drain them and save the water.

2. Brown the mushrooms and onion in 4 tablespoons heated butter. Add 4 tablespoons flour and cook 2 minutes.

3. Add enough water to the reserved soaking water to make 4 cups. Add the dry milk, bouillon cube, and the water to the pot. Stir and cook gently for about 5 minutes.

Cream of Vegetable Soup

This is a very nourishing soup, which can be dinner in itself. The vegetables in the master recipe are a suggested combination which can be varied to include potatoes, green beans, corn, peas, tomatoes, and celery, to name a few. You could also make the soup using a single vegetable. Dried bacon pieces or other dried meat such as beef, ham, or chicken add protein and flavor.

As with all white sauce recipes, try to keep the fire low; anything with milk in it will burn quite easily.

TRAIL INFORMATION

TIME	10 minutes soaking, 10 minutes cooking
WATER	2 cups
EQUIPMENT	1 pot
SERVINGS	2 or 3

PREPARE AHEAD

Ingredients

1 cup dried sliced vegetables, such as a mixture of zucchini, carrots, parsnips, and mushrooms° (see page 34)
½ teaspoon dried minced onion, or 1 tablespoon dried leek°
Small pinch of thyme

½ teaspoon dried parsley°
(optional) 2 tablespoons freeze-dried beef, ham, or chicken
⅓ cup White Sauce Mix (see page 59)

Packing the food

Put into 2 small bags, then package with the trail directions: 1.vegetables, onion, thyme, and parsley, and optional meat; 2.White Sauce Mix.

TRAIL DIRECTIONS—CREAM OF VEGETABLE SOUP

1. Soak the vegetables in 1 cup water in a cookpot for about 10 minutes.
2. Add 1 more cup of water, bring to a boil, and cook 10 minutes. Add ⅓ cup White Sauce Mix and cook slowly until the soup becomes slightly thick, 3 to 5 minutes.

Clam Chowder

As with many recipes in this book, don't hesitate to substitute for dried ingredients fresh onion or potatoes—or clams—depending on your travel plans.

There is no salt given in the recipe because clams and clam juice can be very salty.

Like other homemade soups, clam chowder can make a meal in itself.

TRAIL INFORMATION

TIME	15 minutes
WATER	3 to 4 cups
EQUIPMENT	1 pot, can opener
SERVINGS	4 to 6

PREPARE AHEAD

Ingredients

2 cups (4 ounces) dried sliced
   potatoes*
2 tablespoons dried leek, or 1
   tablespoon dried minced
   onion°
1 tablespoon dried parsley°

2 tablespoons dried bacon pieces°
2 tablespoons butter, or 1½-ounce
   packet Butter Buds
1 cup dry milk
8-ounce can minced clams

*Use the packet of potatoes from a Betty Crocker au gratin potato box, or dry your own.

Packing the food

Put into 2 small bags, then package with the clams and the trail directions: 1. potatoes, leek, parsley, bacon pieces, and Butter Buds, if used; 2. dry milk.

Carry in general provisions, if used: butter.

TRAIL DIRECTIONS—CLAM CHOWDER

1. In a cookpot, combine the contents of the potato bag with 3 cups water and bring to a boil. Simmer, covered, until the potatoes are tender, about 10 minutes.

2. Add the can of clams with their juice, 1 cup dry milk, and 2 tablespoons butter (unless Butter Buds are used). Stir and heat through, but do not boil. Add more water if necessary.

Super Soup

For winter trips, when you need to pack as many calories into your meals as possible (see page 113), make up a soup that positively brims with delicious nutrients. As well as containing plenty of vitamins, carbohydrates, fats, and protein, Super Soup has the advantage of using up the odds and ends of dried vegetables that you have left over from making more refined recipes. And a very tasty soup it is, too! Dumplings (see page 177) make it a complete meal.

Note: Milk does not boil well—it froths and boils over and makes a general nuisance of itself, so add it only in the last few minutes of cooking.

TRAIL INFORMATION

TIME	30 minutes
WATER	4½ cups
EQUIPMENT	1 pot
SERVINGS	6 to 8

PREPARE AHEAD

Ingredients

⅓ cup barley
⅓ cup lentils
⅓ cup Potato Buds, or ¼ cup instant potato powder
2 beef bouillon cubes
1 cup dried sliced vegetables*
(optional) 1 tablespoon dried meat, such as hamburger, ham, beef, or chicken

A pinch each of thyme and marjoram
½ cup dry milk
3 tablespoons butter or margarine
(optional) ¼ cup grated or cut cheese
(optional) 1 cup biscuit mix (see page 174), packed in its own bag and carried with the soup

*Any combination of vegetables, depending on what you have on hand—for instance, a tablespoon each of dried sliced mushrooms, onion, carrots, eggplant, turnips, cabbage, green pepper, and parsley.

Packing the food

Put into one bag everything except the milk, butter or margarine, and optional cheese.

Carry in general provisions: milk, butter or margarine, and optional cheese.

TRAIL DIRECTIONS—SUPER SOUP

1. Put the soup into a pot with $4\frac{1}{2}$ cups water. Bring to a boil, then simmer for $\frac{1}{2}$ hour.

2. During the last 5 minutes, stir in $\frac{1}{2}$ cup dry milk and 3 tablespoons butter or margarine. Add cut or grated cheese if you can spare some from the lunch supply.

3. To make dumplings: Add $\frac{1}{4}$ cup water to 1 cup biscuit mix and make a stiff batter. Form into small balls about the size of ping-pong balls, and float them on top of the soup. Cover so they steam and cook until done, during the last 20 minutes' cooking time.

Watercress Soup, with Wild Watercress

You may hike or canoe regularly in areas where watercress grows abundantly, or you may inadvertently happen into a luxurious patch of this lovely, fragrant, and nutritious green.

Since watercress is delicious eaten plain, you may elect, understandably, to augment your rations with a crisp fresh salad. But this is a wonderful hot soup.

TRAIL INFORMATION

For 2 cups of chopped fresh watercress:
TIME	5 to 10 minutes
WATER	3 cups
EQUIPMENT	1 pot
SERVINGS	4 to 6

PREPARE AHEAD

Ingredients

½ cup White Sauce Mix (see page   Salt to taste
   59), or 2 tablespoons butter or
   margarine, 2 tablespoons flour,
   ¾ cup dry milk

Packing the food

Either put the White Sauce Mix into a small bag with the trail directions,
Or carry extra butter, flour, and dry milk in the general provisions, and put
the trail directions in a place in your pack where you carry other important
papers.

TRAIL DIRECTIONS—WATERCRESS SOUP WITH WILD WATERCRESS

Collect enough watercress to make about 2 cups chopped.

Using White Sauce Mix:

   1. To ½ cup White Sauce Mix add 3 cups water. Stir and heat to boiling.
Cook over low heat until slightly thickened. Salt to taste.
   2. Stir in chopped fresh watercress; heat for a moment longer.

Using butter, flour, and dry milk:

   1. Melt 2 tablespoons butter, add 2 tablespoons flour, and cook for a
minute. Add 3 cups water and ¾ cup dry milk.
   2. Cook until the mixture thickens, which will be about as long as it
takes to come to a boil.
   3. Stir in 2 cups chopped fresh watercress; heat for a moment longer.
Salt to taste.

CAMP BREADS

Camp breads are a welcome part of the wilderness menu. It's hard to describe the rapture a hot, fluffy biscuit with a pat of butter melting in its center can produce in a hiker who has been a week in the backcountry.

Methods of cooking the various forms of camp bread are pan frying, pan baking, burying a pan in the coals for a slow bake, steam cooking (of dumplings), and the old but ingenious trick of cooking on a stick. (I do not backpack with a reflector oven, so I can't offer any suggestions about using this contrivance.)

Except for dumplings, which you can cook right on top of your stew, you may have to do a bit of juggling to make your stove available for the 10 to 15 minutes it takes to cook biscuits; and a longer bake in coals prolongs dinner preparation a little—but the pleasure so added is worth the wait.

Basic Biscuit Mix—Basic Mix for Four Camp Breads

Four kinds of camp bread can be made from one basic biscuit mix: biscuits, bannock, dumplings, and doughboys.

This recipe will make 2½ cups mix, enough for about 15 biscuits, 2 or 3 pans of bannock (depending on the size of the pan), 12 dumplings, or about 6 good-sized doughboys. (Each cup of mix calls for ¼ cup water.)

Individual directions for these four camp breads appear on the following pages.

Note: The biscuit mix is also the basis for pancakes, see page 141.

PREPARE AHEAD

Ingredients

2 cups flour   1 tablespoon sugar
½ teaspoon salt   2 tablespoons dry milk
1 tablespoon baking powder   ½ cup shortening

Preparing and packing the mix

Mix together the dry ingredients. Cut in the shortening with two knives, mixing until the shortening is in tiny pieces (smaller than tiny peas). Put the mix into a plastic bag (not Ziploc), and label it "Biscuit Mix—Add ¼ cup cold water per cup of mix."

Biscuits

Making biscuits in camp is easier than you think. The technique is based on a simple principle—do what you can to produce the illusion that you're using an oven, with the materials at hand. These may be only a pan and a tiny stove. But with a lid (or a piece of foil) for the pan and ten minutes of patient tending, you can turn out biscuits that are golden, sumptuously light, wholesome, and delicious.

I know I'm raving. It's not really easy, especially when you find that producing the illusion of an oven means holding the pan off the flame in order not to burn the biscuit bottoms coal black. Never mind. Have some honey ready, and be prepared for the unbounded gratitude of fellow campers conditioned to think of camp biscuits as coal-like lumps.

Note: If you get dough all over your hands, it will rub off very easily after you have let it dry for a minute, but a good way to prevent the dough from making your hands sticky is to rub a little flour on them before you form biscuits, dumplings, or Doughboys.

TRAIL INFORMATION

TIME	About 15 minutes
WATER	$\frac{1}{4}$ cup
EQUIPMENT	1 bowl, 1 frying pan with lid (or piece of aluminum foil)
SERVINGS	3 (6 biscuits)

PREPARE AHEAD

Ingredients

1 cup biscuit mix
1 teaspoon butter or margarine
1 teaspoon flour

Additional butter, honey, etc., for
  the cooked biscuits

Packing

Pack the biscuit mix with the trail directions. Either pack enough for one meal or measure out for each meal from a larger bag of mix (the master recipe makes $2\frac{1}{2}$ cups).

Carry in general provisions: butter or margarine and flour.

TRAIL DIRECTIONS—BISCUITS

1. Spread a little butter or margarine around the bottom and sides of a cold frying pan. Then coat the pan with flour by shaking a teaspoon of flour inside it.

2. In a bowl add $\frac{1}{4}$ cup cold water to each cup of biscuit mix. Mix the dough. To make it easy to handle, rub some flour on your hands. Shape the dough into thin (about $\frac{1}{4}$ inch high), 2-inch-wide biscuits, and set these in the pan. Cover.

3. Cook over a flame or shove the pan into some hot coals, covering it with coals.

When cooking over heat, the flame must be low. If it isn't, don't despair, simply move the pan around to distribute the heat and hold the pan off the heat part of the time, to keep the bottoms of the biscuits from burning. Cook them 5 to 7 minutes on one side, then turn them with a spatula and cook 5 minutes more. Be patient, and give the baking powder time to work.

Serve with butter and honey.

Bannock

Bannock, a term you might have heard if you hang around with old-timers, is simply pan bread—undifferentiated biscuits.

To make bannock in camp

See biscuit directions. The only difference is that, rather than making individual biscuits, you spread all the dough out in the bottom of the pan to make one huge biscuit, which will take slightly longer to cook than individual ones, about 20 minutes.

Dumplings

Depending on how much you like to slave over a hot stove (take this literally), biscuits may or may not become your forte in the wild kitchen. A wonderful alternative is to make dumplings. These old-fashioned items will make a stunning comeback once backpackers grasp the significance of adding to a meal a fluffy, tasty morsel that needs no care or extra pans, that when cooked soaks up gravy with all the *élan* of a biscuit but requires none of its careful tending. Dumplings are really biscuits cooked by steam. Therefore, to cook them, one forms and sets them on top of a stew or a hearty soup, covers the pot, and waits for about 15 minutes. They double in size, approximately, as they cook, about a fifth submerged in that gravy they later taste so good with.

TRAIL INFORMATION

TIME	20 minutes
WATER	¼ cup
EQUIPMENT	1 bowl, 1 pot in which a stew is already cooking
SERVINGS	3 (6 dumplings)

PREPARE AHEAD

Ingredient

1 cup biscuit mix

Packing

Pack the biscuit mix with trail directions for dumplings. Either pack enough for one meal, or measure out the mix for each meal from a larger bag of mix (the master recipe makes 2½ cups).

TRAIL DIRECTIONS—DUMPLINGS

1. Add ¼ cup cold water for each cup biscuit mix.
2. Mix the dough and, after rubbing a little flour on your hands, form the dough into balls the size of ping-pong balls. Set these on top of a stew or soup and simmer covered for 15 to 20 minutes, or until the middle of the dumplings is dry.

Doughboys

The doughboy is an old scouting invention, but unlike the dumpling is not apt to enjoy a widespread comeback, because of its reliance on conditions impractical in today's crowded camping situations—wood fire and downed sticks. You cook a doughboy by spreading a thick, elongated knob of biscuit dough over the end of a stick and then "toasting" it over the fire. Then— and this is why the doughboy is worth mentioning—you put into the hole left when the stick is pulled out: butter, jam, honey, granola, gorp, or any other delectable meltable or crunchy thing at hand.

TRAIL INFORMATION

TIME	About 15 minutes
WATER	½ cup
EQUIPMENT	A bowl, 4 roasting sticks
	A wood fire is necessary
SERVINGS	4

PREPARE AHEAD

Ingredients

2 cups biscuit mix
Butter or margarine

Jam or honey
Gorp, granola, etc. (see above)

Packing the food

Pack the biscuit mix with the trail directions.

Carry the other ingredients in the general provisions.

TRAIL DIRECTIONS—DOUGHBOYS FOR 4

1. Add ½ cup cold water to 2 cups of mix. Do not add more water than this or the doughboy will fall off the stick.

2. Mix and pat the dough around the ends of 4 sticks (downed sticks about 2 feet long and ½ inch in diameter). Make each doughboy about 4 inches long, ½ inch thick.

3. Hold the doughboys over the fire to toast them slowly for about 10 minutes, or until the inside is done. Turn them as you would a marshmallow you were roasting to perfection, and occasionally pat the dough to keep it evenly distributed. (If it gets lopsided, it will tend to crack apart and fall.)

4. Pull the doughboys off the sticks gently and fill their cavities with butter, jam, or honey; add other ingredients according to whim.

Cornbread and Johnnycakes

TRAIL INFORMATION

TIME	30 to 40 minutes
WATER	¾ cup or less
EQUIPMENT	1 bowl or pot for mixing
	1 flat pan (a frying pan) for baking, with cover
SERVINGS	8 or so

PREPARE AHEAD

Ingredients

¾ cup cornmeal, preferably stone
  ground
¾ cup flour
¼ cup sugar
2 tablespoons dry milk

1 tablespoon dry egg
2 teaspoons baking powder
¼ tablespoon salt
¼ cup shortening

Preparing and packing the mix

Mix together the dry ingredients. Cut in the shortening with 2 knives, mixing until it is in tiny pieces.

Put the mix in a bag with the trail directions.

TRAIL DIRECTIONS—CORNBREAD AND JOHNNYCAKES

1. Grease a frying pan and shake a little flour in it.
2. Add ¾ cup water or less to the mix (2¼ cups), and stir just until mixed.
3. Cook in the covered pan in coals for 20 minutes or until done.

Note: You can make 10 individual johnnycakes (or "journey cakes") from this mix instead of one pan bread.

Mix the batter as usual, stirring only until wet. Heat 2 tablespoons butter or oil in a frying pan and cook the cakes individually, like pancakes, 3 or 4 at a time, depending on the size of your pan.

Oatmeal Bannock

TRAIL INFORMATION

TIME	20 minutes
WATER	3 tablespoons
EQUIPMENT	Shallow pan (frying pan) with lid
SERVINGS	6 to 8

PREPARE AHEAD

Ingredients

¾ cup oat flour (made by grinding rolled oats in the blender)
¾ cup whole-wheat flour
1 tablespoon baking powder
¼ cup sugar
1 tablespoon dry egg
1 tablespoon dry milk
¼ cup shortening

Preparing and packing the mix

Mix together the dry ingredients; cut in the shortening with 2 knives and mix well. Put the mix in a bag with the trail directions.

TRAIL DIRECTIONS—OATMEAL BANNOCK

1. Grease a frying pan and shake a little flour in it.
2. Add 3 tablespoons water to 2¼ cups dry mix, and mix with your hands. Spread out in the pan.
3. Cook slowly, covered, over a low flame for 15 minutes, or set in coals to bake.

Max's Fried Bread and Garlic

In the unlikely event that you near the end of a trip with extra bread which has become stale, don't chide the packer or impulsively feed it to the birds—fry it! Its taste and texture are both wonderful.

TRAIL DIRECTIONS—MAX'S FRIED BREAD AND GARLIC

1. Slice the bread. Smash 2 or 3 cloves of garlic under the flat of your knife, and cut into tiny pieces.

2. In a frying pan heat oil or a combination of oil and margarine to a depth of ¼ inch. Keep the fire medium low, or lift the pan to avoid burning. (You will have oil left over, which you should save and pack out in its original container.)

3. Lightly brown the garlic, and then fry slices of bread until just crisp on both sides.

MAIN DISHES

Dishes with gravy, white sauce, and tomato sauce

A dish with a hearty sauce makes a real feast when combined with one of the basic "energy foods"—noodles, rice or other grains, mashed potatoes, biscuits, or dumplings.

I don't think there is a commercial sauce mix that we can't improve on at home, and thereby avoid the additives, excessive packaging, and expense of those preparations. Your own trail sauces can be instant enough for you to write trail directions that read, "Add water, heat, and serve." (The only mix I do find useful sometimes is an instant gravy mix.) Directions for making your own gravy are on pages 55–6; a recipe for tomato sauce is on page 57; and white sauce is discussed on pages 58–60.

When you're familiar with the procedures behind these three sauces basic to so much cooking, you'll be inclined, I hope, to adapt some of your own home favorites to the trail, and to experiment with your own nourishing trail stews, ragôuts, hashes, and feasts à la king.

Jerky Stew with Dumplings

Properly cooked, jerky stew always gets rave reviews. Proper cooking is easy, as long as you have time—an hour to soak the jerky and an hour to cook the stew. Thickening the gravy and making dumplings or biscuits to soak up the gravy are refinements an old-time woodsman would admonish you to include, because gravy and biscuits are properly within the woodsman's province.

TRAIL INFORMATION

Because of the long cooking time, use a wood fire, or a stove that easily simmers for an hour.

TIME	1 hour soaking, 1 hour cooking
WATER	About 4 cups
EQUIPMENT	1 fairly large cookpot (2½-quart), a bowl
SERVINGS	6

PREPARE AHEAD

Ingredients

6 ounces unmarinated beef jerky (about 1 cup) (see page 39)
½ cup dried sliced carrots
½ cup dried sliced parsnips
¼ cup dried sliced mushrooms

4 ounces (about 2 cups) dried sliced potatoes*
1 package instant beef-gravy mix
1 cup biscuit mix (see page 174)

*Use the potatoes from a package of Betty Crocker au gratin potatoes, or dry your own potatoes.

Packing the food

Put into 4 small bags, then package with the gravy mix and trail directions: 1. jerky; 2. carrots, parsnips, and mushrooms; 3. potatoes; 4. biscuit mix.

TRAIL DIRECTIONS—JERKY STEW WITH DUMPLINGS

1. Soak the jerky in 4 cups water for as long as possible, at least an hour.

2. In a pot, bring the jerky and water to a boil and cook for 1 hour. During the last half hour, add the carrots, parsnips, and mushrooms. Add the potatoes the last 15 minutes. Add water if necessary to keep the ingredients just covered.

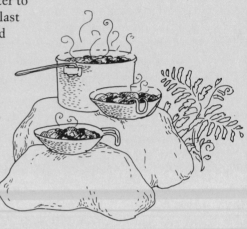

3. Add the gravy mix and stir.

4. To make dumplings: Add ¼ cup water to the biscuit mix and make a stiff batter. Form small balls about the size of ping-pong balls, and float them on top of the stew. Cover so they steam and cook until done, about 20 minutes.

East Meets West Stew

A rich, satisfying stew, for 3 or for a crowd.

TRAIL INFORMATION

TIME	1 hour soaking, 45 minutes to 1 hour cooking
WATER	2 to 3 cups
EQUIPMENT	1 pot (2 if cooking rice)
SERVINGS	3 (easily expanded by doubling or tripling the recipe)

PREPARE AHEAD

Ingredients

2 ounces beef jerky (see page 39)
8 medium or 6 large dried Oriental
    mushrooms (see page 45)

2 tablespoons dried sliced onion, or
    1 tablespoon dried minced
    onion°

1 beef bouillon cube
1 tablespoon flour
Pepper to taste

1 cup biscuit mix,
½ cup rice (see page 174)

Packing the food

Put into 2 separate bags, then package with the trail directions: 1. jerky; 2. mushrooms, onion, and bouillon, unwrapped.

Carry in general provisions: 1. flour; 2. pepper; 3. rice or biscuit mix.

TRAIL DIRECTIONS—EAST MEETS WEST STEW

1. Soak the jerky in water to cover for 1 hour in a pot. The last 30 minutes, add the mushrooms and onions, and more water if necessary.
2. Take out the mushrooms, remove their stems, cut them up, and return them to the pot. Bring the water and contents, plus bouillon, to a boil, cover, and simmer for 30 to 40 minutes.
3. In a cup, mix a tablespoon or so of flour with water to make a thin paste. Stir this into the stew.
4. Set dumplings (made from 1 cup biscuit mix and ¼ cup cold water) on top of the stew. Cover, and cook 20 minutes longer. Or cook ½ cup rice in 1 cup water in another pot.

Note: Do not add salt unless after tasting the stew, you discover it needs some. Pepper is very good, though.

Beef Hash with Gravy

This mashed potato and beef dish isn't a proper hash—but it veers close enough, in the wild kitchen, to collect the name.

TRAIL INFORMATION

TIME	15 minutes
WATER	3 cups
EQUIPMENT	1 pot, 1 frying pan, and a spatula
SERVINGS	4

PREPARE AHEAD

Ingredients

Two 2½-ounce packages cooked
    pressed beef, dried and
    crushed*
1 tablespoon dry milk
2 teaspoons Butter Buds
2 tablespoons dried minced onion°

½ cup French's instant mashed
    potato powder, or 2 cups Potato
    Buds
3 to 4 tablespoons butter or
    margarine
1 package instant brown gravy mix

*Buy this in the lunchmeat section of the supermarket. To dry, see page 42.

Packing the food

Put into 2 small bags, then package with the gravy packet and the trail directions: 1. beef, dry milk, Butter Buds, and onion; 2. potatoes.

Carry in general provisions: butter or margarine.

TRAIL DIRECTIONS—BEEF HASH WITH GRAVY

1. Boil 2 cups water in a pot. Add the contents of the beef bag, cover, and simmer for 2 to 3 minutes.

2. Off the heat, add the potatoes and stir; cover and let sit for a few minutes.

3. Heat 3 to 4 tablespoons butter or margarine in a frying pan. Fry the "hash" over medium heat until browned on one side.

4. Rinse out the pot that the hash was in and boil 1 cup water in it. Add the instant gravy and cook 1 minute.

5. Turn the hash. Pour the gravy over the top. Brown the side that is down.

Creamed Chipped Beef and Mashed Potatoes

A hearty dish for either dinner or breakfast, creamed chipped beef is delicious served over toasted English muffins, as alternatives to mashed potatoes, when your wild kitchen includes a grill. You can serve it over biscuits, too.

Make white sauce from a mix or from trail-carried butter, flour, and dry milk.

TRAIL INFORMATION

TIME	10 to 15 minutes
WATER	2 cups
EQUIPMENT	2 pots
SERVINGS	3

PREPARE AHEAD

Ingredients

One 2½-ounce package pressed cooked beef, dried and crushed (equals ¼ cup)*

⅓ cup White Sauce Mix (see page 60), or 1½ tablespoons butter or margarine, 1½ tablespoons flour, 2 tablespoons dry milk

¾ cup Potato Buds
2 tablespoons dry milk
1 teaspoon Butter Buds or butter from trail supplies

*Buy in the lunchmeat section of the supermarket; to dry, see page 42.

Packing the food

Put into 2 small bags, then package with the trail directions: 1. beef and white sauce mix; 2. Potato Buds, dry milk, and Butter Buds.

Carry in general provisions: Instead of white sauce mix: butter, dry milk, and flour.

TRAIL DIRECTIONS—CHIPPED BEEF AND MASHED POTATOES

With white sauce mix:

1. For the meat: Boil 1 cup water. Add the crumbled beef and white sauce mix, stir, and cook slowly until the sauce thickens. Set aside covered.
2. Potatoes: Boil 1 cup water in a second pot. Add ¾ cup Potato Buds mixture and 1 teaspoon butter, or margarine (if Butter Buds weren't used). Take off the heat, and stir a moment until they are of potato consistency.
3. Reheat the sauce briefly and serve it on the potatoes.

With white sauce made from butter, flour, and dry milk:

1. Melt 1½ tablespoons butter in a pot. Add 1½ tablespoons flour and cook a minute. (Don't burn!) Add 1 cup water and 2 tablespoons dry milk. Stir over heat until thick. Add the ¼ cup beef and let this sit.

2. Potatoes: follow steps 2 and 3 above.

Salmon, Peas, and Noodles or Chicken à la King

For this dinner you can also use freeze-dried chicken, in which case you create Chicken à la King. And we concocted it one temperate Thanksgiving weekend using cold sliced turkey—that was the best!

There are two versions of this recipe. A 1-pot method uses White Sauce Mix. For the slightly more refined 2-pot version, you make a roux out of butter and flour.

TRAIL INFORMATION

TIME	10 to 15 minutes
WATER	2–2½ cups
EQUIPMENT	1 or 2 pots, can opener
SERVINGS	6

PREPARE AHEAD

Ingredients

6½-ounce can salmon or tuna packed in water, or ½ cup (1 package) freeze-dried chicken

⅔ cup White Sauce Mix (see page 60); or ½ cup dry milk, 3 tablespoons butter or margarine, 3 tablespoons flour

2 teaspoons dried parsley°
Small pinch of thyme
½ cup freeze-dried peas
2 cups thin noodles

Packing the food

Put into 3 small bags, then package with the fish or chicken and the trail directions: 1. noodles; 2. White Sauce Mix, parsley and thyme; 3. peas.

Carry in general provisions (instead of White Sauce Mix): butter, flour, dry milk, and herbs.

TRAIL DIRECTIONS—SALMON, PEAS, AND NOODLES OR CHICKEN À LA KING

For White Sauce Mix, using 1 pot

1. Boil 2 cups water and cook the noodles 5 minutes or until just done. Don't drain them.

2. Add the White Sauce Mix and herbs, the salmon, tuna, or chicken, and the peas and cook a few minutes.

For white sauce made from butter, flour, and milk (2 pots)

1. Boil $2\frac{1}{2}$ cups water, add the noodles, and cook 5 minutes or until just done. Stir in freeze-dried chicken or can of fish with juice; add peas, $\frac{1}{2}$ cup dry milk, and a pinch of thyme and parsley. Take off the heat.

2. In another pot, melt 3 tablespoons butter. Add 3 tablespoons flour and cook over low heat for a minute. Add contents of the first pot and stir vigorously. Cook a few minutes until thick, adding a little water if necessary.

Note: If you have 2 stoves available or you're cooking over a wood fire, the noodles can boil in one pot while you put together the sauce and its contents in another. Then drain the noodles and serve the sauce over them.

Spaetzle with Cheese and Croutons

Spaetzle, or tiny rich noodles, make good camping food, as they're both easy to prepare and tasty. (The Familia brand can be found in most supermarkets.) They make an easy side dish, or they're good with cheese as a light supper, accompanied by crisp stir-fried vegetables.

TRAIL INFORMATION

TIME	30 minutes
WATER	1 quart
EQUIPMENT	1 pot
SERVINGS	3 to 4

PREPARE AHEAD

Ingredients

2 cups spaetzle
⅓ cup croutons
1 tablespoon dried parsley°
¾ cup grated (¼ pound) white
    cheese (Swiss, Emmenthal, or
    Monterey jack)

About 1¼ tablespoons dry milk
1 tablespoon butter or margarine
1 teaspoon salt

Packing the food

Put into 3 small bags, then package with the trail directions: 1. spaetzle; 2. croutons and parsley; 3. cheese (or carry in general provisions, ungrated).

Carry in general provisions: dry milk, butter or margarine, and salt.

TRAIL DIRECTIONS—SPAETZLE WITH CHEESE AND CROUTONS

1. Bring 1 quart water with 1 teaspoon salt to a boil. Add the spaetzle, bring to boil again, stir, and take the pot off the heat. Let it sit for 20 minutes, covered, then drain off all but about 1 cup water.

2. Add a generous tablespoon dry milk, 1 tablespoon butter, and ¾ cup grated cheese or cut in an equivalent amount with your knife. Reheat, if necessary, to melt the cheese, and serve with the croutons and parsley.

Beef Ragout

A robust stew to serve by itself or with mashed potatoes.

TRAIL INFORMATION

TIME	1 hour soaking, 40 minutes cooking
WATER	2 to 4 cups
EQUIPMENT	2 pots (with mashed potatoes)
SERVINGS	4

PREPARE AHEAD

Ingredients

4 ounces beef jerky (see page 39)
¼ cup each*:
    dried sliced carrots
    dried sliced mushrooms
    dried sliced parsnips
    dried sliced green peppers
8-by-8-inch piece of dried tomato
    sauce (see page 57)†

1⅓ cups Potato Buds
1 tablespoon dry milk
2 teaspoons Butter Buds, or add 1
    tablespoon butter or margarine
    from general provisions

*Combine vegetables according to what you have on hand. Eggplant, kohlrabi, turnips, green beans, and peas are all good, too.
†This is half the recipe. Cook and dry the whole thing, then tear off what you need.

Packing the food

Put into 3 separate bags, then package with the trail directions: 1. jerky; 2. vegetables and dried tomato sauce; 3. Potato Buds, dry milk, and Butter Buds (or carry butter or margarine in general provisions).

TRAIL DIRECTIONS—BEEF RAGOUT

1. Cover the jerky with 2 cups water and let soak for 1 hour.
2. Bring the water to a boil, cover, and simmer ½ hour. Add the vege-

tables, tomato sauce, and more water if necessary to cover the food. Cook 20 minutes more.

3. Serve with mashed potatoes: In a second pot, boil 1⅔ cups water, add the contents of the potato bag (and 1 tablespoon butter if no Butter Buds were included), stir off heat, and let sit a moment.

Jerky with Peppers

Soaking the jerky a long time and using lots of black pepper are the two secrets to the success of this recipe.

TRAIL INFORMATION

TIME	1 hour or more soaking; ½ or 1 hour cooking, depending on your cook-fire situation
WATER	3½ cups
EQUIPMENT	2 pots
SERVINGS	4

PREPARE AHEAD

Ingredients

4 ounces beef jerky (see page 39)
4-by-6-inch piece of tomato leather (see page 35)
½ cup dried sliced green pepper°
2 tablespoons dried minced onion°

1 cup rice
4 cloves garlic
Black pepper to taste
Salt to taste

Packing the food

Put into 3 small bags, then package with the trail directions and the garlic: 1. jerky; 2. tomato leather, green pepper, onion; 3. rice.

Carry in general provisions: pepper and salt.

TRAIL DIRECTIONS—JERKY WITH PEPPERS

1. Soak the jerky in 1½ cups water for at least an hour.

2. Add the rest of the dried ingredients to the pot, crush the garlic cloves to remove their skins, cut them up, add them, and bring the pot to a boil.

3. Simmer, covered, ½ hour. Add black pepper and salt to taste. Let the jerky sit while you cook 1 cup rice in 2 cups water, then reheat the stew and serve together.

Erie Stew

Use basic tomato sauce and plain dried hamburger to make up this recipe if the dried provisions you have on hand include tomato sauce. (You may have extra tomato sauce, for instance, after preparing a pasta dish; it's the same basic recipe.)

Note: In cool weather, a pound of fresh hamburger packed carefully and eaten the first day tastes great instead of dried meat. Brown the hamburger first, cook the rest of the ingredients for 10 minutes in about 2 cups of water in a second pot, then mix with the browned meat.

TRAIL INFORMATION

TIME	15 minutes
WATER	3 cups or more
EQUIPMENT	1 pot
SERVINGS	4 to 6

PREPARE AHEAD

Ingredients

1⅓ cups dried hamburger, from 1 pound (see page 41)

1 cup Walnut Acres vegetable flakes (see page 272) or dry your own°

8-by-8-inch piece dried tomato sauce (see page 57)*

1 cup tiny macaroni shapes

*This is half the recipe. Cook and dry the whole thing, then tear off what you need.

Packing the food

Pack everything into a bag with the trail directions.

TRAIL DIRECTIONS—ERIE STEW

Add 3 cups water to the contents of the bag in a cookpot. Bring to a boil, covered, then simmer 10 minutes, adding more water if necessary.

Arroz con Pollo (Chicken with Rice)

TRAIL INFORMATION

TIME	20 to 25 minutes
WATER	2½ to 3 cups
EQUIPMENT	1 pot, 1 cup
SERVINGS	4

PREPARE AHEAD

Ingredients

1 cup rice
1 chicken bouillon cube
⅛ teaspoon saffron threads
4-by-4-inch piece of dried tomato
    sauce (see page 57)*

1 package Rich-Moor freeze-dried
    chicken
1 cup freeze-dried peas

*This is one-fourth the recipe. Cook and dry the whole thing, then tear off what you need.

Packing the food

Put into 3 small bags, then package with the trail directions: 1. rice and bouillon cube (unwrapped); 2. saffron; 3. dried sauce, chicken, and peas.

TRAIL DIRECTIONS—ARROZ CON POLLO

1. In a cookpot add 2 cups water to the rice, cover, bring to a boil, and simmer 15 minutes. Meanwhile, crumble the saffron threads into 1 tablespoon water in a cup and let them soak.

2. About halfway through the rice cooking time, add $1\frac{1}{2}$ cups more water, the saffron water, the dried sauce, chicken, and peas. Cover, bring back to a boil, and simmer until the rice is cooked, about 7 more minutes. Add more water if necessary.

Make-Ahead Meals with Ground Beef

Ground beef can be very useful in trail cooking, when you brown and dry it at home first as described on pages 57–58. The ground beef mix given there contains the makings of gravy—flour and beef flavoring, so that you can just add water on the trail. Then you have the basis for several hearty, nearly instant meals.

When you elect simply to brown hamburger and dry it, you can still make gravy on the trail by following the directions on page 58.

OTHER USES FOR GROUND BEEF MIX

• Substitute for ham in Pasta with Ham, Peas, and Mushroom Sauce (see page 206)
• Add it to Lentils with Rice (see page 231)
• Put it into tomato sauce for pasta
• Put it into soups

Mock Shepherd's Pie

TRAIL INFORMATION

TIME	15 minutes
WATER	Almost $3\frac{1}{2}$ cups
EQUIPMENT	2 pots
SERVINGS	3 or 4

PREPARE AHEAD

Ingredients

1⅓ cups Basic Ground Beef Mix
 (see page 57)
(optional) 1 cup freeze-dried peas or
 other vegetable
1⅓ cups Potato Buds

2 tablespoons dry milk
1 tablespoon Butter Buds, or 1
 tablespoon butter
(optional) 2 ounces cheese

Packing the food

Put into 2 small bags, then package with the trail directions: 1. meat mix and optional vegetables; 2. Potato Buds, milk, and Butter Buds if used.

Carry in general provisions: optional cheese and butter, if used.

TRAIL DIRECTIONS—MOCK SHEPHERD'S PIE

1. In one pot, add 1¾ cups water to the meat, cover, and bring to a boil, then simmer 10 minutes.

2. In a second pot, boil 1⅔ cups water. Add the potato mixture and stir vigorously.

3. Reheat the meat, adding a little water if necessary, and serve with the potatoes.

Optional: Put grated or cut cheese on top.

Huron Stew

This is an excellent quick dinner.

TRAIL INFORMATION

TIME	15 to 20 minutes
WATER	2 cups
EQUIPMENT	1 pot
SERVINGS	3 or 4

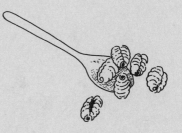

PREPARE AHEAD

Ingredients

1 cup Basic Ground Beef Mix
(see page 57)
4-inch-square piece of tomato
leather (page see 35)
1 cup small macaroni

About 2 ounces cheese (any white
or yellow cheese)
(optional) 1 or 2 tablespoons dried
green pepper
⅛ teaspoon salt

Packing the food

Put into 4 small bags, then package with the trail directions: 1. green pepper if used); 2. beef mix and tomato leather; 3. macaroni; 4. cheese (or carry in general provisions).

TRAIL DIRECTIONS—HURON STEW

1. Add the green pepper to 2 cups water in a pot and bring to a boil. Add the macaroni, boil again, and cook 5 minutes.

2. Add the meat mix and tomato leather and simmer covered 10 minutes more.

3. Add the cheese, turn off the heat, and let sit covered until the cheese melts. Add about ⅛ teaspoon salt.

Vegetable and Ground Beef Stew

A quick, easy trail dinner with the taste of fresh vegetables.

TRAIL INFORMATION

TIME	15 to 20 minutes
WATER	2 cups
EQUIPMENT	1 pot
SERVINGS	4

PREPARE AHEAD

Ingredients

1 cup Basic Ground Beef Mix (see page 57)

1 cup Walnut Acres dehydrated vegetable flakes (see page 272)—or make your own (see page 34)

1 cup biscuit mix (see page 174)

Packing the food

Put into 3 small bags, then package with the trail directions: 1. meat mix; 2. vegetables; 3. biscuit mix.

TRAIL DIRECTIONS—VEGETABLE AND GROUND BEEF STEW

1. Put the meat mix and vegetables into a pot with 2 cups of water. Cover, bring to a boil, and simmer for 10 minutes.

2. To make dumplings: Add ¼ cup cold water to 1 cup biscuit mix to make a stiff dough. Form into 4 small balls and float these on top of the stew while it is cooking. Keep the cover on.

Pasta

What ideal wilderness fare is pasta! It is tasty, easy to carry, nourishing, and nice to look at. Using a sauce made and dried at home, you can prepare a pasta feast in ten minutes and in one or two steps, over the tiniest stove.

The steps are as follows: First heat the sauce; then set it aside (waiting will only enhance its flavors) while you boil water in a second pot and cook the pasta. While draining the cooked pasta, set the sauce back onto the heat for a moment, then serve them together. With a little bit of august, genuine Parmesan cheese cut on top, this elegant, simple dish would please the most discerning Italian palate.

In cases where you must save time and water, or if you have only one pot, cook the pasta first in a little more water than the sauce directions call for. When the pasta is almost done, add the dry sauce to the pot and cook until the sauce has reconstituted. This is not the real Italian way to serve pasta, but if you have a real Italian along, maybe he can carry the extra pot. The reason pasta is flung into a big pot of boiling water is to let it begin to boil as quickly as possible so that it doesn't get mushy.

Two of the sauces for pasta can be made at home and dried in the oven, so that at camp they need only water and a few minutes' heating to reconstitute: Basic Tomato Sauce, which appears on page 57, and Pasta and Home-Dried Meat Sauce on page 201. But, if conditions dictate, you can pack the tomato paste and the flavorings separately, and cook the sauce at camp (see recipe on page 203). This would make sense if you were rushed at home but expected leisure and fuel enough at camp to allow a freshly made sauce to simmer for 20 minutes.

As for cheese—nothing is better than imported Parmesan. But if $9 a pound seems impossibly extravagant, consider that you certainly don't need a whole pound; or try one of the non-Italian "Parmesans," or the Stella brand sold in wedge shapes in the supermarket dairy case. Do *not* buy the already grated stuff in canisters that is called cheese but which tastes like grated cardboard. (Maybe it is grated cardboard.) You can grate your own Parmesan at home, or have the cheese merchant grate it for you. Or you can carry the whole glorious hunk and cut off bits as you want them.

No one knows how many different shapes of pasta there are, but the number is said to run up into the hundreds. For backpacking purposes, the thing to remember is that you want a short cooking time. Choose, there-fore, the skinniest pasta shapes you can find, like vermicelli, linguini, and extra-thin spaghetti. Little seashell shapes, short thin macaroni (whose bigger versions are called ziti), and whatever other mad shapes catch your eye are good, too, especially when you want the bits of meat in the sauce to have something to cling to (or nestle into). It is fun to try different shapes of pasta any time—it's even more fun, somehow, in a wild kitchen.

Happily for the backpacker short on fuel, the worst thing you can do to pasta is to overcook it. After the water has returned to a boil, the re-maining cooking time is generally about 5 minutes. When writing trail directions for someone other than yourself to follow, make it very clear that pasta should not be overcooked. Do this by setting down cooking times a little shorter than you think they really are. Do whatever else you can to get this point across—use the phrase *al dente* (firm to the tooth), use lots of exclamation marks, draw pictures. . . . And stand by to demon-strate, by testing pieces for doneness by biting into them, that mushy pasta is well-nigh inedible pasta. All Italians know this, and the news is spread-ing.

Directions for cooking pasta

1. Bring to a boil in a covered pot enough water to cover generously the pasta you want to cook (certainly less than you would use at home, but boil as much water as you can).

2. Add the pasta, bring the water back to boiling, and time it carefully not to overcook it. After 4 or 5 minutes, extract a piece and chew to see if it is done. It is done when it has *just* stopped being crunchy.

3. Drain immediately and serve with sauce, and with cheese grated or cut on top.

Pasta and Home-Dried Meat Sauce

Makes 2½ cups dried sauce

TRAIL INFORMATION

TIME	15 minutes
WATER	2-pot method: 2½ cups plus 1 potful
	1-pot method: 6½ cups
EQUIPMENT	1 or 2 pots
SERVINGS	6

PREPARE AHEAD

Making and drying the sauce

1 pound lean ground beef	1 teaspoon salt
½ cup finely chopped onion	⅛ teaspoon freshly ground pepper
2 cloves garlic, minced	Two 6-ounce cans tomato paste
2 tablespoons chopped parsley	

Brown the meat and onion together. Set the pan on a slant until the grease collects, then spoon it off. (Unfortunately, some of the meat juices will be lost, so do try to get the leanest meat possible.) Add the garlic, parsley, salt, pepper, and tomato paste, and cook for 5 minutes. (It won't seem much like sauce, since you haven't added any water.)

Divide the mixture, if necessary, into two parts, to spread as thin as possible in shallow pans which have been greased. Dry the sauce in the oven at 140° F. for about 6 hours, with the door propped open a crack. The dried sauce should be crumbly, but be sure not to overdry it.

Note: If you divide the dried sauce to feed fewer people at a time, add water in an equal amount to the dried sauce you use when reconstituting.

Additional ingredients

About 1 pound thin pasta (vermicelli, linguini, etc.)	⅓ cup grated Parmesan cheese

Packing the food

Put into 3 small bags, then package with the trail directions: 1. the dried sauce; 2. pasta; 3. parmesan (or carry in general provisions, ungrated).

TRAIL DIRECTIONS—PASTA AND HOME-DRIED MEAT SAUCE

Two-pot method:

1. Boil 1 pot water. Dip out $2\frac{1}{2}$ cups and add to the sauce in a second pot. (Meanwhile, cover the first pot to keep the water as hot as possible.) Bring the sauce to a boil, stir, and simmer covered for 5 minutes. Set aside.

2. Reboil the first pot of water, adding more if needed to cook the pasta. Drop in the pasta and cook it 5 minutes or until just done. Drain, reheat the sauce for a moment. Serve together with cheese.

One-pot method:

1. Bring 6 cups water to a boil, stirring occasionally. Add pasta, boil again, and cook until almost done, 4 or 5 minutes.

2. Add the dry sauce, heat to a boil again, stir, cover, and simmer 5 minutes. Add more water if necessary. Serve with cheese on top.

Pasta and Home-Dried Tomato Sauce

TRAIL INFORMATION

TIME	15 minutes
WATER	2-pot method: $3\frac{1}{2}$ cups plus 1 potful
	1-pot method: about 6–7 cups
EQUIPMENT	1 or 2 pots
SERVINGS	6 to 8 (see note below about dividing)

PREPARE AHEAD

Making and drying the sauce: see page 57.

Additional ingredients

About 1 pound thin pasta $\frac{1}{2}$ cup grated Parmesan cheese

Packing the food

Put into 3 small bags, then package with the trail directions: 1. the dried sauce; 2. pasta; 3. Parmesan cheese (or carry in general provisions, ungrated).

TRAIL DIRECTIONS—PASTA AND HOME-DRIED TOMATO SAUCE

Two-pot method:

1. Boil 1 pot water. Dip out 3 cups and add to the sauce in a second pot. (Meanwhile, cover the first pot to keep the water as hot as possible.) Bring the sauce to a boil, stir it, and simmer covered for 5 minutes, adding more water if it is too thick.

2. Reboil the first pot of water, adding more to cook the pasta in. Drop the pasta into the boiling water and cook 5 minutes or until just done. Drain pasta, reheat the sauce for a moment, and serve together with cheese.

One-pot method:

1. Bring 6 cups water to a boil, stirring occasionally. Add the pasta and cook until almost done, 4 or 5 minutes.

2. Add the dry sauce, heat to a boil again, stir, cover, and simmer 5 minutes. Add more water if necessary. Serve with cheese on top.

Pasta and Tomato Sauce (to Make in Camp)

This basic tomato sauce is very easy to pack and make, although it needs to cook for 20 minutes in camp. It is very good.

Pack the tomato paste either in the can, or dried to a leather (see page 35); the leather requires twice the amount of water that the canned paste does and therefore feeds more people. To streamline the recipe, substitute 1 teaspoon dried minced garlic and 1 tablespoon Butter Buds and omit step 1 of the trail directions.

There is another tomato sauce, which you cook and dry at home (see page 57) when you want a super-quick spaghetti sauce.

TRAIL INFORMATION

TIME	30 minutes
WATER	Using tomato leather—2 to 3 cups
	Using canned tomato paste—1 to 1½ cups
EQUIPMENT	2 pots, can opener
SERVINGS	Using tomato leather—4 to 5
	Using tomato paste—2 to 3

PREPARE AHEAD

Ingredients

Six-ounce can tomato paste, in the can or dried to a leather (see page 35)
2 cloves garlic
2 tablespoons butter or oil
1 tablespoon dried onion,° sliced into small bits
1 tablespoon dried parsley°

1 tablespoon dried green pepper,° cut into small bits
½ teaspoon sugar
1 teaspoon salt
¼ teaspoon basil
Pinch of oregano
½–¾ pound thin pasta
Parmesan cheese

Packing the food

Pack into 2 bags with the trail directions: 1. garlic, tomato paste, dried vegetables, flavorings; 2. pasta.

Carry in general provisions: butter or oil, Parmesan cheese.

TRAIL DIRECTIONS—PASTA AND CAMP TOMATO SAUCE

1. Smash the garlic cloves with the flat of your knife, slip them out of their skins, and chop them. Cook in 2 tablespoons butter or oil for a moment but don't let them brown.

2. Add the rest of the tomato bag, and 2 cups water with tomato leather, or 1 cup with tomato paste from a can. Bring to a boil, cover, and simmer 15 minutes. Add more water if the sauce is too thick. Cover and set aside.

3. Cook pasta by adding it to a pot of boiling water, bringing it back to a boil, and cooking 5 minutes or until done. Drain it and serve with the sauce and cheese, either grated or cut up on top.

ADDITIONS TO PASTA AND TOMATO SAUCE

The simplest way of serving pasta and tomato sauce, with a generous portion of genuine aged Parmesan over the top, is very good.

The dish does, however, invite the following additions:

CLAMS: In the last 5 minutes of cooking time, add one 6½-ounce can of minced clams with the juice. (For Spaghetti and White Clam Sauce, see page 210.)

SAUSAGE: Slice a few smoked link sausages into the sauce at the beginning of cooking time.

MUSHROOMS: Dried sliced—cook them in butter with the garlic at the beginning of the recipe, or add them to the quick version of the sauce at the beginning of cooking time.

DRIED ORIENTAL MUSHROOMS—soak 30 minutes, discard the stems, and cut the mushrooms into the sauce as it cooks.

MEAT: Dried ground beef, or freeze-dried beef, chicken, or ham can be added to the sauce at the beginning of cooking time. (See page 42.)

Pasta with Ham, Peas, and Mushroom Sauce

TRAIL INFORMATION

TIME	10 to 15 minutes
WATER	3 cups
EQUIPMENT	1 pot
SERVINGS	3

PREPARE AHEAD

Ingredients

⅓ cup freeze-dried peas*
⅓ cup freeze-dried ham (Rich-
    Moor)*
⅓ cup crushed, dried sliced
    mushrooms*
About ½ pound thin pasta

⅓ cup White Sauce Mix (see
    page 59)
⅛ teaspoon salt
Pepper to taste
¼ teaspoon crushed basil
2 ounces grated Parmesan cheese

*Instead of the peas, ham, and mushrooms, you could use 1 cup dried zucchini, broccoli, or whatever combination of things suits you, and make a note in the trail directions to soak them ½ hour first.

Packing the food

Put into 4 small bags, then package with the trail directions: 1. vegetables and ham; 2. pasta; 3. White Sauce Mix and seasonings; 4. cheese (or carry in general provisions).

TRAIL DIRECTIONS—PASTA WITH HAM, PEAS, AND MUSHROOM SAUCE

1. Boil 3 cups water. Add pasta and freeze-dried things or drained soaked vegetables and cook 5 to 6 minutes.

2. Add ⅓ cup White Sauce Mix and seasonings, stir. Add the cheese, let it melt, and serve.

Macaroni and Cheese

Macaroni and cheese can be delicious, with subtle flavorings and a nice balance of textures, or it can be excruciatingly dull. What strikes the balance? Three things—the judicious addition of a few spices (thyme and nutmeg), a good cheese or combination of them (cheddar, Havarti, Italian fontina, Parmesan, Monterey jack asiago), and your steadfast refusal to overcook the pasta.

Two versions follow: a quick 1-pot method using White Sauce Mix, and a slightly more elegant 2-pot version, in which you make white sauce from butter, flour, and dry milk.

TRAIL INFORMATION

TIME	10 to 15 minutes
WATER	3 cups
EQUIPMENT	1 or 2 pots
SERVINGS	4 to 6

PREPARE AHEAD

Ingredients

2 cups small macaroni
⅔ cup White Sauce Mix (see page 59), or 3 tablespoons butter or margarine, 3 tablespoons flour, 4 tablespoons dry milk

2 ounces grated cheese
Pinch each of thyme and nutmeg
½ teaspoon salt

Packing the food

Put into 2 small bags, then package with the trail directions: 1. cheese and White Sauce Mix; 2. macaroni and spices.

Or carry ungrated cheese in general provisions and, instead of White Sauce Mix, butter, dry milk, and flour.

TRAIL DIRECTIONS—MACARONI AND CHEESE

Using White Sauce Mix, and 1 pot:

1. Boil 3 cups water. Add the macaroni and cook for 5 minutes or until it is just done—firm to the tooth when chewed.
2. Add ⅔ cup White Sauce Mix and cheese; stir. Cut in bits of cheese (about ⅔ cup) if cheese has not been included in the package. Add more water if needed, and cook a moment more, until the cheese melts.

For white sauce made from butter, flour, and dry milk (2 pots)

1. Cook 2 cups macaroni in 3 cups boiling water for 6 minutes or until just done. Take off the heat.
2. In a second pot, melt 3 tablespoons butter. Add 3 tablespoons flour and cook over low heat for a minute.
3. Add the contents of the first pot, and stir vigorously. Cook a few minutes until thick. Add about ⅔ cup cut or grated cheese, 4 tablespoons dry milk, ½ teaspoon salt, and a pinch of thyme and nutmeg. Cook a few minutes until the cheese melts.

Spaghetti Carbonara

This simple but elegant pasta dish is perfectly adapted to the wild menu, especially when you keep raccoons from eating your eggs. Whether you inadvertently donate your fresh eggs to the local fauna, as we did one night, use them up early in the trip, or simply don't carry them, Spaghetti Carbonara is delicious without—just use a bit of flour and milk instead. Both versions follow.

TRAIL INFORMATION

TIME	15 to 20 minutes
WATER	1 quart
EQUIPMENT	1 frying pan
	1 pot
SERVINGS	4 to 5

PREPARE AHEAD

Ingredients

¾ pound pasta (linguini or
   vermicelli)
3 cloves garlic
⅓ cup dried bacon pieces°
1 tablespoon flour
1 tablespoon dry milk } or 1 fresh egg

2 tablespoons dried parsley°
½ cup grated fresh Parmesan
2 or 3 tablespoons oil
Salt and pepper

Packing the food

Put into 3 small bags, then package with the trail directions: 1. pasta; 2. garlic cloves, bacon, and parsley; 3. Parmesan cheese (or carry in general provisions, ungrated, and cut it up on the trail).

Carry in general provisions: flour and dry milk or fresh egg, oil, and salt and pepper.

TRAIL DIRECTIONS—SPAGHETTI CARBONARA

1. In a cup, mix 1 tablespoon dry milk with ½ cup water. Have the flour handy.

2. Boil a pot of water, cook the pasta 5 minutes or until just done, drain, and keep warm if possible.

3. Smash the garlic cloves under the flat of your knife blade and chop them. In the frying pan, heat 2 or 3 tablespoons oil, cook the garlic a minute over medium heat. Add the bacon, parsley, and 1 tablespoon flour. Cook about 2 more minutes. Be careful not to burn. Add the ½ cup milk and stir.

4. Add the drained pasta and ½ cup grated cheese and toss. Season with salt and pepper.

Note: To use a raw egg, omit the milk and flour. Add the egg to the cooked, drained pasta along with the bacon mixture, and toss. Then mix in the cheese.

Spaghetti and White Clam Sauce

This elegant dish is one of the rare and simple delicacies that adapts completely to the wild kitchen.

The sauce does not "cover" the pasta, but joins it, rather, in a perfect marriage of subtle and individual flavors.

TRAIL INFORMATION

TIME	10 to 15 minutes
WATER	3 to 4 cups
EQUIPMENT	2 pots, can opener
SERVINGS	2

PREPARE AHEAD

Ingredients

One 6½-ounce can minced clams, which weighs 9 ounces, including juice, which is about ½ cup

2 cloves garlic

1 tablespoon dried parsley°
½ tablespoon flour
About ⅓ pound thin pasta (such as linguini)
2 tablespoons butter

Packing the food

Put into 2 small bags, then package with the can of clams and the trail directions: 1. garlic cloves, parsley, and flour (or carry in general provisions); 2. pasta.

Carry in general provisions: butter or margarine.

TRAIL DIRECTIONS—SPAGHETTI AND WHITE CLAM SAUCE

1. Open the can of clams. Smash the garlic cloves by bringing the heel of your hand down smartly on the flat of your knife blade poised on each one, remove skin, and cut them into pieces.

2. Melt 2 tablespoons butter in a pan. Add the garlic and cook a few

minutes over low heat. Add parsley and $\frac{1}{2}$ tablespoon flour; cook for 3 to 4 minutes but do not brown.

3. Add the clams plus juice, increase the heat to boil the mixture, then simmer, stirring, a few minutes until thickened.

4. Set this aside while you cook the pasta. Bring a pot of water to a boil. Add the pasta, bring to boil again, and cook 5 minutes, or until done. Drain and serve with clam sauce, briefly reheated if necessary.

Dried Oriental Mushrooms in Cream Sauce with Pasta

To enjoy the musky, delicate flavor of dried Oriental mushrooms to its fullest, put them into a cream sauce made from their soaking water; the only other flavoring is a little salt. Green pasta gives the dish an exotic look.

TRAIL INFORMATION

TIME	30 minutes soaking, 10 minutes cooking
WATER	3 cups
EQUIPMENT	2 pots, 1 bowl
SERVINGS	3 to 4

PREPARE AHEAD

Ingredients

About $\frac{1}{2}$ pound thin pasta
10 dried Oriental mushrooms
2 tablespoons butter or margarine

1 tablespoon flour
2 heaping tablespoons dry milk
$\frac{1}{4}$ teaspoon salt

Note: It is possible to use $\frac{1}{3}$ cup White Sauce Mix instead of making a roux of butter and flour.

Packing the food

Put into 2 small bags, then package with the trail directions: 1. pasta; 2. mushrooms.

Carry in general trail provisions: butter, flour, dry milk, and salt.

TRAIL DIRECTIONS—DRIED ORIENTAL MUSHROOMS IN CREAM SAUCE WITH PASTA

1. Put the mushrooms in a pot and cover them with $2\frac{3}{4}$ cups water and soak 30 minutes. Save the water; cut off and discard the mushroom stems, cut the mushrooms into pieces, and set them aside in a bowl.

2. Boil the water from Step 1 and add the pasta; cook 5 minutes or until just done. Return the mushrooms to the pot and stir in 2 tablespoons dry milk and $\frac{1}{4}$ teaspoon salt. Set aside.

3. In a second pot, melt $1\frac{1}{2}$ tablespoons butter. Add 1 tablespoon flour; stir and cook a minute over low heat. Stir in the contents of the first pot and heat through.

Note: It is possible to use $\frac{1}{2}$ cup White Sauce Mix, instead of making a roux out of butter and flour.

Fresh Zucchini and Pasta

TRAIL INFORMATION

TIME	15 minutes
WATER	$2\frac{1}{2}$ cups
EQUIPMENT	2 pots
SERVINGS	4

PREPARE AHEAD

Ingredients

2 small fresh zucchini
About $\frac{1}{2}$ pound thin pasta

2 teaspoons basil
2 ounces Parmesan, grated

½ tablespoon butter or margarine   ¼ teaspoon salt
1 tablespoon flour   Pepper to taste

Packing the food

Put into 3 small bags, then package with the trail directions: 1. zucchini and pasta; 2. basil; and 3. Parmesan cheese.

Carry in general provisions: butter or margarine, flour, salt and pepper.

TRAIL DIRECTIONS—FRESH ZUCCHINI AND PASTA

1. Trim the ends from the zucchini, cut them in half, then into narrow 2-inch strips. Heat 1½ tablespoons butter; add the zucchini and 2 teaspoons basil, and cook slowly 5 minutes or until just tender. Add 1 tablespoon flour, cook another minute, and set aside.

2. In a second pot, boil 2½ cups water. Add the pasta and cook 5 minutes or until just done. Stir in the zucchini, ¼ teaspoon salt, and the grated cheese; heat through.

Note: To use dried zucchini (see page 37), pack ½ cup of it with a note to soak 10 minutes and squeeze the water out before proceeding.

Stir-Fry Dinners

The Chinese technique of cooking foods in a very short time—slicing foods thin, using a small bit of very hot oil, imaginatively combining the ingredients at hand, some of them sun-dried—is easily adapted to backpacking. As a matter of fact, once you master the basic procedure, you may find yourself, as I do, adding more and more stir-fries to your menu plan. (One advantage of "repeating" a meal on a trip, as I mentioned in the menu-planning chapter, is that you can carry the same equipment, staples, and trail directions for several meals. Repeating the procedure can only be helpful, especially when you are tired and want to keep the cooking as simple as possible.)

Even kids are delighted by the crunchy whole nuts, bright colors, glossy sauce, and plain rice accompaniment of a stir-fry. (Naturally, anything this good seems a positive *miracle* under trail conditions, which adds to the fun.) Using your own ideas and food preferences, you can vary the ingredients of a basic stir-fry endlessly and not get bored. Most stir-fry meals are balanced in carbohydrates, protein, fats, roughage, and vitamins, all of which a hiker's diet is supposed to include and usually the last thing to which you give much deep thought after the challenge of simply collecting enough food that weighs under two pounds per person per day. Another advantage is that with the food on hand at home it's not complicated to throw together several stir-fry meals at the last minute.

For successful stir-frying on the trail:

Combine your own home-dried jerky and vegetables with Oriental dried foods. Learn where to find the latter: dried Oriental mushrooms (Chinese or Japanese), mo-er (cloud ears—a black fungus), tiger lily buds, tiny dried shrimps, and sliced, dried bean curd (see pages 45–7).

Find sources of excellent whole nuts—almonds that taste like almonds (try California ones) and fresh whole unsalted cashews and peanuts. They're expensive but you use only a few at a time. Try health-food stores and nut stores.

Learn how to make your own jerky (see page 39) because buying it is expensive. You might be able to find a good source in a Chinatown, if you look very hard.

Become familiar with and learn how to use fresh garlic cloves and ginger root (see pages 62–3).

Learn how to cook rice (see page 224).

Learn the basics of stir-frying technique:
- When you dry your own food, slice it very thin, so that it will cook fast and evenly.
- In your trail kitchen, have everything ready before you begin; that is, the soaked ingredients wrung out and stems cut off dried Oriental mushrooms, the garlic cut, and the rice cooked (or almost cooked and sitting off the heat), and the sauce ready.
- Heat the pan before adding oil.
- Cook the garlic and ginger first.
- Stir the food and shake the pan with enthusiasm (style will ensue).
- Add delicate foods last.
- Prepare at home a basic finishing sauce for thickening and flavor (see page 60), or simply season your stir-fry with soy sauce.

Each of the three stir-fry dinners that follow uses a different form of meat—jerky, dried hamburger, and freeze-dried chicken. Depending on your store of dried foods, try variations within the basic theme of meat, vegetables, and seasonings. There is room for experimentation and substitutions in the wild kitchen, where delicate refinements are usually not possible. For a detailed, tempting exploration of Chinese stir-fry techniques, see *The Key to Chinese Cooking*, by Irene Kuo.

Note: Peanut oil is the traditional stir-frying oil since it can be heated to very high temperatures without burning. Other kinds of oil will work, as long as you are careful not to get them *too* hot.

Beef and Vegetable Stir-Fry

To buy dried Oriental foods, see page 273.

TRAIL INFORMATION

TIME	½ hour (includes soaking and rice), 5 minutes for stir-fry
WATER	3 to 4 cups
EQUIPMENT	1 bowl, 1 cup, 1 frying pan
SERVINGS	3

PREPARE AHEAD

Ingredients

½ cup beef jerky (see page 39)
6 dried Oriental mushrooms
About 2 tablespoons each
   Mo-er (cloud ear fungus)
   Tiger lily buds
   Dried sliced parsnips, carrots,
     or other vegetable°
   Freeze-dried peas
(optional) 6 tiny dried Japanese
   shrimp

2 cloves garlic
10 or 12 whole nuts (almonds,
    cashews, or peanuts)
¾ cup rice
2 tablespoons peanut oil
3 tablespoons thickening-seasoning
    sauce (see page 60), or soy
    sauce

Packing the food

Put into 3 small bags, then package with the trail directions: 1. jerky, vegetables, and shrimp if used; 2. garlic and nuts; 3. rice.

Carry in general provisions: oil, and seasoning sauce or soy sauce.

TRAIL DIRECTIONS—BEEF AND VEGETABLE STIR-FRY

1. Soak the jerky and vegetables for ½ hour. Meanwhile, cook ¾ cup rice in double the amount of water for 15 minutes, or until almost all of the water is absorbed, and let sit, keeping it warm if possible.

2. Squeeze the water out of the soaked food and cut the hard stems off the mushrooms and discard; cut the mushrooms into pieces. Smash the garlic cloves under flat of your knife, take off skins, and chop them. If you are using a thickening-seasoning sauce, mix 3 tablespoons of it with double the amount of water in a cup, and have this ready, too. (Shake this mixture well before you measure it.)

3. Heat a frying pan, put in a tablespoon or so of oil, and add the garlic. Cook a moment, then add the beef and vegetables and stir-fry them for 3 to 5 minutes, adding the nuts toward the end. Add your prepared sauce, or a few tablespoons of soy sauce, swirl around in the pan; then serve the stir-fry with the rice.

Ground Beef and Green Bean Stir-Fry

This is a very pretty dish, with the beans very green and the beef a glossy mahogany on the white rice.

TRAIL INFORMATION

TIME	½ hour (includes soaking and rice), 5 minutes for stir-fry
WATER	About 3 cups
EQUIPMENT	1 bowl, 1 cup, 1 frying pan
SERVINGS	3

PREPARE AHEAD

Ingredients

1 cup dried green beans (see page 37)

(optional) 1 tablespoon dried leeks or scallions°

¾ cup dried hamburger, plain (see page 41), or Ground Beef Mix (see page 57)

2 cloves garlic

A few shavings of fresh ginger

¾ cup rice

1 to 2 tablespoons peanut oil

3 tablespoons thickening-seasoning sauce (see page 60), or soy sauce

Packing the food

Put into 3 small bags, then package with the trail directions: 1. green beans and leeks; 2. meat, garlic, and ginger; 3. rice.

Carry in general provisions: oil and seasoning sauce or soy sauce.

TRAIL DIRECTIONS—GROUND BEEF AND GREEN BEAN STIR-FRY

1. Soak the beans and leeks for 30 minutes. Cook rice in double the amount of water for 15 minutes, or until almost all of the water is absorbed, and let sit, keeping it warm if possible.

2. Squeeze the water out of the vegetables. Smash the garlic cloves under the flat of your knife, take off skins, and chop them. If you are using a thickening-seasoning sauce, mix 3 tablespoons of it with double the amount of water in a cup, and have this ready too. (Shake this mixture well before you measure it.)

3. Heat a frying pan, put in 2 tablespoons oil, and add the garlic and ginger. Cook a moment, then add the beef, beans, and leeks, and stir-fry for 3 to 5 minutes over high heat, taking care not to burn the beans. Add your prepared sauce, or a few tablespoons soy sauce, swirl around in the pan; then serve the stir-fry with the rice.

Chicken and Vegetable Stir-Fry

TRAIL INFORMATION

TIME	½ hour (includes soaking and rice), 5 minutes for stir-fry
WATER	About 3 cups
EQUIPMENT	1 bowl, 1 cup, 1 frying pan
SERVINGS	3

PREPARE AHEAD

Ingredients

⅓ cup Rich-Moor freeze-dried chicken

⅓ cup freeze-dried peas

⅓ cup dried sliced parsnips or other vegetables°

6 dried Oriental mushrooms

Few shavings of fresh ginger

10 or 12 whole nuts (almonds, cashews, or peanuts)

¾ cup rice

2 tablespoons peanut oil

3 tablespoons thickening-seasoning sauce (see page 60), or soy sauce

Packing the food

Put into 4 small bags, then package with the trail directions: 1. chicken, peas, parsnips, and mushrooms; 2. rice; 3. ginger (or carry in general provisions); 4. nuts.

Carry in general provisions: oil and seasoning sauce or soy sauce.

TRAIL DIRECTIONS—CHICKEN AND VEGETABLE STIR-FRY

1. Soak the dried food for 20 to 30 minutes. Cook ¾ cup rice in double the amount of water for 15 minutes, or until almost all of the water is absorbed, and let sit, keeping it warm if possible.

2. Squeeze the water out of the food; cut the stems off the mushrooms and discard, and cut the mushrooms up. If you are using a thickening-seasoning sauce, mix 3 tablespoons of it with double the amount of water in a cup and have ready, too. (Shake the mixture well before you measure it.)

3. Heat the frying pan and add 2 tablespoons oil. Crush the ginger in and cook a moment. Add the chicken and vegetables and stir-fry, adding the nuts at the end. Add the prepared sauce, or a few tablespoons soy sauce; swirl around in the pan; then serve the stir-fry with the rice.

Mexican Dinners

You can easily make Mexican dinners on the trail by filling warmed tortillas with a variety of good foods—easily reconstituted bean or meat fillings, cheese, your favorite hot seasonings, and crunchy greenery, whether packed or foraged.

An easy way to warm tortillas is to put them one at a time under the lid of the cookpot. Big, 10-inch Piñata-brand flour tortillas will fit most pots; the overhang keeps them from falling into the sauce warming underneath. (We even warm smaller corn tortillas similarly, using our skinny second pot.) You can also heat tortillas in a little oil in a frying pan, or first oil them and then grill them quickly on your camp grill or by holding them with sticks (if you can figure out a way to keep them from falling off the sticks).

Two recipes follow. One is for a meat sauce to use for tacos; the other is for refried beans to use in burritos. Both mixtures are dried in the oven at home and reconstituted quickly with water on the trail.

Note: Refried beans easily become soup when you add dry milk, a few spices, and water (see recipe for squash soup, page 161).

Meat Tacos

Makes 1½ cups dried sauce

TRAIL INFORMATION

TIME	10 minutes
WATER	1 cup or more
EQUIPMENT	1 pot, skillet (optional)
SERVINGS	3

PREPARE AHEAD

Making and drying the filling

1 pound lean ground beef
½ onion, finely chopped
2 cloves garlic, minced
Black pepper

1 teaspoon chili powder
¾ teaspoon salt
8-ounce can tomato sauce

Brown the meat and pour off any fat. Add the onion and garlic, grind in some black pepper, and cook for a few minutes. Add the rest of the ingredients, cover, and simmer 5 minutes.

Spread the sauce thin in a greased shallow pan and dry it in the oven at 140° F. for 6 hours or until crumbly.

Additional ingredients

6 corn tortillas
6 ounces sharp cheese, grated or
   whole

(optional) Fresh chopped onion
(optional) Hot sauce

Packing the food

Put into 3 or 4 small bags, then package with the trail directions: 1. meat sauce; 2. tortillas; 3. cheese, grated (or carry ungrated in general provisions); 4. (optional) onion.

Carry in general provisions: optional hot sauce.

TRAIL DIRECTIONS—MEAT TACOS

1. To the dry sauce add an equal amount of water, cover, and cook for 10 minutes.

2. Meanwhile, warm the tortillas under the lid of the pot, or fry them lightly in a little oil in a separate pan.

3. Serve the meat sauce in the tortillas with cheese, hot sauce, and sliced onion.

Burritos

Refried beans are cooked beans that you fry only once, really, with garlic, salt, and pepper to give them flavor. Do this at home and dry them; then reconstitute them on the trail to roll inside flour tortillas with cheese and onions to make delicious, quick burritos.

TRAIL INFORMATION

TIME	10 minutes
WATER	1 cup
EQUIPMENT	1 pot, skillet (optional)
SERVINGS	3

PREPARE AHEAD

Ingredients

1 cup dried refried beans (see page 237)
3 or more flour tortillas
3 ounces cheese, to make about ½ cup grated

(optional) Fresh chopped onion
(optional) Hot sauce

Packing the food

Put into 3 or 4 small bags, then package with the trail directions: 1. refried beans; 2. tortillas; 3. cheese (or carry in general provisions); 4. (optional) onion.

Carry in general provisions: optional hot sauce.

TRAIL DIRECTIONS—BURRITOS

1. To the dry refried beans add an equal part of water and cook for 10 minutes.

2. Meanwhile, warm the tortillas under the lid of the pot, or fry them lightly in a little oil in a separate pan.

3. In the tortillas roll the beans, cheese, and hot sauce and onions (if used).

Quick Chili

Makes about 2 cups dried chili

TRAIL INFORMATION

TIME	15 minutes
WATER	1½ to 2 cups
EQUIPMENT	1 pot
SERVINGS	4

PREPARE AHEAD

Making and drying the chili

1 pound ground chuck (medium-lean beef)
½ cup finely chopped onion
2 cloves garlic, minced
⅓ cup finely chopped green pepper
Big pinch of oregano

Small pinch of powdered cumin
1 tablespoon chili powder
½ teaspoon salt
6-ounce can tomato paste

Brown the meat and spoon the fat off. Add the onion, garlic, green pepper, spices, salt, and tomato paste. Stir and cook for 15 minutes. Let it sit for an hour if you can—this enhances the flavor.

Spread the chili on a greased shallow pan and dry in the oven at 140° F. with the oven door propped open a crack.

Packing the food

Put the dried chili in a bag with the trail directions:

TRAIL DIRECTIONS—QUICK CHILI

Add 2 cups water to the 2 cups dried mix, stir, cover, and bring to a boil. Cook slowly for 10 minutes.

Rice, grains, lentil, and bean dinners

In the recipes for rice in this book, trail directions will specify, in the interest of simplicity, twice as much water as rice. Generally, the more rice you're cooking, the lower the portion of water to rice. The Chinese way of calculating water amount fits the wild kitchen perfectly: lay your hand flat on the rice in the pot, and pour in cold water until it comes three-quarters of the way up your hand.

Although it's better not to peek at simmering rice under normal cooking conditions, the backpacker with an intractably hot stove had better not only peek from time to time, but stir as well. (Don't forget that a pot getting too hot over a flame that you can't adjust can be held off the heat, or removed for a moment.)

The cooking times I give for rice are shorter than in most recipes. The rice will continue to cook and to absorb water for five minutes or so after it's removed from the heat—thus freeing the heat for another pot, or simply conserving fuel. But, if you observe that the water hasn't been almost absorbed after 15 minutes of cooking, let the rice simmer for another 5 minutes.

As far as the amount of rice to cook is concerned, keep in mind that 1 cup of raw rice feeds 4 people.

The type of rice to use for general purposes is long-grain. (Short-grain rice, with a creamier texture, is the kind used for puddings.) But don't worry if you get hold of the wrong kind—the wilderness has a way of letting you do what haute cuisine might frown on. Brown rice, with a cooking time of 45 minutes, seems unsuitable for backpacking menus; so does "wild rice"—but soaking these nutritious foods first will shorten their cooking time. Minute Rice, which is precooked and stripped of all its nutrients, is hardly food, in my opinion, but for the super-streamlined cooking situation, it at least fills you up for a while.

Plain Rice

TRAIL INFORMATION

TIME	20 minutes
WATER	2 cups
EQUIPMENT	1 pot
SERVINGS	4

PREPARE AHEAD

Ingredients

1 cup raw rice
(optional) 1 teaspoon butter or
    margarine

Salt to taste

Packing the food

Put the rice into a small bag with the trail directions.

Carry the butter and salt in general provisions.

TRAIL DIRECTIONS—PLAIN RICE

1. Put 1 cup rice and 2 cups water into a pot. Cover, bring to a boil, and simmer 15 minutes or until most of the water is absorbed. Stir occasionally if necessary to prevent burning.

2. Let the pot sit off the heat for 5 minutes, covered. Fluff it up, add optional butter, and salt to taste.

Rice Pilaf

The items added to rice in this recipe are merely suggestions—your own cupboard and imagination will yield many different combinations. (See Note for possible additions besides the ones in the recipe.)

A pilaf makes a meal, especially when you provide protein in the form of meat, seafood, or cheese.

TRAIL INFORMATION

TIME	20 minutes
WATER	1 cup
EQUIPMENT	1 pot
SERVINGS	2 to 3

PREPARE AHEAD

Ingredients

½ to ¾ cup rice
1 clove garlic
2 tablespoons sliced home-dried
    mushrooms,° crumbled*
1 tablespoon dried sliced leeks°
½ tablespoon dried parsley°

1 to 2 tablespoons whole or sliced
    almonds or other nuts
(optional) Pinch of thyme
1 to 2 tablespoons butter or
    margarine

*Home-dried mushrooms don't need presoaking, but imported dried Oriental mushrooms need to be soaked ½ hour and to have their hard stems cut off, so adjust trail time and directions accordingly.

Note: Other possible additions are sunflower seeds, raisins, wild rice, celery, cheese, bacon pieces or sausage, canned shrimp or tuna packed in water, freeze-dried meats. Herbs and spices could be cloves, marjoram, thyme, saffron (a few threads, soaked in water first), curries (a combination of spices). The amount of various foods to add to a basic recipe of ⅓ cup raw rice is about 2 tablespoons and a pinch each of whatever spices you choose.

Packing the food

Put into 2 small bags, then package with the trail directions: 1. rice; 2. garlic, vegetables, nuts, herbs.

Carry butter in general provisions.

TRAIL INGREDIENTS —RICE PILAF

1. Take out the garlic clove. Put it under the flat of your knife and give it a good whack. Slip it out of its skin and chop it.

2. Melt 2 tablespoons butter. Slowly cook the garlic a minute. Add the rice and stir to coat all the grains. Add the other ingredients.

3. Add twice as much water as rice, cover, bring to a boil, and simmer 12 to 15 minutes, stirring occasionally. Let it sit off the heat for about 5 minutes to absorb the flavors.

Rice with Potato and Bacon

TRAIL INFORMATION

TIME	20 minutes
WATER	1¾ cups
EQUIPMENT	1 pot, 1 frying pan
SERVINGS	4

PREPARE AHEAD

Ingredients

1 cup rice
1 chicken or beef bouillon cube
1 tablespoon dried bacon pieces°
1 tablespoon dried minced onion°
1 teaspoon dried parsley°

1 small whole potato
1 or 2 ounces cheese, cut small or grated
2 or 3 tablespoons butter or margarine

Packing the food

Put into 3 small bags, then package with the potato and the trail directions: 1. rice and boullion, unwrapped; 2. bacon pieces, onion, and parsley; 3. cheese (or carry in general provisions).

Carry butter in general provisions.

TRAIL DIRECTIONS —RICE WITH POTATO AND BACON

1. Put 1 cup rice and bouillon with 1¾ cups water into a pot, cover. Bring to a boil, then simmer for 12 to 15 minutes or until the water is

almost absorbed; then take the pot off the heat and let it sit for about 5 minutes until the water is absorbed.

2. Meanwhile, slice the potato as thin as you can. Heat 2 or 3 tablespoons margarine in a frying pan, heat the onion, parsley, and bacon for a moment, then fry the potatoes until they are just done, but still crunchy, like water chestnuts.

3. Add the rice, and cut in an ounce or two of cheese, stir, and let sit a moment until the cheese softens.

Rice with Dried Oriental Mushrooms

TRAIL INFORMATION

TIME	30 minutes soaking, 20 minutes cooking
WATER	2¼ cups
EQUIPMENT	1 pot, 1 bowl
SERVINGS	3–4

PREPARE AHEAD

Ingredients

8 to 10 dried Oriental mushrooms
2 tablespoons dried leeks°
¾ cup rice

3 ounces Parmesan cheese
3 tablespoons butter or margarine

Packing the food

Put into 3 small bags, then package with the trail directions: 1. mushrooms and leeks; 2. rice; 3. cheese (or carry in general provisions with the butter or margarine).

TRAIL DIRECTIONS —RICE WITH DRIED ORIENTAL MUSHROOMS

1. Soak the mushrooms in 2¼ cups warm water for ½ hour. Squeeze out the water and save it; put the mushrooms aside to add to the rice.

2. Heat 3 tablespoons butter in a cookpot, add the leeks, then ¾ cup

rice, and cook a minute, stirring well. Add the mushroom water (it should be double the amount of rice) and bring to a boil. Cut in the mushrooms.

3. Simmer covered for 12 to 15 minutes until the water is absorbed. Add cut Parmesan and stir to melt it.

Wild Rice with Peas and Chicken

Wild rice is not really rice at all but a wild grass harvested from shallow lakes in Minnesota by Indians, who whack the grains into their boat with long sticks. It sometimes costs $4 per 4-ounce box—a dollar an ounce! How can any self-respecting, budget-keeping backpacker justify such an extravagance?

Its preparation time is long, too: it needs to soak for an hour before cooking 15 minutes.

But, to offset these serious drawbacks are two pluses of considerable note.

First, wild rice earns half its name, anyway, with its wonderful taste. It's definitely a wild taste—a clean, intact, utterly special flavor due, no doubt, to the fact that it can only be harvested from those great blue, wind-ruffled lakes of the north Midwest.

And second, wild rice is spectacularly nutritious. It has, for instance, nearly twice the protein, more than double the iron, and more than ten times the riboflavin of its not-even-remote cousin, brown rice.

Two ounces of wild rice will make two generous servings when stretched with other ingredients.

This recipe is an elegant trail meal with a crunchy texture and the special flavor of wild rice.

TRAIL INFORMATION

TIME	1 hour soaking, 20 to 25 minutes cooking
WATER	2 cups
EQUIPMENT	1 pot, 1 bowl or second pot
SERVINGS	4

PREPARE AHEAD

Ingredients

⅔ cup (4 ounces) wild rice
⅔ cup chopped hazelnuts or
slivered almonds
2 tablespoons dried parsley°
½ teaspoon thyme
Pinch of rosemary
Tiny pinch of ground cloves

⅔ cup freeze-dried peas, home-dried
peas,° or raisins
⅔ cup Rich-Moor freeze-dried
chicken
4 tablespoons butter or margarine
Salt and pepper to taste

Packing the food

Put into 3 small bags, then package with the trail directions: 1. rice; 2. nuts, parsley, herbs, and cloves; 3. peas and chicken.

Carry in general provisions: butter or margarine and salt and pepper.

TRAIL DIRECTIONS —WILD RICE WITH PEAS AND CHICKEN

1. Soak ⅔ cup wild rice in 1⅓ cups water for 1 hour. If using home-dried peas, soak and cook them with the wild rice.

2. In a pot cook the nuts and flavorings slowly in butter for 3 to 4 minutes. Add the rice and soaking water and cook 8 to 10 minutes. Add the chicken, freeze-dried peas, raisins, and an additional ⅔ cup water; cook another 8 to 10 minutes. The dish will be crunchy. Add salt and pepper to taste.

Note: To use regular rice, omit the soaking. Add ½ cup rice and 1 cup water after cooking the nuts, then proceed as above.

Couscous

Couscous, durum wheat semolina, is the staple grain of North Africa. Steamed over stews fragrant with spices and the flavors of lamb and vegetables, it's wonderful, although not a practical trail meal.

A quick-cooking version of the grain is available, however; in 5 minutes' time it becomes a rather nice grain side dish to absorb gravies or otherwise accompany meat dishes.

To make a pilaf out of couscous, follow the directions for Rice Pilaf (see page 224) but be sure all the additions are cooked before you add the couscous, because it cooks fast.

Couscous is sold in fancy markets. Double-check the box to make sure you buy the quick (precooked) version for backpacking.

TRAIL INFORMATION

TIME	5 to 10 minutes
WATER	1 cup
EQUIPMENT	1 pot
SERVINGS	3 to 4

PREPARE AHEAD

Ingredients

2 teaspoons butter   ⅔ cup instant (precooked) couscous

Packing the food

Put the couscous into a small bag with the trail directions.

Carry the butter in general provisions.

TRAIL DIRECTIONS —SIDE DISH OF COUSCOUS

1. Melt 1 teaspoon butter in a cookpot. Add ⅔ cup couscous and stir to coat all the grains.

2. Add 1 cup water and bring to a boil. Cook over medium heat, stirring, until the water is absorbed—about 3 minutes.

Lentils with Rice or Mashed Potatoes

With slightly sharp Parmesan and plain rice or potatoes to complement their dusky flavor, lentils are good backpacking fare and earn their 40-minute cooking time. Part of that "cooking time" is really soaking—when you let them sit for 20 minutes after an initial boiling they actually cook in about 15 minutes, and that saves fuel.

Any crunchy fresh vegetable, like onion, celery, or cucumber, is a welcome contrast in texture. Link sausages make a hearty meal out of this simple fare.

TRAIL INFORMATION

TIME	About 45 minutes
WATER	About 2 cups
EQUIPMENT	2 pots
SERVINGS	3

PREPARE AHEAD

Ingredients

½ cup lentils
½ tablespoon dried minced onion°
1 teaspoon dried parsley°
½ teaspoon powdered beef bouillon, or ½ beef bouillon cube
(optional) 1 tablespoon dried minced carrot°

2-inch square tomato leather (see page 35)
⅓ cup rice, or ¾ cup Potato Buds, 2 tablespoons dry milk, 1 teaspoon Butter Buds, butter, or margarine
2 ounces Parmesan cheese

Packing the food

Put into 3 small bags, then package with the trail directions: 1. lentils, onion, parsley, bouillon, and optional carrot and tomato; 2. cheese (or carry in general provisions); 3. rice, or Potato Buds with dry milk and Butter Buds.

Carry butter, if used, in general provisions.

TRAIL DIRECTIONS —LENTILS WITH RICE OR MASHED POTATOES

1. In one pot bring the lentils and 1¼ cups water to a boil, covered. Take off the heat and let sit for 20 to 25 minutes.

2. Meanwhile, in a second pot, bring ⅓ cup rice and ⅔ cup water to a boil, covered. Simmer for 12 to 15 minutes; take off the heat and let sit.

3. Put the lentils back on the fire and simmer 10 to 15 minutes. Serve with reheated rice and Parmesan cheese cut on top.

To use mashed potatoes:

1. Cook the lentils for 20 minutes, then let sit while you boil 1 cup water for mashed potatoes in a second pot.

2. Add the potatoes, stir, add 1 teaspoon butter or margarine if Butter Buds weren't included, and serve with the lentils and Parmesan cheese cut on top.

Lentils with Eggplant and Noodles

Cinnamon and oregano turn this vegetarian dish into an exotic creation. It may not appeal to the typical Boy Scout troop, but the "epicure" will love it.

Serve it with a crunchy salad if you can.

TRAIL INFORMATION

TIME	About 45 minutes
WATER	1½ cups plus 1 potful
EQUIPMENT	2 pots
SERVINGS	3 to 4

PREPARE AHEAD

Ingredients

½ cup lentils
¾ cup dried sliced eggplant, cut into strips*
1 tablespoon dried minced onion°

1 clove garlic
2-inch square piece of tomato leather (see page 35)
½ teaspoon cinnamon

Pinch of oregano
2 cups noodles
⅓ cup White Sauce Mix (see page 60)

2 ounces Parmesan cheese (⅓ cup when grated)

*From 1 medium eggplant (see page 37 for drying instructions)

Packing the food

Put into 4 small bags, then package with the trail directions: 1. lentils, eggplant, onion, garlic, tomato paste, cinnamon, and oregano; 2. noodles; 3. white sauce mix; 4. cheese (or carry in general provisions).

TRAIL DIRECTIONS —LENTILS WITH EGGPLANT AND NOODLES

1. Find the garlic clove in the lentil bag, smash it under the flat of your knife blade, remove its skin, and chop it. Put the contents of the lentil bag in a cookpot with 1½ cups water and the garlic pieces. Cover, bring to a boil, and then simmer for 20 to 30 minutes. Add more water if necessary.

2. Meanwhile, boil a potful of water for the noodles. Add them when the water boils, cook 5 minutes (until just tender), and drain.

3. While the noodles cook, add about ⅓ cup Parmesan cheese, grated or cut up, to the lentils. Heat until the cheese melts, then serve the lentils with the noodles.

Shrimp or Tuna and Barley Pilaf

Although pearled barley, with both its hull and germ removed, is not as nutritious as whole barley, its faster cooking time makes it feasible wilderness fare, and a welcome change from rice and noodles.

TRAIL INFORMATION

TIME	25 minutes
WATER	1¼ cups
EQUIPMENT	1 pot, can opener
SERVINGS	6

PREPARE AHEAD

Ingredients

½ cup pearled barley, toasted＊
¼ cup dried mushrooms, broken
    into pieces°
1 tablespoon dried minced onion,
    or 2 tablespoons dried leek°
1 teaspoon dried minced green
    pepper°

¼ cup slivered or sliced almonds
Pinch each of thyme and sage
1⅛-ounce package commercially
    freeze-dried peas
1 can shrimp, or 1 can tuna, packed
    in water
1 tablespoon butter or margarine

＊To toast barley, spread it on a cookie sheet and set it in a 350° F. oven until lightly
brown, about 10 minutes.

Packing the food

Put into 2 small bags, then package with the can of shrimp or tuna and the
'trail directions: 1. barley, mushrooms, onion, green pepper, nuts, thyme,
and sage; 2. peas.

Carry in general provisions: butter or margarine.

TRAIL DIRECTIONS —SHRIMP OR TUNA AND BARLEY PILAF

1. Melt 1 tablespoon butter or margarine in a pot. Add the contents of
the barley bag and stir over medium heat for a few minutes.

2. Add 1¼ cups water, bring to a boil, then simmer covered for 20
minutes. During the last 5 minutes, add the peas.

3. Add the shrimp or tuna and cook a few more minutes to heat it
through.

Kasha (Buckwheat Groats)

TRAIL INFORMATION

TIME	20 minutes
WATER	1 cup
EQUIPMENT	1 pot, a second pot or frying pan
SERVINGS	3

PREPARE AHEAD

Ingredients

½ cup buckwheat groats
1 tablespoon dry egg (see page 52)
(optional) 2 tablespoons dried leeks
    or onion°

(optional) 1 tablespoon dried green
    pepper°
Generous tablespoon butter or
    margarine

Packing the food

Pack the dry ingredients in one small bag with the trail directions.

Carry the butter or margarine in general provisions.

TRAIL DIRECTIONS —SIDE DISH OF KASHA

1. Boil 1 cup water.

2. Add 1½ to 2 tablespoons cold water to the buckwheat mixture in the bag you brought it in and mix it up.

3. Melt 1 generous tablespoon butter in a frying pan or second pot, add the buckwheat mixture, and stir until the grains are coated and separate. Add 1 cup boiling water, cover, and simmer 15 minutes or until the water is absorbed.

Polenta and Sausages

TRAIL INFORMATION

TIME	25 minutes
WATER	3½ cups
EQUIPMENT	1 pot
SERVINGS	3 to 4

PREPARE AHEAD

Ingredients

1 cup cornmeal, preferably stone
    ground
1½ teaspoons salt

2 tablespoons butter or margarine
3 or 4 smoked link sausages
⅓ cup Parmesan cheese

Packing the food

Put the cornmeal and salt into a bag with the trail directions.

Carry in general provisions: butter, sausages, and cheese.

TRAIL DIRECTIONS —POLENTA AND SAUSAGES

1. Boil 3½ cups water. Pour in 1 cup cornmeal in a thin, steady stream, stirring as you pour. Cook slowly, stirring occasionally, for 20 minutes, until the polenta is stiff and comes away from the sides of the pan when you stir. If no salt was added at home, salt to taste (as much as 1½ teaspoons).

2. Stir in 2 tablespoons butter, about ⅓ cup cheese, cut into pieces or grated, and 3 or 4 link sausages, and heat these through before serving.

Note: To make the pot easier to clean, put water in it to soak it while you are eating.

Beans

Dried beans have been a traditional camp food because they're light, non-perishable, and full of vitamins and protein. In the old days, when camps were stationary and firewood was plentiful, beans were a basic food, in spite of an increasing awareness that they cause flatulence.

Modern backpackers, no less determined to make beans a camp staple, are apt to learn quickly that dried beans don't fit the hiking schedule. I've met several hikers who have tried, rather unsuccessfully, to soak and cook dried beans on the trail, and to their mournful experiments I add my own.

But your can cook and dry beans at home, or dry out a can of cooked beans, to produce a fast, nourishing trail meal. Beans prepared in this way re-enter the camping menu in all the ways they're good at home—with sausages or hot dogs; mixed with ground beef and tomato sauce; with rice; and stuffed with cheese into warm tortillas or pita.

In the recipes that follow, your source of beans can either be dried beans that you soak and cook, or a 16-ounce can. Generally, the amount of cooked beans produced from a pound of dried ones is equal to that from three 16-ounce cans. For drying canned beans, see page 36.

To make and dry refried beans

Makes 5 to 6 cups

1 pound dried kidney, black, or navy beans	1 tablespoon salt
	Pepper to taste
(optional) 1 large onion, chopped	6 tablespoons oil
6 to 7 cups water	6 cloves garlic

Soak the beans overnight in 6 cups water. Or you can put them in a pot with 6 cups water, bring to a boil, turn off the heat, and let them sit for an hour. Then add the optional onion and simmer for about 2 hours, until they are soft. Add salt, and pepper to taste. Purée in the blender, a little at a time, adding a few tablespoons water if necessary with each batch to keep the beans from clogging the blades.

To fry the beans with garlic before drying:

Lightly sauté 2 cloves finely chopped garlic in 2 tablespoons hot oil. Over medium heat fry one-third of the mashed beans, turning once to cook the other side. Repeat this process with the rest of the beans.

Spread the beans on a greased flat pan and dry them in the oven at 140° F., with the door propped open a crack, for 6 to 8 hours, until they are crumbly. Pack in a plastic bag, labeled "Dried Cooked Beans: Reconstitute with an equal amount of water."

Note: To make the "baked" bean recipe on page 238, dry the canned beans without mashing them.

Quick "Baked" Beans

TRAIL INFORMATION

TIME	10 minutes
WATER	3 cups
EQUIPMENT	1 pot
SERVINGS	3 or 4

PREPARE AHEAD

Ingredients

1⅓ cups dried cooked beans (see page 237) or two 16-ounce cans beans, dried (see page 36)
2 teaspoons dried bacon pieces°

2 teaspoons brown sugar
1 teaspoon Butter Buds, or 2 teaspoons butter or margarine

Packing the food

Pack into a bag with the trail directions: beans, bacon, sugar, and Butter Buds, if used.

Carry butter or margarine, if used, in general provisions.

TRAIL DIRECTIONS —QUICK "BAKED" BEANS

1. Add 2 cups water to the contents of the bean bag and bring to a boil. Add butter or margarine, if used.

2. Cover and simmer for 5 minutes, adding more water if necessary.

Black Beans and Rice

This nourishing, inexpensive meal is easy to prepare on the trail. It is possible to use other beans, like navy or pinto beans.

TRAIL INFORMATION

TIME	25 minutes
WATER	$1\frac{2}{3}$ cups
EQUIPMENT	2 pots
SERVINGS	3 to 4

PREPARE AHEAD

Ingredients

1 cup dried cooked black beans (see page 237) or 16-ounce can of beans, dried (see page 36)
1 beef bouillon cube
2 teaspoons dried minced onion°
¼ teaspoon dry mustard
1 clove garlic
(optional) 2 tablespoons jerky (see page 39)

(optional) 1 tablespoon each dried green pepper and parsley°
⅓ cup rice
(optional) ⅓ cup grated cheese
2 teaspoons butter or oil
(optional) 4 smoked link sausages

Packing the food

Put into 3 small bags, then package with the trail directions: 1. beans, bouillon, onion, mustard, garlic, optional jerky, green pepper, and parsley; 2. rice; 3. optional cheese (or carry in general provisions, ungrated).

Carry in general provisions: butter or oil and optional sausages.

TRAIL DIRECTIONS — BLACK BEANS AND RICE

1. Smash the garlic clove with the flat of a knife to remove its skin. Cut it into little bits and cook it for a few minutes in 2 teaspoons butter or oil.

2. Add the other contents of the bean bag, the optional sausage, and 1 cup water, and cook 10 minutes, adding more water if necessary.

3. To cook rice, add ⅔ cup water to ⅓ cup rice in another pot, bring to a boil, and simmer for 12 to 15 minutes, covered. Let sit off heat 5 minutes. Reheat the beans and serve over the rice, with about ⅓ cup cheese cut or grated on top.

SALADS AND VEGETABLES

Although camp meals often have to be cooked in one pot, it's wonderful when you can offer the contrast of taste, texture, and color of a vegetable presented "on the side." The salads offered here are easily made from gossamer-light dried ingredients; the stir-fried vegetables capture color and vivacity from dried provisions; and fresh vegetables have been known to render backpackers speechless with appreciation.

Tabbouleh Salad

The glory of Lebanese tabbouleh salad is the absolutely fresh and individual taste of its raw vegetables, imbued with olive oil and lemon. It's an excellent trail salad as long as you use the best dried ingredients you can—your own dried parsley, tomatoes, and leeks give you this assurance. And, if you find fresh mint in your travels, you'll surely be blessed.

Pure olive oil is the best choice, although any vegetable oil will do. A fresh lemon will give you the best juice, but the reconstituted juice in one of those little plastic lemons is all right and might be useful as well in other salads and soups, or on fish.

TRAIL INFORMATION

TIME	30 minutes to soak (no cooking)
WATER	1 cup
EQUIPMENT	1 pot or bowl
SERVINGS	4

PREPARE AHEAD

Ingredients

½ cup bulgur wheat
4 tablespoons dried minced parsley°
2 tablespoons dried leeks°
4 dried tomato slices°
Scant ⅛ teaspoon salt

(optional) 1 teaspoon dried mint
  (add fresh mint on the trail if
  you find some)
1 tablespoon olive oil
2 teaspoons lemon juice

Packing the food

Mix all the dry ingredients and put them into a bag with the trail directions.

Carry in general provisions: oil and lemon juice.

TRAIL DIRECTIONS — TABBOULEH SALAD

1. Soak dry mix in 1 cup cold water for 30 minutes, and drain.
2. Add 1 tablespoon olive oil and 2 teaspoons lemon juice, mix well, and serve.

Cole Slaw

Cabbage dries well and reconstitutes into a crunchy salad. The sweet-sour dressing that follows is a generous amount (it will cover 2 cups dried cabbage), which you can diminish according to the number in your party and the amount of cabbage you use.

Substitute red or Chinese cabbage if you prefer. And you can add sunflower seeds and dried parsley, onion, or carrot to the salad to make it more interesting.

TRAIL INFORMATION

TIME	20 to 30 minutes (soaking)
WATER	2 cups or less
EQUIPMENT	1 bowl, 1 cup or additional bowl
SERVINGS	5 or 6

PREPARE AHEAD

Ingredients

1 cup dried cabbage° (from 1 small cabbage)
(optional) 1 tablespoon freeze-dried chives

½ tablespoon sugar
½ tablespoon white vinegar
½ tablespoon oil
½ teaspoon salt

Packing the food

Put the cabbage and optional chives in a small bag with the trail directions.

Carry in general provisions: sugar, vinegar, oil and salt.

TRAIL DIRECTIONS —COLE SLAW

1. Soak 1 cup of cabbage in cold water for 20 to 30 minutes.
2. Make up the dressing out of ½ tablespoon each of sugar, vinegar, and oil; ½ teaspoon salt; and 1 tablespoon water.
3. Drain the cabbage, squeeze the water out of it, and mix with dressing.

Carrot and Raisin Salad

This is a simple fresh-tasting salad that children will appreciate. The sweet-and-sour dressing is the same as on page 61.

TRAIL INFORMATION

TIME	20 to 30 minutes
WATER	About ¾ cup
EQUIPMENT	1 bowl
SERVINGS	3

PREPARE AHEAD

Ingredients

½ cup dried grated carrot° (from 3
   carrots)
¼ cup golden or dark raisins
1 teaspoon sugar

1 teaspoon vinegar
1 teaspoon oil
¼ teaspoon salt

Packing the food

Put the carrot and raisins in a small bag with the trail directions.

Carry in general provisions: sugar, vinegar, oil, and salt.

TRAIL DIRECTIONS —CARROT AND RAISIN SALAD

1. Soak ½ cup carrot and ¼ cup raisins in water to cover for 20 to 30 minutes.

2. Make a dressing from 1 teaspoon each sugar, vinegar, and oil; ¼ teaspoon salt; and 1 tablespoon water.

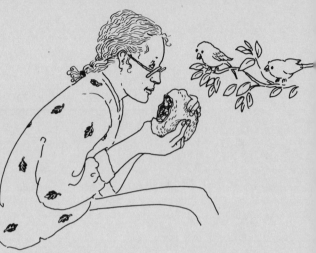

Stuffed Pita Bread

Pita, Lebanese "pocket" bread, can be stuffed with a variety of delicious mixtures and combined with soup for a satisfying supper. The recipe for pita is on page 80.

Here are a few stuffing ideas for pita:

One of the best and simplest ways to fill pita is to put tabbouleh salad in it as the Lebanese do (see page 240 for Tabbouleh Salad recipe). Actually, any salad is delicious inside pita.

The traditional Greek souvlakia, grilled lamb with seasonings, is a trail possibility. First combine yogurt with minced garlic. Let that sit to mingle flavors while you slice a fresh onion and grill some lamb or beef jerky. To this zesty filling add vegetables such as foraged greenery or a cucumber that you've sneaked into your pack.

Combine pieces of salami, cheese, and a crunchy vegetable. Soaked dried cabbage will add crunch, as will zucchini and carrots.

Use leftover cooked lentils, rice, or beans (carried in cool weather) a few slices of salami or cheese, and any crunchy vegetables you can muster. Reconstituted, briefly heated Ground Beef Mix (see page 57) or any of the quick fillings—refried beans (see page 237), taco filling (see page 219), baked beans (see page 238)—will fill the pita nicely, too.

These are just a few of the many combinations possible. When you make or heat up a soup to go with it, stuffed pita can be a satisfying trail meal.

Vegetables with Butter and Herbs

TRAIL INFORMATION

TIME	10 minutes
WATER	1 cup
EQUIPMENT	1 pot
SERVINGS	3 to 4

PREPARE AHEAD

Ingredients

1 cup dried sliced vegetables*
(optional) Pinch of rosemary,
   thyme, tarragon, or dill

2 teaspoons butter or margarine
Salt and pepper to taste

*Carrots, parsnips, kohlrabi, beets, zucchini, summer squash, peas, or green beans (see pages 36–7 for vegetable chart and drying instructions)

Packing the food

Put the vegetables and optional herbs into a small bag with the trail directions.

Carry in general provisions: butter or margarine, salt and pepper.

TRAIL DIRECTIONS —VEGETABES WITH BUTTER AND HERBS

    1. Cover the vegetables with water in a cookpot, cover, bring to a boil, and simmer until just tender—5 to 10 minutes.

    2. Drain, add 2 teaspoons butter, and salt and pepper to taste.

Creamed Vegetables

TRAIL INFORMATION

TIME   15 minutes
WATER   1½ to 2 cups
EQUIPMENT   1 pot
SERVINGS   3 to 4

PREPARE AHEAD

Ingredients

1 cup dried sliced vegetables*
⅓ cup White Sauce Mix (see page 60)
Pinch of one or more of the following:
  dried parsley or chives
  thyme
  tarragon
Salt and pepper

*Some combination of the following: carrots, parsnips, peas, zucchini, green beans, or mushrooms (see pages 36–7)

Packing the food

Put into 2 separate bags, then package with the trail directions: 1. vegetables; 2. white sauce mix and seasonings.

TRAIL DIRECTIONS —CREAMED VEGETABLES

1. Cook the vegetables in 1 cup water for 10 minutes.
2. Add ⅓ cup white sauce mix and stir until dissolved. Add more water to make a consistency of heavy cream, and simmer, covered, for a few minutes. Flavor with spices, if not already included, and salt and pepper.

Note: For Cream of Vegetable Soup, see page 168.

Harvard Beets

While dried beets can be cooked simply and deliciously in water to cover and flavored simply with butter or margarine, your hiking taste buds might yearn for a sweet-and-sour taste. Harvard beets are better eaten 30 minutes after cooking, so you can prepare them first if you are working over a single camp stove, then let them "rest" while you cook the rest of the dinner.

TRAIL INFORMATION

TIME	15 to 20 minutes
WATER	2 cups
EQUIPMENT	1 pot, 1 cup
SERVINGS	4

PREPARE AHEAD

Ingredients

1 to 1½ cups dried sliced beets (from 2 pounds beets—see page 36)

⅓ cup sugar

¼ cup white vinegar

1½ teaspoons cornstarch

(optional) 1 teaspoon butter or margarine, added on the trail

Packing the food

Either combine the cornstarch, sugar, and vinegar in a leakproof container, or carry them separately in the general provisions. Put the beets into a small bag with the trail directions.

TRAIL DIRECTIONS —HARVARD BEETS

1. In a covered pot, cook 1 to 1½ cups beets in 2 cups water for 10 minutes or until tender.

2. In a cup, mix ¼ cup sugar, 1 tablespoon vinegar, and 1½ teaspoons cornstarch. Pour ½ to ⅔ cup beet water into the cup and mix.

3. Drain the beets, put the sauce mixture in, cook 5 minutes, until the sauce has thickened. Let the beets sit for 30 minutes before eating.

Puréed Squash

TRAIL INFORMATION

TIME	5 to 10 minutes
WATER	½ to ¾ cup
EQUIPMENT	1 pot
SERVINGS	4 to 6

PREPARE AHEAD

Ingredients

½ cup dried squash (from a 2-pound   Salt to taste
    butternut squash—see page 35)

Packing the food

Put the dried squash in a small bag with the trail directions.

TRAIL DIRECTIONS —PURÉED SQUASH

Add ½ to ¾ cup water to ½ cup dried squash in a cookpot. Stir and heat until the lumps are gone. Add salt to taste.

Stir-Fried Vegetables

Trail stir-fried vegetables are light, colorful, crunchy, and tasty, because most dried vegetables reconstitute to their original color and regain considerable crispness, too. If you are unfamiliar with the general stir-fry procedure, refer to the basic directions given on page 214.

    Fresh foraged vegetables might adapt themselves to stir-frying, depending on what they are. In most cases, I suspect their chief contribution will be a fresh "accent," depending on their nature and on your taste buds.

    Two recipes follow that stir-fry well after drying. (For drying instructions, see pages 34–7.)

    Soak the dried vegetables a half hour and squeeze the water out before stir-frying them. Some of the vegetables are good alone or combined with another one—most fare very well in and contribute nicely to a general mix like the Beef and Vegetable Stir-Fry recipe on page 215. The drying and soaking process blurs the distinctions somewhat between individual vegetables that in their original state can be cooked in a number of delicious individual ways, with more precise timing and a more delicate matching of seasonings. (See, for example, the vegetable chapter in Irene Kuo's *The Key to Chinese Cooking.*)

Stir-Fried Carrots and Zucchini

TRAIL INFORMATION

TIME	$\frac{1}{2}$ hour soaking, 5 minutes cooking
WATER	About 1 cup
EQUIPMENT	1 bowl, 1 frying pan
SERVINGS	3

PREPARE AHEAD

Ingredients

$\frac{1}{3}$ cup dried, thinly sliced
    carrots°
$\frac{1}{3}$ cup dried, thinly sliced
    zucchini°

2 tablespoons oil
$\frac{1}{4}$ teaspoon slivered fresh ginger
    (see page 63)
Pinch of salt

Packing the food

Pack the vegetables in a small bag with the trail directions.

Carry in general provisions: oil, salt, and ginger.

TRAIL DIRECTIONS —STIR-FRIED CARROTS AND ZUCCHINI

1. Soak the vegetables for $\frac{1}{2}$ hour in cold water. Drain them and squeeze the water out.

2. Heat a frying pan. Add 3 tablespoons oil and get it hot, then add a few slivers of ginger and press them into the pan for a moment. Add the vegetables and stir-fry for a minute or two. Season lightly with salt.

Stir-Fried Sweet-and-Sour Red Cabbage

TRAIL INFORMATION

TIME	30 minutes (includes soaking)
WATER	About 1½ cups
EQUIPMENT	1 bowl, 1 frying pan with lid
SERVINGS	4

PREPARE AHEAD

Ingredients

1 cup dried sliced cabbage°
1 clove garlic
2 tablespoons oil
Pinch of salt

2 teaspoons white vinegar
2 teaspoons sugar
2 teaspoons soy sauce

Packing the food

Pack the cabbage in a small bag with the trail directions.

Carry in general provisions: garlic, oil, salt, vinegar, sugar, and soy sauce.

TRAIL DIRECTIONS —STIR-FRIED SWEET-AND-SOUR RED CABBAGE

1. Soak the cabbage for ½ hour in cold water. Drain it and squeeze the water out. Smash a garlic clove under the flat of your knife and have the rest of the ingredients at hand.

2. Heat the frying pan. Add 2 tablespoons oil, heat, and then add the garlic and stir it around, pressing it with a spoon. Add the cabbage, sprinkle with salt, cook a little, and add 2 teaspoons vinegar. Add 2 teaspoons sugar and stir-fry for a few minutes. Add a scant ¼ cup water, cover, and cook over rather high heat until the water is just gone, for about 3 minutes.

3. Uncover the pan and add 2 teaspoons soy sauce. Stir.

Mashed Potatoes with Cheese and Parsley

These tasty potatoes go well with stews, lentils, or beans; they'll also substitute in the sausage and potato recipe on the next page.

TRAIL INFORMATION

TIME	5 minutes
WATER	2 cups
EQUIPMENT	1 pot
SERVINGS	4 to 6

PREPARE AHEAD

Ingredients

1½ cups Potato Buds
2 tablespoons grated cheese
   (Parmesan or cheddar)
2 teaspoons dried parsley°

2 teaspoons Butter Buds
4 tablespoons dry milk
½ teaspoon salt

Packing the food

Put all ingredients into one bag with the trail directions.

Note: Because of the cheese, store this bag in the refrigerator if you pack it ahead.

TRAIL DIRECTIONS — MASHED POTATOES WITH CHEESE AND PARSLEY

1. Boil 2 cups water.
2. Add the contents of the potato bag, stir, cover, and let sit off the heat for 1 minute.

Serve with grilled sausages, stews, lentils, or beans.

Knockwurst and Hot Potato Salad

This spicy potato dish makes a meal when you add knockwurst, hot dogs, or smoked link sausages. Either grill the meat or add it to the potatoes as you begin to cook them.

TRAIL INFORMATION

TIME	15 minutes
WATER	1¼ cups
EQUIPMENT	1 pot
SERVINGS	3 or 4

PREPARE AHEAD

Ingredients

4 ounces (about 2 cups) dried sliced potatoes*
2 tablespoons dried bacon pieces°
2 tablespoons dried leeks, or 1 tablespoon dried minced onion°
1 packet instant beef bouillon, or 1 bouillon cube

1 tablespoon dry egg
4 hot dogs, knockwurst, or smoked link sausages
2 or 3 tablespoons white vinegar
½ teaspoon salt
Pepper to taste

*Use the potatoes from a package of Betty Crocker au gratin potatoes, or dry your own.

Packing the food

Put into 2 separate bags, then package with the trail directions: 1. potatoes, bacon, leeks or onion, bouillon, and egg; 2. sausages.

Carry in trail provisions: vinegar and salt and pepper.

TRAIL DIRECTIONS —KNOCKWURST AND HOT POTATO SALAD

1. Cook the contents of the potato bag and the sausages in 1¼ cup water for 10 minutes.

2. Add 2 or 3 tablespoons vinegar, ½ teaspoon salt, and pepper to taste; stir and simmer for 2 minutes.

Note: If you are using a wood fire, consider grilling the sausages and serving them separately.

Roasted Fresh Potatoes

TRAIL INFORMATION

TIME	About 40 minutes
WATER	None
EQUIPMENT	Aluminum foil
SERVINGS	1 potato per person

Note: You need a wood fire.

PREPARE AHEAD

Ingredients

1 medium-small potato (4 ounces)   Butter or margarine
    per person

Packing the food

Wash and dry the potatoes. Carry them in your pack along with the aluminum foil.

Carry the butter or margarine in general provisions.

TRAIL DIRECTIONS—ROASTED FRESH POTATOES

When you have a good bed of coals from a wood fire, wrap the potatoes in foil and bury them in the coals. A medium potato will take about 40 minutes to cook—test the inside with a sharp stick or a fork. Put butter or margarine on the roasted potato.

Fried Potatoes

Made from raw potatoes rather than from leftover cooked ones as fried potatoes often are, these will take longer to cook—about 15 minutes. But the result is wonderfully crunchy—excellent with eggs or grilled sausages. They also make unusual potatoes au gratin with a bit of White Sauce Mix, water, and cheese.

TRAIL INFORMATION

TIME	20 minutes
WATER	None or ½ cup (see variations)
EQUIPMENT	1 frying pan
SERVINGS	4

PREPARE AHEAD

Ingredients

¾ pound fresh potatoes (2 medium potatoes)
1 fresh scallion or very small fresh onion
4 tablespoons butter or margarine
Salt and pepper

(optional) 2 or 3 smoked link sausages or 2 tablespoons dried Ground Beef Mix (see page 57) or ¼ cup White Sauce Mix (see page 60) and 3 tablespoons cheese

Packing the food

After washing the potatoes and drying them well, put them in the bottom of your pack. Do not put them into a plastic bag, because it's better for them to have all the air they can get. (Moist potatoes think they're in the ground, and grow.)

Carry in general provisions: onion, butter or margarine, salt and pepper, optional white sauce mix, optional cheese, optional sausages or ground beef mix.

Carry the trail directions in some important-paper section of your pack.

TRAIL DIRECTIONS—FRIED POTATOES

1. Find the potatoes and the onion. Get a frying pan and 4 tablespoons butter ready. Find a cutting board and slice the onion and 2 medium potatoes very thin. (Don't peel the potatoes. Cut them in half lengthwise, then slice, to make it easier.) Put them in cold water if you don't use them immediately.

2. Heat the pan to melt the butter. Cook the onion a few minutes until soft, then add the potatoes and fry over medium-low heat until just softened, about 15 minutes, turning often. Fry in batches rather than overcrowd the pan.

Variations:

1. Add 2 or 3 cut smoked link sausages to the potatoes after a few minutes. Or add a few tablespoons dried Ground Beef Mix the same way.

2. At the end of the cooking time, mix ¼ cup White Sauce Mix with ½ cup water in a cup, and cut about 3 tablespoons cheese; add these to the potatoes, and heat to melt the cheese.

Grilled Fresh Vegetables

These are a great treat, but not for long trips, when packing fresh vegetables in quantity is impractical. You need to use a wood fire.

TRAIL INFORMATION

TIME	20 minutes
WATER	None
EQUIPMENT	Grill, bowl
SERVINGS	6

PREPARE AHEAD

Ingredients

1 Spanish onion
2 green peppers
2 medium zucchini
(only for mycologists) Fresh foraged
    mushrooms

(optional) Beef jerky (see page 39)
Olive oil
Salt and pepper

Packing the food

Package the vegetables and the optional jerky together; carry the olive oil and salt and pepper in general provisions.

TRAIL DIRECTIONS—GRILLED FRESH VEGETABLES

1. Prepare the vegetables: halve the onion through its equator, slice the zucchini lengthwise. (Leave the green peppers whole.) Get out the oil, salt and pepper, and a bowl.

2. Have your cookfire burned down to hot coals. Here is the order of cooking, according to the time needed for each ingredient:

Onion	15 to 20 minutes, turn once
Peppers, zucchini	10 minutes, turning over and over
Jerky	As long as it takes to heat through, a few minutes
Mushrooms	1 minute to a side

Arrange the food on the grill according to this order.

3. As the vegetables are cooked, transfer them to the bowl, put a little olive oil on them, and salt and pepper to taste.

Fresh Zucchini with Cheese

A fresh zucchini makes a nice surprise on the trail. It will keep a few days and doesn't weigh much.

The dish works with dried zucchini as well. Simmer 5 to 10 minutes to soften it, then add the cheese.

TRAIL INFORMATION

TIME	5 to 10 minutes
WATER	A few tablespoons
EQUIPMENT	1 pot or frying pan with a lid
SERVINGS	2 or 3

PREPARE AHEAD

Ingredients

1 whole fresh zucchini, fairly small   Salt and pepper
2 tablespoons butter or margarine
¼ cup grated or cut Parmesan
    cheese, or mozzarella, or
    Monterey jack

Packing the food

Carry the zucchini in your pack with the trail directions.

Carry in general provisions: butter or margarine, cheese, salt and pepper.

TRAIL DIRECTIONS—FRESH ZUCCHINI WITH CHEESE

1. Cut the zucchini into thin slices.
2. Melt 2 tablespoons butter in a pot, add the zucchini and a few table-spoons water and bring to a boil, covered. Simmer for 3 minutes or so.
3. Add cheese, grated or cut into small pieces, and cook, covered, a moment longer, until the cheese melts. Do not overcook or the zucchini will turn to mush.

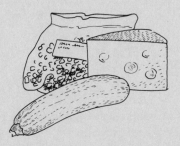

Cucumber Surprise

Serve this great backpacking classic simply with a little salt.

PREPARE AHEAD

Sneak a fresh cucumber into your pack.

TRAIL DIRECTIONS—CUCUMBER SURPRISE

About the fourth day out, take out the fresh cucumber, cut it into slices, and serve with a little salt on a flat dish.

CAMP DESSERTS

A few dried apricots, half a chocolate bar, a cup of hot chocolate are plenty of dessert for most trip menus.

But some menus require more elaborate desserts: in large groups, for instance, when dessert can be an event, or on trips with children, when it might be considered a reward. Out comes Camp Cake, with a fancy frosting waiting in the wings, or popcorn fresh from the frying pan, or a berry betty made from biscuits and fresh berries. Some wilderness cooks will lavish attention and time on memorable camp desserts; they putter and hum, and add and stir, long after I can barely keep my eyes open. These people mystify me, and I respect them and give them space (literal and figurative).

There is something about a gelatin dessert that entrances the wilderness appetite—even when the promised "pudding" texture is never reached. Often it isn't, whereupon the wild cook calmly pours warm raspberry junket over cornbread and pronounces a New Dessert.

Once we successfully put together a Betty Crocker cheesecake at a lakeshore so primitive we had to cross moose tracks to get to our refrigerator (the lake). The response to this culinary feat was exuberant, and we felt as proud as the legendary inventor of ice cream, to whom the enthusiastic king turned over the keys to his kingdom.

When selecting instant puddings and pies for the wild kitchen, stand in the store and read the directions, note the milk needed, and try not to get involved with those that require egg. The idea is to keep the dessert cooking simple—I think.

Mixed Fruit with Brandy

TRAIL INFORMATION

TIME	20 minutes
WATER	About 1½ cups
EQUIPMENT	1 pot
SERVINGS	6

PREPARE AHEAD

Ingredients

½ pound dried fruit, some combination of peaches, apricots, figs, and prunes

Sugar or honey to taste (optional) ⅓ cup (3 ounces) brandy

Packing the food

Pack the fruit in a bag with the trail directions. Carry sugar or honey and brandy separately.

TRAIL DIRECTIONS—MIXED FRUIT WITH BRANDY

1. Cover the fruit with water in a cookpot and bring to a boil. Cook gently, uncovered, for 10 to 15 minutes.

2. Sweeten to taste, and add the brandy at the last minute, with flourish.

S'mores

America's own camping dessert, named in the old days by Scouts who worried neither about the wood supply nor about their waistlines. S'mores are traditionally made over a campfire.

PREPARE AHEAD

Ingredients

Marshmallows—allow at least 4
    per person
Graham crackers—1 box for 10
    people
Chocolate in bar form—Hershey
    bars are traditional.
    However, sweet cooking
    chocolate works equally well
    and (to risk being heretical)
    tastes better.

TRAIL DIRECTIONS—S'MORES

Equipment

One 16-inch roasting stick per person. Fashion these from *downed* branches of trees by cutting a point on the skinny end with a knife. If your only source of sticks would be a living tree, have s'mores another night.

    Have ready a piece of chocolate, poised between two graham cracker squares. Roast two marshmallows at once over the fire (in it if you are one of those persons who loves the taste of charred food), and squeeze them off the stick between the crackers. Being hot, they will partly melt the chocolate, to make a gooey, sticky, altogether terrific dessert.

Chocolate Pudding

TRAIL INFORMATION

TIME	10 minutes cooking, and an optional hour of cooling in a stream
WATER	3 cups
EQUIPMENT	1 pot
SERVINGS	6 to 8

PREPARE AHEAD

Ingredients

½ cup unsweetened cocoa
1 cup sugar
¼ teaspoon salt
¼ cup cornstarch

½ cup dry milk
2 tablespoons Butter Buds, or 2
   tablespoons butter or
   margarine, added on the trail

Note: The total volume of the recipe is 2¼ cups mix, to which you add 3 cups water for 6 servings. For 3 servings: Divide the mix into 2 equal parts, of 1 cup plus 2 tablespoons each; then add 1½ cups water to each.

Packing the food

Mix all the dry ingredients together and put them into a plastic bag with the trail directions.

TRAIL DIRECTIONS—CHOCOLATE PUDDING

1. Add 3 cups water to the mix in a pot. Stir and bring to a boil. Add 2 tablespoons butter if the mix doesn't include Butter Buds. Cook slowly for a few minutes, stirring, until the pudding is thick.

2. Cool the pudding in a stream by putting the pot where it will not fall over or be swept off by the current. (Prop it carefully between rocks, for example.)

Note: Add granola, muesli, or gorp to the pudding for variety.

Apple Dumpling Dessert

This excellent trail dessert is just as good with other dried fruits, like apricots or pears. Throw in a handful of raisins if you have them.

To use fresh berries, simply omit the soaking time, cut down on the water, and vary the amount of sugar to suit your taste. (See below.) Serve with a little milk, yogurt, or—if you want to be totally elegant about it—some ultrapasteurized cream carried in a leakproof container.

TRAIL INFORMATION

TIME	1 hour soaking, 20 minutes cooking
WATER	2¼ cups
EQUIPMENT	1 pot, 1 bowl
SERVINGS	6

PREPARE AHEAD

Ingredients

1 cup biscuit mix (see page 174)
1 cup dried apples°
½ cup sugar
¼ teaspoon salt

½ teaspoon cinnamon
2 tablespoons butter or margarine (optional, for topping) milk, yogurt°, or cream

Packing the food

Put into 3 small bags, then package with the trail directions: 1. biscuit mix; 2. apples; 3. sugar, salt, and cinnamon.

Carry in general provisions: butter or margarine and optional milk, yogurt, or cream.

TRAIL DIRECTIONS—APPLE DUMPLING DESSERT

1. Cover the apples with 2 cups water in a pot and let them soak 1 hour. Then bring them to a boil and simmer, covered, while you make the dumpling.

2. To make dumpling: Add ¼ cup water to the biscuit mix and form into one piece of dough.

3. Add the sugar-spice mixture and 2 tablespoons butter or margarine to the apples. With a spoon spread the dumpling dough over them. Simmer, covered, for 15 to 20 minutes, until the dumpling is done; it will be dry in the middle.

Suggested amounts of sugar and water for blueberries:

2 cups fresh blueberries   ⅓ to ½ cup sugar
¼ cup water

Camp Cake

This cake without eggs manages to have a sweet, crumbly texture. A basic recipe is given here, with a list of things to put in as you pack.

Allow for camp variations, too, though you'll find that this basic cake invites freshly picked berries, a sauce made of rum or whiskey (see page 264), or a mad topping of muesli and peanut butter when creative urges strike you miles from civilization.

TRAIL INFORMATION

TIME	20 to 40 minutes
WATER	1 cup
EQUIPMENT	1 pot or bowl, shallow pan (a frying pan) with cover
SERVINGS	8 to 10—or use half the mix at one time

PREPARE AHEAD

Ingredients

2 cups flour   ¼ teaspoon salt
1¼ cups sugar   2 tablespoons dry milk
2 tablespoons baking powder   ¼ cup shortening

Optional additions to the basic camp cake mix:

Spices	$1\frac{1}{2}$ teaspoons cinnamon $\frac{1}{2}$ teaspoon mace $\frac{1}{2}$ teaspoon cloves
Raisins	$\frac{3}{4}$ to 1 cup
Nuts	$\frac{3}{4}$ cup, chopped
Chocolate/coffee	$\frac{1}{3}$ cup cocoa, 1 teaspoon cappucino or instant coffee (optional), and increase the shortening to $\frac{1}{2}$ cup

Preparing and packing the mix

Mix the dry ingredients, including the optional ones, then cut in the shortening with two knives. Package the mix with the trail directions.

TRAIL DIRECTIONS—CAMP CAKE

1. Prepare a frying pan or other baking pan by coating it with margarine and dusting it with flour.

2. Stir 1 cup water into the mix (to halve the recipe, use $\frac{1}{2}$ cup water). Using a lid or aluminum foil to cover the pan, cook the cake slowly by setting it in the coals left after your regular cooking fire has burned down. It will take about 20 minutes to cook. You can tell it is done if you push the center with your finger and it springs back a little.

Rum or Whiskey Sauce for Camp Cake

This is a hot topping to serve over cake. It is not the same as frosting, which means you don't have to worry about losing "frosting consistency" by adding too much liquid.

It can be served over any home-baked cake as well.

TRAIL INFORMATION

TIME	5 minutes
WATER	$\frac{1}{2}$ cup
EQUIPMENT	1 pot
SERVINGS	8 to 10

PREPARE AHEAD

Ingredients

1 cup brown sugar
1 tablespoon Butter Buds

1 35-mm film can rum or whiskey
(1 ounce)

Packing the food

Pack the brown sugar and Butter Buds together in a small bag. Package it with the film can of spirits and the trail directions in a larger bag.

TRAIL DIRECTIONS—RUM OR WHISKEY SAUCE FOR CAMP CAKE

In a small cookpot combine the dry ingredients with $\frac{1}{2}$ cup water. Heat but do not boil. Off heat, add one ounce (or so) of spirits. When each person has his cake, spoon the hot sauce over it.

Note: When using only half a cake mix, use $\frac{1}{2}$ cup frosting mix with $\frac{1}{4}$ cup water.

Camp Frosting

This is enough to frost one whole camp-baked cake.

TRAIL INFORMATION

TIME	5 minutes
WATER	A few tablespoons
EQUIPMENT	1 bowl
SERVINGS	8 to 10

PREPARE AHEAD

Ingredients

1 cup powdered sugar
1 tablespoon dry milk

1 tablespoon Butter Buds

Note: For chocolate frosting, add $\frac{1}{4}$ cup cocoa to the basic mix.

Preparing and packing the mix

Mix the ingredients together and put them into a small plastic bag with the trail directions.

TRAIL DIRECTIONS—CAMP FROSTING

Add 1 tablespoon cold water to the dry mix and stir. *Very slowly*, add 1 to 2 teaspoons more cold water, stirring, until you have frosting consistency. (It very easily becomes too wet.)

To use half, for half a cake, use ½ cup frosting mix and start with 1 teaspoon water.

Indian Pudding

It's possible to carry molasses, instead of honey or sugar, as your sweetening "staple." In that case, consider making Indian pudding, an old-fashioned dessert. Its wholesome flavor is delicious with yogurt, or with "ultrapasturized" cream, which can be carried in cool weather.

TRAIL INFORMATION

TIME	30 minutes*
WATER	1½ cups
EQUIPMENT	1 pot with lid
SERVINGS	6 to 8

*Prepare the pudding first and let it sit while you prepare and eat dinner.

PREPARE AHEAD

Ingredients

¼ cup cornmeal, preferably stone
   ground
½ cup dry milk
2 tablespoons dry egg

⅛ teaspoon salt
¼ teaspoon cinnamon
⅓ cup molasses

Packing the food

Mix and pack into a small bag the cornmeal, dry milk, dry egg, salt, and cinnamon. Carry the molasses separately in a leakproof container inside a Ziploc bag.

TRAIL DIRECTIONS—INDIAN PUDDING

1. Add 1½ cups water to the dry ingredients in a pot. Add molasses. Bring to a boil, then cover and simmer 20 minutes, stirring occasionally.

2. Let the pudding sit off the heat to cool for at least 10 minutes before you eat it. Serve plain or with yogurt, milk, or cream.

APPENDIXES

How to tie a bear bag/Mail-order suppliers of dried foods/Where to buy Chinese and other Oriental dried foods/Mail-order suppliers of backpacking equipment/ Reconstituting information

How to tie a bear bag

All kinds of bears are dangerous. The totally wild ones are unpredictable, and so are the ones that are used to humans—but the ones used to humans are used to eating their camping food, and that makes them particularly worrisome when you retire for the night.

Never keep food in your tent, and be very careful that neither it nor you—including your clothes—smells like food, because a bear won't stop to ask questions.

The only safe thing to do with your food at night in bear country is to tie it 15 feet in the air.

NEEDED

2 large plastic bags, one inside the other (use more bags if you have a lot of food)

20 or more feet of strong nylon line

A piece of wood, 8 to 10 inches long, or a stone you can tie the end of the line around

LOCATE

A tree limb 15 feet off the ground and unobstructed enough so you'll be able to throw a line over it.

PROCEDURE

Put all the food into the double plastic bags, filling the bags only half full.

Tie a knot in the top of the bag, or simply twist the top around itself, to be secured with the line.

Tie one end of the line securely around the top of the bag, knotting it and making a few loops around the bag itself if there's plenty of line.

Coil the line.

Tie the wood or stone to the other end of the line.

Holding the coiled line in your (left) hand, throw the stick over the branch you have chosen. (Be patient, you'll get it.)

Pull the bear bag up so it's flush with the branch.

Secure the bag by tying half hitches around: (a) another branch on the tree, or (b) the tree trunk.

Coil the extra line so it's neat.

Sleep well: your food will be safe from raccoons and other varmints as well as from bears.

Additional reading on bears can be found in:

"Roaming Their Last Domains, Grizzlies May Clash with Man," by Robert C. Gildart, in the August 1981 issue of *Smithsonian*.

Coming into the Country, by John McPhee.

Mail-order suppliers of dried foods

Alpine-Aire
P.O. Box 926, Nevada City, CA 95959. 916-272-1971

Their food is expensive, but they have dried some things, without additives, that are useful for cooking: potato flakes, tomato flakes, and tomato powder, for instance.

Eastern Mountain Sports, Inc.
Vose Farm Road
Peterborough, NH 03458
Basically an equipment source, but some freeze-dried foods are available.

Harrington's in Vermont, Inc.
Richmond, VT 05477
This is a good mail-order source of cheeses and smoked meats.

Recreational Equipment, Inc.
P.O. Box C-88125
Seattle, WA 98188
Basically an equipment source, but some freeze-dried foods are available.

Rich-Moor Corporation
P.O. Box 2728, Van Nuys, CA 91404
Send for a list of their products, which they only sell through sporting-goods dealers. They'll send you a list for your area. Useful are diced freeze-dried meats and pilot biscuits. (I wouldn't bother with the jerky or the "meat bar"—you can do much better.)

Stow-A-Way
166 Cushing Highway, Cohasset, MA 02025
They supply individual freeze-dried vegetables and fruits, as well as freeze-dried orange-juice crystals. Four and a half ounces of orange-juice crystals, enough to make a quart, costs $1.10.

Walnut Acres
Penns Creek, PA 17862. 717-837-0601
This is an organic farm with an extensive mail-order system. They obtain some foods from other sources, too, and they are careful to note just which products are absolutely "organic" and to what degree others aren't. Many dried foods and other products—dried milk, honey, grains, nuts, flour—are available at prices better than stores' (maybe not better than co-ops'), although you do have to pay shipping charges. There is truck delivery, too. It is a friendly and efficient outfit, and the products are excellent.

Williams-Sonoma
Mail Order Dept.
P.O. Box 3792
San Francisco, CA 94119

Their catalog, mostly for cooking equipment, does offer pure maple sugar granules as well as other possible trail foods, like herbs, chocolate, and olive oil.

Where to buy Chinese and other Oriental dried foods

A Chinese, Japanese, or Korean food store in your own area is the best place to buy dried Oriental foods. You'll be able to see what you're buying, to ask questions, and to compare prices.

But, if you haven't such stores near you, you can order by mail. The Chinese Grocer, 209 Post Street, San Francisco, CA 94108, has a shopping list–catalog and an order-by-phone number, 800-227-3220.

Kam Kuo Food Products, Inc., in New York's Chinatown, 7 Mott Street, New York, NY 10013 (212-571-0330), also sends dried items when you specify the amount and the brand name, if you know it. If you don't know either one, approximate the amount, and authorize Kam Kuo to choose the brand name. They will send items C.O.D.

From Kam Kuo, standard amounts and 1981 prices of a few sample packages are:

black mushrooms	8 ounces	$6.75
tiger lily buds	8 ounces	.95
black fungus (small version)	4 ounces	3.50
dried sliced bean curds	8 ounces	1.00

These are large amounts, which will last a long time: don't order more than one package if you are unfamiliar with the item.

Mail-order suppliers of backpacking equipment

L. L. Bean, Inc.
Freeport, Maine 04033

Eastern Mountain Sports, Inc.
Vose Farm Road
Peterborough, New Hampshire 03458

Recreational Equipment, Inc.
P.O. Box C-88125
Seattle, Washington 98188

Eddie Bauer
Fifth & Union
Seattle, Washington 98124

Early Winters, Ltd.
110 Prefontaine Place South
Seattle, Washington 98104

Mountain Safety Research
625 South 96th Street
Seattle, Washington 98108

Send for a catalog of "high tech" equipment which, though mostly available through retailers, M.S.R. will mail if you can't find.

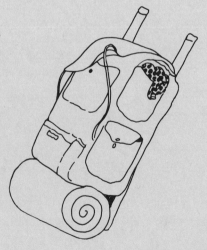

Reconstituting information

BISCUIT MIX

Add $\frac{1}{4}$ cup water per 1 cup mix for 6 biscuits.

BUTTER BUDS

1 packet (8 teaspoons) Butter Buds plus $\frac{1}{2}$ cup water = $\frac{1}{2}$ cup melted butter flavor. (*Note*—Do not try to fry things in reconstituted Butter Buds, since they contain no fat.)

DRY EGGS

2 tablespoons dry egg mix plus 3 tablespons water = 1 fresh egg in volume if not in taste.

DRY MILK

2 tablespoons to $\frac{1}{3}$ cup dry milk plus 1 cup water = 1 cup milk.
1 cup dry milk plus 1 quart water = 1 quart milk.

HOME-DRIED SAUCES

Generally, add an equal amount of water to a dried sauce. If this isn't enough, add more after a little cooking.

INSTANT POTATOES

Potato Buds—Use $\frac{3}{4}$ the amount of Potato Buds to water. For example, $\frac{3}{4}$ cup Potato Buds and 1 cup water.
Instant potato powder—Use 4 times the amount of water as potato powder. For example, $\frac{1}{4}$ cup powder and 1 cup water.
To this amount of each of the above, which feeds 3 people, add 2 tablespoons dry milk, 1 teaspoon Butter Buds or butter or margarine, and $\frac{1}{4}$ teaspoon salt.

KOOL-AID

1 scoop (almost $\frac{1}{4}$ cup) = 1 pint of sweetened drink.

MAPLE SYRUP GRANULES

Although the best way to use these on the trail is simply to sprinkle them on your food (including pancakes), you can make a syrup by mixing 1 part boiling water to 2 parts granules: for instance, ¼ cup boiling water with ½ cup granules for 8 servings (3 ounces).

WATER AMOUNTS NEEDED TO COOK

Cereals—Note the directions on the box.
Cornmeal—Use almost 4 times as much water as cornmeal.
Pasta—See cooking directions.
Rice—Use twice as much water as rice.
Other grains—Generally, use 2 to 3 times as much water.

WHITE SAUCE MIX

Use ⅓ cup mix per 1 cup water for a medium-thick sauce.

Index

A NOTE ABOUT THE AUTHOR

Gretchen McHugh was born and raised in Michigan, and
was graduated from Wellesley College. She has backpacked
in various regions of the United States, and lives in
New York with her two children.

A NOTE ON THE TYPE

The text of this book was composed in a film version of
Trump Mediæval. Designed by Professor Georg Trump in
the mid-1950s, Trump Mediæval was cut and cast by
the C. E. Weber Type Foundry of Stuttgart, West Germany.
The roman letter forms are based on classical prototypes,
but Professor Trump has imbued them with his own
unmistakable style. The italic letter forms, unlike those of
so many other type faces, are closely related to their
roman counterparts. The result is a truly contemporary
type, notable for both its legibility and its versatility.

Composed by Centennial Graphics, Inc.,
Ephrata, Pennsylvania. Printed and bound by
Halliday Lithographers, Inc., Hanover, Massachusetts

Typography and binding design by Judith Henry